THE LOST GROVE

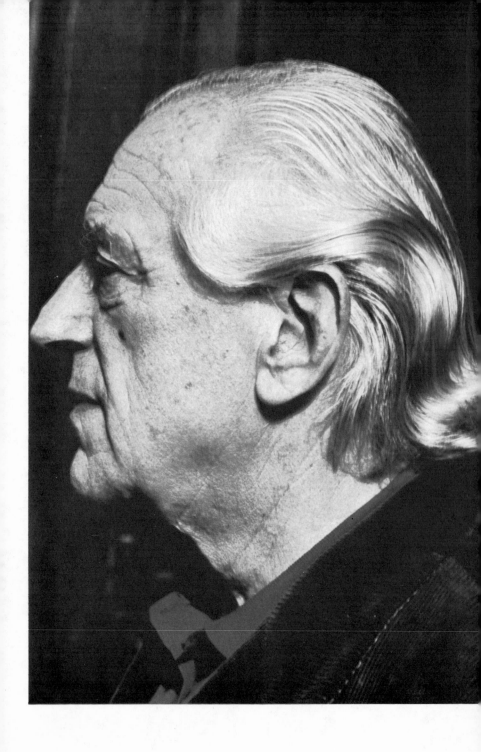

RAFAEL ALBERTI

The Lost Grove

Translated and edited by Gabriel Berns

*I cannot imagine how anyone can
go through life without carrying
the memories of his childhood
on the surface of his soul*

MIGUEL DE UNAMUNO

UNIVERSITY OF CALIFORNIA PRESS

BERKELEY   LOS ANGELES   LONDON

University of California Press
Berkeley and Los Angeles, California

University of California Press, Ltd.
London, England

Primera edición: *La arboleda perdida,* por
Rafael Alberti, © 1959 by Compañía General
Fabril Editora, S.A., Bs. As.

First English translation copyright © 1976 by The Regents
of the University of California with permission

ISBN 0-520-02786-8
Library of Congress Catalog Card Number: 74-79760

Designed by Wolfgang Lederer
Printed in the United States of America

CONTENTS

ACKNOWLEDGMENTS
AND
TRANSLATOR'S NOTE

I WISH TO EXPRESS here my deepest appreciation to Aitana Alberti without whose kind help and intercession this translation of her father's memoirs would not have been possible. I am grateful to the Faculty Research Committee of the University of California at Santa Cruz for granting me the funds which allowed me to visit Rafael Alberti and his daughter in Italy and Spain during the summer of 1974. Certainly worthy of mention here are my colleagues Joseph H. Silverman and John Wilkes who were extremely generous with their time and their constructive comments on this manuscript. Mrs. Eileen Beeby's highly professional and conscientious work on the transcription of tapes and the preparation of the first draft of this translation helped me through some difficult moments. I take this opportunity to formally thank her for her technical assistance as well as for her intelligent comments on the text. To Mrs. Phyllis Halpin, Mrs. Charlotte Cassidy and particularly Mrs. Elaine Dilts I am greatly indebted for their assistance in typing this manuscript more than once. Important contributions were also made by Peggy Smith, Joseph Chadwick and Barbara Hull. My wife Arlette showed unusual tolerance and patience during the two years it took to complete this translation, reading sections of it on so many different occasions, that she even committed some of them to memory. I thank her for the needed encouragement she furnished me so often.

As for the translation itself, George Steiner writes in his *After*

Babel (1975), that "a true translator knows that his labour belongs to oblivion (inevitably, each generation retranslates), or 'to the other one, his occasion, begetter, and precedent shadow.' He does *not* know 'which of us two is writing this page'." I can only hope the reader of the following pages will not suffer from such doubts, but will instead feel that here it is the voice of Rafael Alberti which can be heard, communicating directly from among the branches of his *Lost Grove.*

TRANSLATOR'S
INTRODUCTION

THE LOST GROVE is an apt title for the
autobiography of the Spanish poet-in-exile, Rafael Alberti.[1] In the
young Andalusian growing up in Puerto de Santa María on the
shores of the Bay of Cádiz, there always seems to have existed a
deeply entrenched feeling of loss, of separation from a previously ex-
istent state of grace or vaguely intuited paradise. The poetry of
Rafael Alberti was later to display consistently this strong element of
longing, and his poems are often an attempt to bridge the distance,
whether it be physical or psychic, which he feels separates him from a
former state of bliss. For Alberti, whose life has been spent in
productive wandering since his forced departure from Spain as a
result of the Spanish Civil War more than thirty-five years ago, the
loss is more than partially real. But on reading the early poetry of
Alberti and following the autobiographical account which comprises
this present work, one becomes acutely aware that an extremely fertile imagination is at work here. The possibility suggests itself that
the poet's nostalgia may conceivably be for things, people and places

[1]The original title in Spanish is *La arboleda perdida*. Book I (1902–1917) first
appeared in Mexico in 1942, and it was published again with the addition of Book II
(1917–1931) in Buenos Aires in 1959. A new Spanish edition was published by Seix
Barral in Barcelona in 1975. Sections of this work in English translation have been
published under the title of *The Vanished Grove* in *Rafael Alberti, Selected Poems*,
edited and translated by Ben Belitt (Berkeley: University of California Press, 1966).

3

that exist primarily in his mind or, even more significantly, in his gently tempered memory.

The Lost Grove is, in many ways, the story of a paradise imagined, lost and subsequently regained through the written word. We find here the memories which Alberti has resurrected or recreated of his formative years in Andalusia after the turn of the century, and of his beginnings first as a painter and then as a poet in Madrid from the year 1917 to 1931. For a poet, the past is of greater significance both to him and the readers of his poetry than it would be for those whose lives are primarily a constant projection forward. For those of the latter group, a dwelling on the past might have the adverse effect of retarding the desired forward movement. But in looking backward, the poet is of course also looking inward in an effort to discover the origins of his particular response to life. The poet's responsiveness and the nature of his responses are the basis for his particular poetic activity. The poetic imagination reacts to stimuli that may appear to come from sources external to him, but they set off a series of inner signals "installed" somewhere in the past. Such signals are not completely engaged, not activated, until much later when the poet's own engagement with the world, "his successive collisions with circumstances,"[2] bring these signals into full play.

For the artist or poet in exile who, as in the case of Rafael Alberti, continues to live physically removed from the land which nurtured him culturally, spiritually and linguistically, the written document that describes scenes from this past as well as the frame of mind within which the previous existence is actualized or brought fully into the present are of special importance. The diaspora of Spanish artists and intellectuals created by the holocaust of the Spanish Civil War is not yet over. A full account of this long exile with its almost biblical dimensions is yet to be written, but Rafael Alberti represents, perhaps more than any other Spaniard living today, the way in which the strong will to create and to remember can transform a personal tragedy into an artistically fruitful experience. Alberti continues from his present exile in Rome to draw from his cultural heritage, from a revitalized past intimately tied to Spanish soil. This autobiography, this *Lost Grove*, whose second volume was completed some sixteen years ago, serves as a kind of lifeline which transmits

[2]Roy Pascal, *Design and Truth in Autobiography* (Cambridge: Harvard University Press, 1960).

4

sustenance to the poet, fortifying his present and strengthening his already potent creative drive.

Displacement can be a source of creativity, and a sense of separation may give rise to a way of looking at all things in a very special light. Exile for some artists is not only inspirational, but may also constitute the only viable condition under which their existence becomes tolerable. In an interesting study on the poetry of Rafael Alberti, Solita Salinas de Marichal suggests that the poet had always made ample use of memory even in his earliest poetry, and she mentions that Alberti's desire to return to the past through memory transformed can be seen clearly in his first book of poems, *Marinero en tierra (Sailor on Land)*.[3] In this collection of sonnets, sea ballads and songs, the emptiness of the poet's daily existence removed from the scenes of his childhood is filled with a reworking of the past. The very title of this book, for which Alberti received the National Prize for Literature in 1925 and that also launched him on his poetic career, expresses this sense of displacement. Living in Madrid, landlocked and far removed from that beloved "blueness" of the Andalusian sea and sky, Alberti composes a seascape that never really was. The Bay of Cádiz becomes mythologized, glorified and exalted in these poems. The physical separation from the Cádiz of his childhood serves to generate a free flow of the poet's imagination:

> *How good it would be*
> *to live on a farm in the sea*
> *apart, with a little girl-gardener!*
>
> *In the smallest of carts, drawn*
> *by a salmon—what delight*
> *to call under sea-salt, love,*
> *a gardener's harvest for all!*
>
> *"Here's algae! Fresh algae! Get*
> *your algae still wet with the sea!"*[4]

[3]Solita Salinas de Marichal, *El mundo poético de Rafael Alberti* (Madrid: Editorial Gredos, S. A., 1968).

[4]"Pregón submarino" ("Underwater Street Cry") is the title of this poem which appears here in a translation included by Professor Luis Monguió in his excellent introduction to the poetry of Rafael Alberti in *Rafael Alberti, Selected Poems*, op. cit.

In his autobiographical narrative, however, Rafael Alberti does not really mythologize the past, but he *does* "poeticize" it. To the casual reader approaching this text without any previous knowledge of Alberti, it should soon become obvious that this is the work of a poet. *The Lost Grove* is not autobiography that tries to disguise itself as objective biography in order to "tell it like it was." The creation of a somewhat rarefied atmosphere, of a mood tinged with bittersweet longing, is of prime importance to Alberti as evidenced by the opening paragraphs:

> In the city of Puerto de Santa María, province of Cádiz, on the right hand side of a road, lined with prickly pear cactus, that leads down to the sea and proudly bears the name of an old bullfighter—Mazzantini—there was a melancholy place, covered over with yellow and white Spanish broom, called The Lost Grove.

> Everything there was like a memory: birds circling trees that had disappeared long ago, furiously seeking vanished branches on which to sing; the wind moving through the clumps of Spanish broom sighing longingly for tall, green treetops to rustle, so as to hear its own voice; mouths, hands and foreheads searching for patches of cooling shade, to rest there amorously. Everything brought back sounds of the past, of an ancient forest that no longer existed. Even the light in that grove was like a memory of light; and the games we played there as children, when we would cut our classes, echoed those sounds of things past.

Loss, longing, nostalgia and a sense of separation are the primary emotions strongly conveyed on the very first page. The language itself floats in a detached way like the birds encircling those vanished branches. This approach to the past has, of course, its basis in the present, and the sense of loss which we have suggested as being a constant in the works of Alberti is felt to exist here with a particularly strong impact as the poet begins to recapture a temporally distant past from the vantage point of a physically distant exile. What is established here and is maintained throughout *The Lost Grove* is "a balance between past experience and the present self,"[5] and it is

[5]Roy Pascal, op. cit., p. 57.

6

worth noting at this point that the seventeen years which elapsed between the writing of Book I of these memoirs and Book II had little intrinsic effect on the overall tone of the completed work. For Alberti, the main purpose or need for writing these memoirs remains the same from the early years of exile in Paris in 1939 to his long residence in Argentina where Book II was finally finished in 1959: to make of the past a living presence and an inspiration for continued creativity. During the period from 1948 to 1956, Alberti composed a series of poems under the collective title of *Retornos de lo vivo lejano (Return of the Distant, Living Past)* in which the memories of past events are distilled and poured into formal poetic molds. Alberti's friends from the Jesuit school in Puerto de Santa María, his cousins, his mother, his first loves, the sand dunes along the bay, are all recalled here as living essences. In the edition of his Collected Poems first published in 1967, Rafael Alberti introduces the poems of *Retornos de lo vivo lejano* with a statement which could be equally applied to *The Lost Grove:*

> During those years of exile in Argentina, the most minute details of my distant life in Spain became clearly defined and they are now memories—places, people, desires, loves, moments of sadness and joy . . . —which invade my very being hour after hour, making of the poem not an elegy for dead things, but, on the contrary, a living presence that has returned in spite of the apparent distances which separate me from them. A book that has no end since it is like the chronicle of the best or worst moments of my life, moments for whose return I will be forever waiting.[6]

And so, Rafael Alberti attempts both in his poetry and in prose to give the past a living presence, but the writing of the prose version is a long, difficult process. The reasons for this are manifold, but part of the delay can be attributed to Alberti's constant travels during the years 1944 to 1959, including two trips to China and the Soviet Union, as well as visits to Poland, Czechoslovakia, Rumania, Germany, France and Italy. Moreover, Alberti is the first to recognize the problems he has in writing prose which, he claims, often eludes him and threatens to become pure poetry in spite of efforts to prevent this from occurring. In a passage from the second book of *The*

[6]Rafael Alberti, *Poesía (1924–1967)* (Madrid: Aguilar, 1972), p. 899.

Lost Grove, Alberti gives vent to his dismay when faced with this dilemma:

> How slowly I work! A simple page of prose is as difficult or even more difficult than an entire poem. Everything I do turns out to be too rhythmical. I struggle against this. I make corrections and even mutilate a sentence to make it sound less like a verse of poetry. I read it carefully and find that I don't like it at all. What else can I do but continue with the Grove as I have up until now and apologize for my inability to keep from getting lost among its branches; for filling it with the same musical, metrical and jaunty gusts of air that have shaken these same branches ever since the opening chapter.

In *The Lost Grove*, we obviously have the autobiography of a man and a poet for whom "events become important ... not in themselves, but for what he puts into them."[7] Our reaction as readers is similar in that we are more interested in the poet's responses to the events chronicled than to the occurrences themselves, and this would particularly apply to the English-speaking reader whose familiarity with many of the incidents and people mentioned in these pages would be slight or non-existent. Such a reader can and probably will be fascinated by the way in which the narrator's imagination is kindled by the personalities and incidents which are woven into the fabric of a life and of a book which recounts this life.

As we read about Alberti's childhood under the strict tutelage of the Jesuits and the watchful eyes of all those bigoted but strangely endearing aunts and uncles who spy on him from everywhere, as we follow his account of how he came to form an integral part of the exciting and slightly mad artistic circles of Madrid, we are given an opportunity which only literature and particularly autobiography can adequately offer—the chance to see the particular way in which one observant and talented young man becomes actively engaged with the world around him. In presenting this work in book form to an English-reading public for the first time, however, certain questions are bound to arise which would most probably never have occurred to the Hispanic reader.[8] How exotic and removed from our own ex-

[7]Roy Pascal, op. cit., p. 133.

[8]*La arboleda perdida* in its entirety has to date been translated only into Russian. This translation appeared in Moscow in 1968.

perience is this world of Spain in the early part of the twentieth century as it is seen through the eyes and filtered through the memory of Rafael Alberti? Can his approach to and his exiled vision of the world be of interest to those who are not yet familiar with Alberti's poetry nor fully aware of its significant place in contemporary Hispanic literature?[9] In an amusing but penetrating article which deals with the validity of autobiography, the American novelist Herbert Gold quotes from a novel by Brock Brower:

"I'm writing an autobiography," Brock Brower has a character declare.

"Good. I hope you find a subject worthy of it," answers a friend.[10]

In one sense, of course, every life is a worthy subject of autobiography. The overwhelming desire to tell one's own story constitutes one of the most startling and enjoyable aspects of a work considered by many critics to be the first truly modern European novel—Cervantes' *Don Quixote.* The individual episodes themselves which comprise such a life story may be of varying interest, but the vantage point and narrative style of the "autobiographical subject" are the elements that keep the reader or listener in a constant state of anticipation. Rafael Alberti's life, as recounted by him in the pages of his *Lost Grove,* takes on a certain novelistic and even picaresque quality. He remains well within an established Spanish literary tradition when he describes his youthful activities and his feeble attempts to destroy the social fabric of the Spain he knew as a child, in a style reminiscent of the early Spanish *pícaros* or rogues in their encounters with the society of their time.

Alberti's life is filled with a sense of tension, of unrest, of a feeling that he has been placed somewhere "between the carnation and the

[9]In his Introduction to *Rafael Alberti, Selected Poems,* which has already been cited, Professor Luis Monguió lists the various English translations of Alberti's poetry which had appeared prior to 1966. Subsequently, the poet Mark Strand published a series of translations of Alberti's poems in *The Owl's Insomnia* (New York: Atheneum, 1973).

[10]Herbert Gold, "Why 'I'?", *Saturday Review* (February 8, 1975), pp. 18–21.

sword."[11] This becomes evident in *The Lost Grove* when we discover tender, lyrical passages that are in jarring proximity to harsh and even perhaps rather offensive descriptions of the pranks and games played by the young painter-poet in the company of other members of his generation. But this tension and restlessness are also the primary ingredients of his poetry as well as of his subsequent creative activities. They continue to form an integral part of his daily existence. He is now, as he apparently always was, an indefatigable seeker in pursuit of his own form of creative expression and of what he considers to be his particular place in the world of arts, letters *and* social injustice.

This state of perpetual motion, of insistent striving, can be gleaned from the pages of these memoirs, but *The Lost Grove* is merely an introduction into the life and times of Rafael Alberti. The years covered here are, after all, the most tranquil in what was later to become an extremely peripatetic and active existence. The main body of the narrative concludes in the year 1931, and yet Rafael Alberti continues to be alive, well and highly productive in Italy some forty-four years later. It might be assumed by anyone who reads these pages, that there is still much to come and that a life which showed such momentum during the early years of growth and development was not fated to become subsequently either restful or sedentary. His travels and long periods of residence outside of Spain were to bring Alberti into close contact with many of the outstanding literary figures of the twentieth century. As one looks at the Autobiographical Index which serves as a preface to his Collected Poems, it is apparent that the rhythm of his activities increases in the years that follow the one with which he concluded the second book of his *Lost Grove.*

In Paris, during the winter of 1931, he became friendly with Picasso and he was admitted to the literary world of other expatriate authors such as César Vallejo, Miguel Angel Asturias and Alejo Carpentier. In 1932, on his trip to Russia, he met Boris Pasternak and Louis Aragon; when he returned to Moscow in 1934, Alberti established contact with Gorki, Eisenstein and Prokofiev, as well as with André Malraux. Alberti is obviously pleased to include such people among his friends and acquaintances, but his Index also points to his own abundant creative work produced in the years 1931 to 1970. Since establishing permanent residence in Rome in 1963

[11]*Entre el clavel y la espada (Between the Carnation and the Sword)* is a collection of poems by Alberti dedicated to Pablo Neruda and published in 1941.

where he now lives with his wife of many years, the novelist María Teresa León, Rafael Alberti has returned to the dual life of painter-poet which he describes so well in the *The Lost Grove*.

Rafael Alberti is well known not only in the Trastevere section of Rome where he and María Teresa have their apartment, but also among Italy's foremost artists and intellectuals. He has even become a familiar figure to the nation's television viewers. To a large number of politically oriented Romans with a strong sense of history, Rafael Alberti is considered to be Italy's "very own" most distinguished exile from the Spanish Civil War and, for them, his presence in Rome is a constant source of pride. Thus, they acknowledge him primarily as an important political figure who represents a stubborn refusal to accept dictatorial repression, while also recognizing him as the talented poet and artist he is. Such an accolade would undoubtedly please Alberti. There are many instances in *The Lost Grove* where the reader is made aware that Rafael Alberti's awakening consciousness of himself as a poet was followed only a few years later by the stirrings of his political consciousness.

Alberti's complete devotion to the Spanish Republic is not detailed in the main narrative of these memoirs. But the highly charged parenthetical statements which Alberti intersperses throughout the text and which place before the reader a suffering Alberti who cannot totally obliterate the present, *do* show his passionate involvement in the struggle. In spite of his driving need to immerse himself in a distant past in an attempt to block recent events from his mind while giving shape and coherence to his life, the immediate past forces itself upon his consciousness. But in these first books of his memoirs, Alberti refuses to comment at length on these intrusions. There are two moments in *The Lost Grove* when he indicates his desire to push aside the painful consequences of the Spanish Civil War and his subsequent exile so that he may more freely return to the grove of his youth. The first one occurs in Book I in Alberti's brief description of his experience as a refugee in Paris:

> *With my soul filled with the memory of so much blood and my ears ringing from the explosions they had heard, I walked the streets of Paris and lived with the truly great and human Pablo Neruda, a veritable guardian angel of the Spaniards, in his home on the banks of the Seine; 31 Quai de l'Horloge. Toward the middle of August and in order to keep from dying of hunger, as well as to avoid being*

any further burden to the fearful and not overly generous French, María Teresa and I accepted an offer from the Paris-Mondial radio station to translate their broadcasts to Latin America into Spanish. We obtained the job through the auspices and on the recommendation of Pablo Picasso. What did I actually accomplish during all these months? What did I produce? Hardly anything at all. I only saw many good Spaniards die of starvation and persecution, and I witnessed the departure from Europe of many close friends. But some day I will talk about all this. The present is too harsh, too sad to write about now. I wish to go back to those other days of my childhood on the shores of the Gulf of Cádiz letting the undulating pine trees along the coast clear my mind, and feel my shoes fill with sand, the blonde sand of the burning dunes shaded here and there by clumps of Spanish broom.

When (some fifteen years later) in the spring of 1954, Rafael Alberti decided to begin the second book of memories, as he sat in the garden of his home in Buenos Aires, he made the leap back to his childhood with greater ease. He continued to "suffer the unbearable nostalgia of his lost country,"[12] but he and María Teresa were settled in Argentina, their daughter Aitana, born in Buenos Aires in 1941, was a joy to them both as well as the subject of many of Alberti's poems of the period, and his physical surroundings now allowed for a smoother transition into the past:

> *I emerge from my fifty-one years and passing over so many horrifying events and so much sadness, I fly toward those other years when humor, joy, transparent faith and enthusiasm had only been slightly dampened by those pure first tears which never blind but rather illuminate even more the beauty, grandeur and profundity of life.*

Rafael Alberti's name has frequently been linked with that of another Andalusian poet whose international reputation is well established; Frederico García Lorca. Alberti shares with Lorca a very special approach to popular or traditional themes and imagery of an

[12]In Alberti's brief introduction to *Pleamar* (1942–1944) in *Poesía (1924–1967)*, op. cit., p. 545.

Andalusia that both poets recreated in their respective works. A certain playfulness often tinged with surrealistic fantasy and oneiric mystery imbues their writings and their art with a distinctive coloration that makes it quite natural for them to be discussed together and for critics to indulge in that unending search for "influences and imitations."

In his autobiography, Alberti devotes many pages to Lorca and he prepares us for his eventual meeting with this highly original poet from Granada at the Residencia de Estudiantes in Madrid very early in his narrative. As a result, feelings of suspense are created prior to their meeting and the significance of this personal encounter for the young Rafael Alberti as well as for the mature autobiographer is clearly apparent. The scenes describing García Lorca at the Residencia surrounded, as he almost always was, by an admiring throng of poets and artists that often included Salvador Dalí and Luis Buñuel, constitute some of the most delightful and lingering episodes of The Lost Grove. Alberti greatly admired Lorca as a poet and experienced a profound sense of identification with him. The minor literary skirmishes between the "albertistas" and the "lorquistas" which took place in Spain during the early 1930's never damaged the friendship which existed between these two poets. In fact, one cannot help but sense that the comparison with Lorca might well have been highly flattering to the youthful Alberti.

Lorca's poetry was popular because it captured and conveyed the underlying inventive imagination of Andalusia and its people. But although his execution in Granada in 1936 was apparently carried out under the orders of anti-government forces, Lorca was never as immersed as Alberti in political activity, neither in his writings nor through personal participation in the cause of the Spanish Republic. Alberti, on the other hand, began to conceive of himself in 1933 as "un poeta en la calle," a poet of the streets, and he appeared at political rallies and before groups of workers gathered in the public squares of Spain where he would recite his satirical, "incendiary" poems to appreciative audiences. Alberti and María Teresa founded the revolutionary journal Octubre in 1934, and that same year they were invited to Moscow as guests of the First Congress of Soviet Writers. They remained active participants in the events which preceded the outbreak of the Spanish Civil War in 1936 and continued to serve the Republic until they left Spain to begin their long exile, which has not yet come to an end. Alberti's chronicle of those years is still to be written and in a recent interview in Rome[13] he indicated his strong desire to complete his memoirs, to return to *The Lost Grove*. Memory, for Alberti, continues to be of great significance and this is borne out by his remarks on the subject of exile:

> The great enemy is not the country where one happens to be, but rather the onslaught of arteriosclerosis, the loss of memory when your head becomes filled with blank spaces. When the right language is not accessible. If language is there, and if you pull at it as if it were a string, thousands of things will come to you from unknown sources.[14]

But Rafael Alberti's active schedule in Rome and elsewhere throughout Italy has consistently forced him to postpone this project. He now devotes himself primarily to painting and graphics, although he has never totally abandoned his poetry nor his interest in writing for the theater. In many ways, his energy resembles that of his friend Pablo Picasso, several of whose works line the walls of his apartment in Rome. Since establishing his residence in Italy, he has written and published some books of poetry, including the delightful *Roma, peligro para caminantes (Rome: Dangerous for Pedestrians)* and one dedicated to Picasso, *Los 8 nombres de Picasso (The 8 Names of Picasso)*, which was published in Barcelona on the occasion of the artist's eighty-ninth birthday.[15]

In his Epilogue to the second volume of *The Lost Grove*, Alberti speaks of his return to Spain while he plants his new grove in Argentina:

> . . . *there is something in my country that is on the verge of collapse. Among us, the Spanish exiles, there are breezes circulating which sing to us a song of return. In the meantime . . .*

Almost two decades have passed since that statement, and "in the meantime" Rafael Alberti has continued to draw on his Andalusian

[13]Luis Pancorbo, "Entrevista con Rafael Alberti," *Revista de Occidente* (July 1975), pp. 41–77.

[14]Ibid., p. 71.

[15]This work was published by Editorial Kairós in 1970. Alberti insisted that it appear in Spain and in an inexpensive paperback edition.

childhood and his lost grove for inspiration. The recent publication in Spain of *La arboleda perdida* is, in a significant way, Alberti's homecoming since he has not himself set foot on Spanish soil in thirty-seven years. But his active, full life bridges the distances which separate him from his country and his beloved Bay of Cádiz and also carries him into a future filled with projects and hope. Indeed, recent events in Spain may soon entice Alberti back to the land he abandoned so long ago, but such a return is bound to be anticlimactic. What is more essential is that he clearly appears before the reader in the pages of *The Lost Grove* not only as a man of unusual talent, but as one who has drawn fully from life whatever it had to offer. He does not tell all, but he tells enough for us to feel his presence strongly, with all its human weaknesses and strengths, as well as the presence of the world around him. As a poet and as an autobiographer, his creative act has brought to consciousness the nature of his own existence, "transforming the mere fact of existence into a realized quality and a possible meaning."[16] It is for each reader to determine for himself just what that possible meaning might be, but Rafael Alberti offers us here what Herbert Gold has eloquently described as "an example of sufficiency before the common fate and his unique recognition of it."[17]

[16]James Olney, *Metaphors of Self* (Princeton: Princeton University Press, 1972), p. 44.

[17]Herbert Gold, op. cit., p. 21.

Book
One
1902–1917

In the city of Puerto de Santa María, province of Cádiz, on the righthand side of a road, lined with prickly-pear cactus, that leads down to the sea and proudly bears the name of an old bullfighter —Mazzantini—there was a melancholy place, covered over with yellow and white Spanish broom, called The Lost Grove.

Everything there was like a memory: birds circling trees that had disappeared long ago, furiously seeking vanished branches on which to sing; the wind moving through the clumps of Spanish broom sighing longingly for tall, green treetops to rustle, so as to hear its own voice; mouths, hands and foreheads searching for patches of cooling shade, to rest there amorously. Everything brought back sounds of the past, of an ancient forest that no longer existed. Even the light in that grove was like a memory of light; and the games we played there as children, when we would cut our classes, echoed those sounds of things past.

Now as I retreat further and further into myself, becoming smaller and smaller, a distant point along the road that will eventually lead to that "gulf of shadows" which waits to close in upon me, I hear the muted sound of footsteps behind me—the inexorable, advancing invasion of that remembered lost grove of my youth.

It is then that I begin to hear with my eyes, see with my ears, my head making my heart spin but without causing me to fall out of step as I obediently move forward. The forest too continues to

17

advance day and night, overtaking me and my dreams that are released drop by drop, while the faded light, the dead shadows of words and cries, take on shape and form.

Some day, when the final moment of land's end has been reached, when the conquest is finished and when we have dissolved into the oneness of all things in that gulf of open darkness inevitably prepared for us, who can say if on the righthand side of another path that also leads down to the sea I will not once again stretch out to rest beneath the yellow and white Spanish broom and remember, . . . becoming totally transformed into the lost grove that lives and pulsates inside of me.

And a long memory of which no one will ever hear will be written fleetingly on the air; driven definitively off its course —definitively lost.

CHAPTER *I*

1902—YEAR of great agitation and activity among the peasant masses of Andalusia, a year of preparation for the revolutionary uprisings still to come. December 16—the date of my birth, on an unexpectedly stormy night, as I heard my mother once say, and in one of those port towns overlooking the perfectly shaped Gulf of Cádiz: Puerto de Santa María—formerly known as the Puerto de Menesteos—at the mouth of the Guadalete River, the River of Forgetfulness.

Both my grandfathers were Italian. As a small boy I remember hearing this language spoken at home. One of my grandmothers came from Ireland and the other was born in the city of Huelva. I can only recall seeing my paternal grandfather once, his long dark body stretched out in bed, a small cap—like the kind mailmen wear today—pulled down over his eyes. I can't remember his face at all, nor will memory serve to help bring back his voice. His wife, my paternal grandmother, does come back to me, sitting sad-faced and motionless on a very high-backed chair set in the corner of a darkened room, her fallen hand clutching a reed-like walking stick. Don Agustín, my mother's father, exists for me through a faded, yellowish photo which for years has been lying at the bottom of an old bureau drawer or in one of those dusty old packing crates that are falling apart piece by piece down in the basement. I know he has light-colored eyes and that blonde Italian sideburns frame and sharpen his smile. Beginning at his left shoulder and cutting across the front of his buttoned morning-coat, he wears a wide, multicolored sash which had been conferred on him by His Gracious Majesty Alfonso XII. His wife, my maternal grandmother, is sitting in the garden at sunset while the church bells toll for the dead, fanning herself in front of a jasmine bush beside a low fountain where a pitcher receives the running water like an open flower. She died in South America. My father was sick in bed with a livid case of jaundice when he was urgently called to my uncle's house. My mother and I and all my brothers and sisters were returning from a stroll along the riverbank where the steamboat was docked when we turned a corner and saw Papa all disheveled and green in the face. My grandmother Josefa had just died on her children's ranch about five or six kilometers outside of Buenos Aires.

My grandfathers were wine merchants, great middle-class proprietors of vineyards and wine cellars, Catholics to the point of extravagant madness and crushing tyranny. It was they, along with a few other powerful families who were the true owners of the Puerto at the turn of the century. Throughout my childhood, whether in our home or at my uncle's house, I always heard vacuous and annoying comments about "the good old days," that *belle époque* replete with luxuries as well as anecdotal voyages to Russia, Sweden and Denmark, to which my grandfathers exported their wines. Up until a few years ago some of the old bottle-labels, engraved in gold lettering but by then having taken on the color of dry leaves and partially eaten away by dampness and rats, would unexpectedly fall out of old pieces of furniture in my house in Madrid. These labels, with their golden inscriptions, had embossed medallions that depicted the kings of Sweden and Denmark, presided over by the profile of Czar Alexander II, killed by revolutionary terrorists in the streets of St. Petersburg. Inscribed below these three effigies was the caption: "Merello Brothers, Purveyors to Their Majesties the Kings of . . ." —and there followed the names of those countries which filtered through my imagination night after night as long, desolate, icy plains covered with dark pine forests. But those "good old days," with their Becquerian harps placed in sitting-room corners, their long and tedious chanting of the rosary in late afternoon, their lyre-shaped sofas and mother-of-pearl fans, were slowly disappearing between the covers of books, stiffly and lifelessly stretching out like dead branches, reaching into the present in an endless nightmare of aunts, uncles, cousins, great-aunts and great-uncles: bigots, cranks, drunks —rich, poor, frightening.

My father was always away, traveling in the north of Spain as a representative, no longer of his own wines, but of those of another important firm in town. We were still quite young and living with my mother, and it was then that the tyrannical reign of aunts and uncles began in my life. I ran into them everywhere. They would suddenly appear in the most unexpected places—from behind a rock, for example, when math class had been converted into a happy morning of fishing somewhere between La Pólvora Castle and Santa Catalina, across the bay from Cádiz; or from behind a pyramid of salt one afternoon when it was Latin that induced me to wander along the shore under the pine trees in the direction of San Fernando. Aunts and uncles to the north, to the east, to the west, to the south—everywhere in town, twenty-four hours a day: at noon, at three in the afternoon, in the blistering heat of the most oppressive days. I met them coming around the corner, standing still in the most unlikely doorway, at eight o'clock at night seated on a stone bench along an empty boulevard, or kneeling and speaking to themselves in a dark corner of some out-of-the-way church. They were the ones who snitched to my mother that I had a girlfriend who lived in an attic room somewhere in town, those old aunts of mine who wrote to the rector of San Luis Gonzaga, the elegant Jesuit school I attended at the time, telling him of my total lack of concentration during daily Mass—aunts and uncles who were successful in having me spectacularly expelled from this religious center of learning and, as a result, caused me to lose my entire fourth year of studies. I finally gave up school altogether and devoted myself to painting when my family moved to Madrid in 1917.

But I did not really perceive this hysterical tyranny, this fanatical and well-meaning power, nor did it wound me until years later when I had acquired what we call the use of reason, a faculty forcefully and angrily instilled in me, naturally under the guise of moral assistance, by the good fathers of the Society of Jesus. The tyrannical rule of my Uncles Fernando, Miguel, José María or Guillermo had not yet shown itself while I was learning to read and write in the school run by the Carmelite Sisters. The real figure of authority in those days, even more so than my mother, was Paca Moy, the old servant who had been present at the birth of all the children in the family and even treated my parents with great informality, scolding them at times, and tolerated our relentless teasing with saintly patience.

> "Hag, nag,
> Skinny old bag!"

Every afternoon when the nuns left, a chorus of fifteen or twenty little devils, all classmates under my leadership, would take up this cruel cry. On other occasions, turning our smocks into bullfighters' capes, we would surround Paca Moy and, screaming and shouting at the top of our lungs, would try to incite her to make passes at the capes as we danced around like *toreros* until the poor woman was beside herself and made us scatter by threatening us with a stone. Later, when we arrived home one by one, there was Paca Moy still indignant and mumbling to herself. I always feared the inevitable punishment that would ensue when my mother heard about what we had done, but this kind old servant would only mutter to herself as she crossed the patio: "That devil of a child!"

The following afternoon we would repeat the same chorus of insults as well as the bullfight game or else, for a change, we might decorate the back of poor Moy's shawl with a ridiculously fat doll cut out of newspaper, which she then wore down the street until our howls and shrieks of "Drop it, drop it, drop it—it's not yours!" shouted at the street-crossing made her stop and take off her shawl. When she discovered this insolent prank, she would tear the paper doll into a thousand pieces. The love she had for me always made her forgive everything, even the gang under my leadership, and out of gratitude and affection I obeyed her and actually feared her at times more than I would an angry, rusty old sword.

The day of my First Communion, on a rainy morning in March, Paca Moy opened the window of my bedroom slightly and sent an awakening slit of light across my bed. She was ecstatic: "Today is the happiest day of your life; you are going to receive the Lord."

"Yes, but what about my pieces of chocolate?"

"What are you talking about, child?"

"My usual breakfast . . ."

"The Carmelite Sisters will give you doughnuts and hot chocolate later, afterwards."

"I don't want their chocolate. I want what mama always leaves on the table for me every night."

"You little devil!"

"Don't call me a devil. I won't go to Communion without my chocolate."

Seeing my determination, Paca Moy left the bedroom, scandalized and confused. She returned immediately, carrying the chocolate, still wrapped in its silver paper. "Here you are; but you know, child, you can only receive the Lord on an empty stomach."

While the old woman held the chocolate in her hands and I put on the ridiculous sailor-suit that had been made just for that occasion, my mother appeared excitedly on the scene and kissed me. "Today is the happiest day of your life, my son. Isn't this a pretty ribbon Aunt Josefa has embroidered for you?"

That ribbon must at the time, in fact, have seemed *very* pretty to me, because I still remember how proud I felt as I walked down the still-empty streets in the early morning on my way to the convent. Before I had left the room, and while my mother's back was turned to us, Paca Moy handed me the bar of chocolate, which I immediately broke into small pieces and hid in the pockets of my sailor suit.

In the church of the Carmelites, Mass was sung and a little preparatory talk was offered for those who were to receive Communion for the first time. There were just a few of us, perhaps five in all, and I must have been the oldest. In order to set an example for the smaller children, we heard Mass on our knees, never lifting our eyes from the prayerbooks, sometimes lapsing into deep meditation which we made even deeper by squeezing our noses against the pages of the book until we could hardly breathe. The sermon, in keeping with what priestly intelligence imagines a poor, fasting child is capable of understanding, was probably long-winded and full of inanities. I say this because I soon forgot that this was the happiest day of all the days which awaited me in my lifetime, and a certain sense of boredom coupled with acute hunger made me yawn a number of times in a most unedified way. Finding it impossible to meditate because of the sermon, unable any longer to resort to covering my constantly opening mouth with my prayerbook, my only recourse was to take on an innocent look, as if I had just been deeply moved by the priest's words. So I cupped my face in my hands and stopped up my ears with my thumbs. Hunger continued its tickling torture while a truly satanic aroma of chocolate began to surge from my pockets, creeping up through my sleeves. When, after I don't know how long, the priest ended his talk by saying "And now, my dear children, prepare yourselves to receive the Lord," my left hand, trying to ignore what my right hand had just done, proceeded to unwrap the silver paper surrounding the second square of chocolate. The infernal aroma had become more and more irresistible.

Despite the remorse which haunted my sleep for many nights afterwards, no one ever knew about this sacrilege. I never mentioned it to any of my confessors, and I am not sure if I have been living in mortal sin since that day. To placate Paca Moy, I went up to her during the breakfast which the Carmelite Sisters had prepared for the five of us on the happiest day of our lives and gave her the remaining chocolate square: "This is for your snack." She was really touched and kissed me, sniffling back her tears.

Of all the memories of my childhood years in that convent school, I remember most a pebbled garden in which there was a toilet—a tiny place known as "the little room"—where lovely Sister Jacoba and the refined Sister Visitación would take the smaller children, both women often returning to the classroom with their ugly nun's shoes sprinkled with pee. That garden, with its four whitewashed walls covered only by a bushy *báncigo* tree and at certain hours of the day filled with more sparrows than flowers, must certainly still contain the echoes of my first games, those first cries and chants that now resound with such delightful clarity in the recesses of my awakening memory.

> *Las hermanas carmelitas,*
> *con delantales azules,*
> *se parecen a los cielos*
> *cuando se quitan las nubes.*

> *The Carmelite Sisters,*
> *With their blue mantles on,*
> *Are like the clear heavens*
> *When the rain clouds are gone.*

My childhood in Puerto de Santa María was shaped and filled with many shades of blue. And I mentioned them over and over again, almost to the point of losing my voice, in the songs of my first books of poetry. But they are now reborn, and I am immersed in them once more. In the midst of all those different blues—blue smocks, blue sailor-suits, blue skies, blue river, bay, island, boats, breezes—I opened my eyes and learned to read.

I cannot remember now exactly when the letters came together to form words, nor the precise instant when these words became linked to each other, revealing their special meaning to me. So many sleepless nights filled with dark terror, so many tears shed while I stood punished in the corner of the room, so many unhappy meals with no dessert! I feel now with dread the stirring of those memories that have been pounding inside of me from that distant morning when I repeated, over and over again, "*P-A, P-A,*" until that difficult but marvelous day when my eyes, wide open before the pages of some forgotten book, concentrated the force of their being on my tongue, making it spew out violently—as if a wire that held it down had suddenly been severed—an entire sentence! "The soldiers went forth into battle, marching nine hours without stopping to rest. . . ." What an astonishing day! A wondrous moment in which silence erupts into speech, syllables are formed from the air, strung together into words that roll down the mountains into the valleys, and from the sea come hymns disintegrating into sand and sea spray!

But that same afternoon the child cries and knows nothing; he dreams all night long of huge, bloated letters that pursue him, heavy letters trying to close in on him or trap him in a corner where spiders spin their webs, gray and thick like the capital letters which threaten to engulf him. Since the schoolboy is too old to wet his bed, his mother scolds him for it the following morning and he is punished. During the bullfight game, Paca Moy threatens to tell the whole story to the boys in the gang.

What was my mother like in that distant past? Tall and fair; very beautiful. Her name was María. I remember her now looking like certain Italian women I have seen in museums or perhaps in films and magazines that no longer exist.

My mother had almost always lived alone since, as I have already mentioned, my father was constantly traveling in Madrid, Galicia, San Sebastián, Bilbao—on the road at times without coming home for more than a year and a half. I can truthfully say that I had very little to do with him, nor did I know what he was like, until the last years of his life when the whole family had moved to Madrid. During this period of my childhood I am convinced that my mother was a delightful woman, although somewhat melancholy—probably because of the continuous separation during the first years of her young marriage, as well as because of the family's economic decline.

The daughter and sister of fanatic Catholics, maniacal religious bigots of Andalusia, it was only natural that she would seek refuge from her loneliness and misfortunes in the daily Masses that were held at the Convent of the Holy Spirit and in the pious murmurings of the nuns that issued forth from behind the spiked gates of the cloister. She would take me to dark chapels for Eucharistic Thursdays, the Third Order, and to recite prayers for the souls of the dead. I remember the Chapel of Santo Tomás de Villanueva where we went almost every afternoon. We would reach the place by passing through those mysterious church aisles, almost always arriving at the precise moment when the bellringer—a yellowish man with the face of an executioner—was tugging at the creaking bell-cords as if they were hangman's ropes, sending forth as far as the sleeping sea the moaning of the bells which rang out for all the souls in torment. Standing before the closed iron grating that separated us from the saint, both of us with our hands open in penitent supplication, my mother made me repeat the prayer whose opening and closing verses are all I can now remember.

>*Santo Tomás de Villanueva,*
>*santo querido de Dios,*
>*esa bolsa que en tu mano tienes*
>*el Señor te la envió*
>*para socorrer a tu bienhechor.*
>*Ese soy yo . . .*

>*Saint Thomas of Villanueva,*
>*Saint beloved of God,*
>*That purse you have in your hands*
>*Was sent to you by the Lord*
>*To help your benefactor. I am that one . . .*

I have never been able to reconstruct the following lines. But the beautiful ending, filled with elegance and grace, has always echoed in my ears, and only later did I realize how these final lines opened that window through which the popular Andalusian soul was to enter my own so completely.

>*. . . y por esas olitas de la mar*
>*que van y vienen,*

26

lléname mi casa
de salud y bienes.

. . . And through those little ripples of the sea
That come and go,
Fill my house
With health and wealth.

The good and most beautiful part of my mother's religious faith stemmed from its innocence, contaminated as it was by popular beliefs. For this reason, as I remember it today, her devoutness doesn't wound or offend me as does the ugly, inflexible, dirty and unpleasant bigotry displayed by the other members of my family. As a typical Andalusian woman educated within the confines of white-washed patios and gardens, my mother cultivated flowers; she knew all about grafting and pruning rosebushes, she knew by heart the often reinvented legends and myths about the narcissus, the passion-flower, the anemones and the stonecrop moss; she remembered the names of hundreds of small wildflowers which she would point out to me as we strolled through the fields on Sundays: the willow herb, the virgin slipper, St. Joseph's staff, foxtail, man's-word; during the month of August, she used to like to fall asleep at night at the foot of the jasmine, to the accompaniment of buzzing mosquitoes. I never did understand how she could possibly enjoy this, but I later discovered that it was a common enough pleasure among Andalusians.

She was, then, a strange and delicate woman who loved her saints and virgins as much as she loved her plants and fountains, the songs of Schubert—which she played on the piano—and the popular ballads and songs of southern Spain that she sang to me alone, perhaps because I was the only person in the house who felt an affinity for her tastes and beliefs.

During those years, we lived on Santo Domingo Street in a house with a red-tiled patio surrounding a huge orange tree that sprouted in the center. The tree was so tall that I always remember it as having its top branches pruned so they wouldn't tear the awning we had put up to protect us from the hot summer sun. The base of the tree was embraced by various rings of flowerpots, all filled with dark and succulent aspidistra. In a narrow cavity beneath the stairway which led from the patio to the second floor crouched the coal-bin, the dark and gloomy room where I first learned about punishment and terror.

Opposite this, but always locked, was the Nativity room, which was only opened a few days before Christmas by the one person who kept the key all year long—Federico.

Federico was a man from the village who used to decant wines in my father's ancient wine cellar. He was highly imaginative and also very fond of the liquid content in the barrels he himself crafted and polished. When Christmas Eve drew near, Federico, his eyes all bloodshot from imbibing so much sherry, would come to our house to take us to the woods along the coast in search of juniper, pine and mastic which were later to grow again on the miniature mountains and valleys which he had dreamed up and devised in his own mind. We were also accompanied by Centella, a little black dog with white markings on her forehead and paws who had been born the same day I was, but in the corner of a waterless cistern. Those woods belonged to the Duke of Medinaceli, as did many other palaces and mansions in the Puerto. The Duke of Medinaceli: how mysterious this name was to our budding imaginations!

"Who was he, Federico?"

The old man knew everything and he never kept any of it to himself.

"Well, the Duke of Medinaceli was a nobleman who singlehandedly, with his broad sword, went like this—whoosh—and drove all the Moors from the Puerto."

"And where did he send them?" we asked in amazement.

"Where do you think? Into the sea. The whole bay is filled with Moors, and that big pine tree over there, well—whoosh—he also cut it down with one fell swoop. Everything came tumbling down —towers, weathervanes, chimneys, birds' nests . . ."

"And why doesn't he come now with his sword to cut down that pine tree again?"

"Because the King won't let him; he's holding him prisoner in his own palace in Madrid."

We all remained silent, but not for long.

"Do you know the Duke?"

"Naturally! I've known him for more than a hundred years."

"Well how old are *you*, Federico?"

"You want to know how old I am, children? Fifty-seven, that's how old I am."

There was another moment of silence. Then; "Does papa know him, too?"

"No, because the Duke never went to Galicia."

"Where is Galicia?"

"Across the sea. Far away from where the Duke lives."

"But papa also goes to Madrid."

"Only *I* know the Duke. But he'll never come back to the Puerto or even write to me again. The King has thrown him in jail."

"Didn't you say he was in his palace?"

"In his palace, yes, but it has been turned into the Ceuta Prison."

Baffled by his hermetic reply but afraid that Federico would refuse to answer any new questions, we followed along silently picking rosemary and breaking off mastic branches, all of us finally dividing up the load according to the size of each one's shoulders.

So we headed back home—my younger sister, whom we called Pipi, my sister Milagros and I, crushed by the weight of our bundles of Christmas branches, watched over by Federico who walked more slowly behind us, his head crowned with long pine branches like some Shakespearean warrior from the Birnam Wood. In this way we crossed over to the other side of the river on the San Alejandro Bridge and, like children of the forest, we walked along the main streets of the Puerto until we reached home. Naturally, Centella was still with us and always led the way.

In the evenings after dinner, the Nativity crèche was assembled. Federico was very proud of this Nativity scene which was entirely of his own invention. He would not accept anyone else's ideas, not from the children nor from the adults, and he became really angry when anybody dared to make a suggestion. The only assistance he accepted from us was to let us carry the shepherds and other figurines when he took them out of their boxes, and he would also allow us to place the trees and bushes or spread the sand along the fields and roads as long as we carefully followed his instructions; but when it came to the rest—keep your suggestions to yourself! And so that theatrical set made of paper glued to a wooden frame began to take shape before our astonished eyes like some divine miracle: ruffled mountain ridges which a brush dipped in white lead splattered with snow; that scene where a few miniature clay figures represented the mystery of the birth of Christ. The crèche conceived by Federico, the old man who decanted wines, appeared before us like a delicate and exquisite creation of pure Andalusian ingenuity.

My mother got along very well with Federico, but Paca Moy was afraid of him because he used to take off his coat and blacken his face with burnt cork in a perfect imitation of her that made us all laugh. Federico, sweaty and always a little drunk, looking at his Nativity, his whiskers covered with soot, would reinvent or improvise dances and Christmas carols to the accompaniment of a makeshift drum with all the skill and uneven spontaneity of a primitive minstrel. I remember a song from those days whose first lines I didn't understand until much later. The old man used to shout it out while he kicked his feet in the air in front of the portal of the newborn child of clay:

> *Acuéstate en el pozo,*
> *que vendrás cansado,*
> *y de mi no tengas*
> *penas ni cuidados.*

> *Come, lie down in the dew;*
> *You must be tired and weary.*
> *My pains and cares are few,*
> *No need for you to worry.*

Whenever this little stanza came back to me during my early youth and adolescence, I never could figure out why the Virgin Mary would tell her husband St. Joseph to lie down on the wet ground.

Come, lie down in the dew . . .

Finally its meaning became unexpectedly clear to me one day. I was leafing through the book *Popular Spanish Folk Songs* by Francisco Rodríguez Marín, and stopped to look at the section devoted to Christmas songs and carols. Suddenly, on turning the page, I came across the same verse that Federico had re-composed in that absurd and poetic style so typically Andalusian:

> *Acuéstate, esposo,*
> *que vendrás cansado . . .*

> *Come, lie down, my husband, do,*
> *You must be tired and weary . . .*

Federico had unconsciously made this unexpected transformation and thus created a surprising variant, the basis of the freshness and diversity of all truly popular literature.

30

In those days I also learned a ballad which contained a word with a particular ending that made a great impression on me:

Más arribita hay un huerto
y en el huerto un naranjel . . .

A little ways up there's an orchard,
And in the orchard an orangel . . .

Orangel! Orangels! A delicate Andalusian variant which we, García Lorca and I, would use so often in our early poems!

Christmas, with its Nativity scenes, occupies extensive, hazy zones in my childhood dreams.

We had a great-uncle—the brother of Don Agustín, my mother's father—who was a marvelous crackpot, inventive, affable, eccentric: Uncle Vicente! Never will I grow tired of remembering him and finding in him endless inspiration and material for my theatrical poetry, both lyrical and dramatic.

My Uncle Vicente willingly spent sleepless nights worrying about his daughter whose advanced state of spinsterhood was leading her slowly but surely in the direction of a strange love for saints and for the poor gypsies who lived in the shabbier sections of town. Every year my uncle made a Nativity crèche for Aunt Josefa and her ragged students, since out of sheer pity she had started a school for gypsies which was housed in a little room on the ground floor of her own house. This crèche was surely the strangest, most extraordinary one to be found in the entire Puerto in those days. Uncle Vicente himself, with his flat, yellow fingers, molded the clay figures—the shepherds and their flocks, the Holy Family, the Three Wise Men—as well as the vegetation which was to serve as the scenic background for the presentation of the Mystery. He later set the clay figures on the terrace to dry and harden. All of us—Paquillo, the coachman's son, my brothers, sisters, cousins, and I—helped him to color the strange prehistoric figures that his hands were turning out, using oil paints diluted with turpentine. I remember one afternoon when I took advantage of my uncle's temporary absence to model a camel on my own. I then timidly showed it to him. It must have struck him as being not too bad, because that very night it was included in the group of kings he had made which were lined up along the road leading to the stable of the newborn God-child.

31

My great-uncle's Nativity crèche was completely different from Federico's. In the old peasant's creation, the mastic trees, the pines, the rivers that flowed with real water or water simulated by pieces of quartz, the shiny stars made from candy wrappers, the cotton or white-lead snow, all glowed in a warm, intimately poetic atmosphere which even today I remember with nostalgia. In Uncle Vicente's Nativity, however, everything was harsh and frozen, hard as a petrified planet. Only mud trickled through his torpid little rivers and streams; the trees and plants on the hillside were pale and insipid, as were the cereal-like grasses that cast a muddy color over the orchards strewn with rocks and encircled everywhere by footpaths. What a sad Nativity, made from mud hardened by a merciless sun! How unappetizing was this birth of Christ which the gypsies stared at night after night with blank expressions in their huge dark eyes!

My Uncle Vicente lived in a quiet, rundown house on Fernán Caballero Street. The family was progressively occupying less and less space while cracks and crevices were opening everywhere in the house. They withdrew little by little during the period I describe here, until finally they only had use of two or three bedrooms, a hallway, and an ugly dining-room that looked out on a large terrace. The rest of the house, the living-room and the other bedrooms where several of my uncle's nieces and nephews had lived before they had gone off to get married, were now just mounds of rubble through which one could descend to a dark cellar that had become the lair of horrendous spiders. A gloomy, mysterious house full of frightening things! None of us dared to go there alone, and we would only appear if Mama was with us or if we were accompanied by some other adult who helped us overcome our sense of panic as we climbed up that dark, creaking stairway blanketed by layers of sand which had fallen from the ceiling. That house, like the family that lived within it, fell apart bit by bit, more and more each day, until it finally reached a state of complete ruin. When in 1919 I returned to the Puerto after a three-year absence, I discovered that Uncle Vicente's old house was only a single wall with its windows open to the sky. At that time I thought again about my uncle who to me had always been an extraordinary figure—full of dignity and at the same time half crazy. Standing before the ashes of his past, my eyes became filled with the shadow of his presence. A patchwork of memories and stories of his life which he himself would tell us in the late afternoons, as he played with that eternal parrot of his, resounded in my ears. My Uncle Vicente had traveled from one end of Europe to the other in a stagecoach, on his way to Russia.

"In the olden days, children, just like now in the Sierra Morena around Córdoba, there were bands of robbers all over the world. I was on my way to the court of the Russian Czar on a business trip for the winery. After making my way through Spain, France and Germany, having changed mules and horses thousands of times at the post-stations along the way, I reached the first Polish inn. Poland is now a part of Russia and it is very far away. It was winter. At dawn I was to continue my trip. After dinner the innkeeper accompanied me to my room, and I asked him to awaken me a half-hour before the stagecoach was due to leave. I was very tired. But when by candle-light I pulled down the cover on the bed where I was supposed to sleep, I saw with disgust that the sheets were torn and dirty. I decided then to sleep in a big, broken-down armchair that had been placed in a corner of the room. It was so uncomfortable that in spite of my fatigue I couldn't get to sleep, although I kept my eyes closed as long as I could.

"There I am, exhausted but wide awake, when suddenly I hear a strange noise nearby, a scratching sound—but I can't figure out where it's coming from. I opened my eyes. The wick end of a candle I had inadvertently left burning threw a flickering light onto the bed. Suddenly an object fell right in the center of the bed and disappeared silently. Then something else fell on the pillow and slid down. I could not imagine what it was. I brought the candle over closer to the bed. Horrors! [My uncle used to speak like a character in a romantic novel.] Two large daggers. The first had penetrated the bedcovers up to the hilt, and the second one was stretched out like a cross between the pillow and the open covers; that is, the first one had been aimed at my heart and the other one at my belly. I spent the rest of the night reciting Hail Marys and offering up other prayers to Our Lady of Miracles for having saved me from that catastrophe.

"I left my room at dawn without waiting for the innkeeper's knock and I then paid him what I owed, cheerfully, as if nothing had happened. At the last moment, right before the sleigh pulled out on its way to Warsaw, I merely gave him the following piece of advice: 'My friend, be sure your sheets are a little cleaner when I come back this way.' And I disappeared, leaving him standing there in the snow, stupefied."

Uncle Vicente knew many different languages, including Arabic and Hebrew. He tried to teach me English, using as a text a grammar book divided into forty lessons which told the story of the Sultan Mohammed. This sultan, from what I can remember, wanted to learn the marvelous language of the birds from his vizier who understood it perfectly. Even today, at the age of 36, I can still repeat from memory the first seven or eight chapters of that book: "We are told that the Sultan Mamuth ..."

During these classes my uncle often spoke to me of things which were somewhat unsuitable for a boy of my age, but I didn't understand their meaning or his intentions until much later. He was a bitter enemy of Voltaire, whom he denounced as being "godless"; he was obsessed with what he claimed were the sacrilegious activities perpetrated by the Masons; but the man who revolted him most was Emile Zola. One day he joyfully and vividly described the death of this great writer:

"He was suffocated by the fumes of a brazier, sitting there in his own shit, just as he had lived. All his filthy, disgusting novels have been banned by the Catholic Church and are on the Index. I am telling you this for your own good, just in case you ever come across them."

My poor naive and fanatical uncle! I can see you now, tonight, while the war rains down on us, half-dead with cold as you move through the heavenly spheres, with your head framed by a halo of birds and that old imperial parrot you loved so much perched on your shoulder. You are frightened. If you look down on Spanish soil, that land you traversed so many times by stagecoach when you were young, you will see it now full of brilliant lights, you will hear it now rocked by explosions, torn open by immense craters echoing the sounds of blood. Perhaps Zola and Voltaire are pursuing you, waiting to ask you certain harsh and ironic questions which you are afraid to hear, so you try to dodge them by quickening your airy pace. I too would like to say something to you, uncle: What? You won't listen? You're covering your ears? This is your nephew shouting to you. From Madrid. You won't come down? Are you on your way to Cádiz? To Sevilla or Burgos? (Barcelona has fallen tonight.) Are you going away? You don't even want to see me! You are ashamed of me, uncle! My poor, sad uncle! Adieu! Voltaire and Zola understand me.

It is probably becoming obvious that what worried my family

most was our religious education, our formation within the most rigid principles of the Catholic faith with all its annoying consequences. My parents, aunts, uncles and all the other relatives preferred a perfect recitation of a Hail Mary or The Lord's Prayer to a decent demonstration of our ability to read or write, skills they considered secondary to the salvation of one's soul. This explains why my Uncle Javier, for example, when he was in his twenties, knew to perfection all the obligations of a Christian even though during Mass he held the prayerbook upside down while his illiterate forehead was tightly creased in an expression of sweet suffering. A pupil would come out of those Andalusian schools, both on the elementary and secondary levels, with his head crammed only with The Lord's Prayer, the memory of horrifying sermons, and such an accumulation of spelling mistakes and misinformation that even when I reached the age of twenty, having already spent five of those years in Madrid, I would blush with shame when I discovered the elementary knowledge possessed by any eleven-year-old kid who had attended the *Instituto* or some other respectable educational institution. Sad, pitiful generations of young Spaniards trained in such dens of corruption, incubated in these filthy and mediocre caves of learning!

Even though I now detest and despise stupid, anti-religious boasting, which if not worse is at least as unpleasant and unenlightened as the most narrow-minded religious bigotry, I am compelled once more to put in writing the repugnance I feel for this Spanish Catholic spirit, this reactionary and savage Catholicism that darkened the blueness of the sky from the days of our childhood, covering us with layers and layers of gray ashes which only served to muffle any real creative intelligence we might have had. How many arms and anguished lungs have we seen struggling frantically and hopelessly to escape from these depths, without ever having grasped even a momentary fistful of sun? How many entire families drowned or buried alive? What a hideous inheritance of rubble and suffocation! Those whom I loved most during my childhood and adolescent years float at the bottom of those sad ashes, lost forever, and I have now abandoned all hope of one day seeing them standing firmly on the surface of the light. All of them flounder in those unhappy seas, gasping for breath—my brothers and sisters, my cousins, swarms of former school friends and, even worse, admired teachers, members of my literary generation, people whose echoing presence I still feel within myself and whose voices and gestures I recognize in my own being. Ultimately, the fate of Ortega y Gasset and Pérez de Ayala, former students of Jesuit schools, was no different than that of my slightly demented Aunt Josefa or any Falangist or right-wing cousin of mine, all of whom were disciples of the Society of Jesus and also great admirers of Francisco Franco. Such a sad descent of the stars, of lights we thought were stars, which, having dizzily fallen to the level of latrines, finally disappeared, accompanied by the sounds of gushing water and the pulling of chains, into well-deserved black wells!

But I was by this time too grown up and "manly" to be in school with girls and have the beautiful Sister Jacoba and the always happy Sister Visitación take me to the little back room and pull down my pants so that I could pee or even do other, grosser things. For that reason my mother sent me to Doña Concha's school. What I remember most about Doña Concha was her hatred for the Carmelite Sisters and all the other elementary schools in town. This old lady believed, economically speaking, that all the children in the Puerto should be pupils of hers. With Doña Concha I learned something about religious history, and was very impressed with the story of Joseph who was sold by his brothers to the merchants of Egypt; I found out about addition and multiplication, but nothing at all about division and subtraction; I even managed to recite Ripalda's Catechism with a crisp Castilian pronounciation, a very difficult feat for any Andalusian child. The strongest criticism my new teacher had for the little nuns stemmed from just that: the lack of proper diction on the part of all those innocent children who had been under the protection and tutelage of the "blue aprons." Diction was important; if not, why did the Catechism mention this in its first section? To poke fun at it?

> . . . *To be well pronounced,*
> *Well believed and well performed,*
> *Let us say it as follows:*
> *"Our Father," etc. . . .*

"Well pronounced! Well pronounced! Do you hear?" she scolded me in her unpleasant way. "If the Catechism itself demands it, how could an Order that claims to be religious allow all those z's or *th* sounds to be pronounced like s's; and all those obvious b's, as in *book*, to sound like v's?"

Mientras la niña lavaba,
A la abuela se le caía la baba.

While the little girl washed,
The grandmother drooled.

"Those lines," this disagreeable woman continued, "which any student of mine can recite to perfection, could never be said correctly by a disciple of the Carmelites."

And this was the truth, although it wasn't really our fault. It seemed to me and the other children, accustomed as we were to the free Andalusian pronounciation, that it was all totally ridiculous, that it was sad and comic to hear ourselves reading aloud in front of the imposing and somewhat mustachioed Doña Concha any passage from the Holy Scriptures or from one of those idiotic fables that filled our fresh, infantile imagination with so much hot air:

Jugando Pepe en la huerta
con su hermanito Lisardo,
cogió del suelo un erizo*
que se cayó del castaño . . .

While Pepe was playing in the garden
With his little brother Lisardo,
He picked from the ground a hedgehog
That had fallen from a chestnut tree . . .

Wrapped in a gummy green smock which she had inherited from her beloved godmother, an old·lady long since deceased who watched over the school from the heights of a ghastly portrait, Doña Concha used to observe me during the long hours of silence with a special gray look in her eyes which I could barely stand. At other times she would come zooming up behind me like an arrow to catch me drawing those boring little sketches, products of an infantile melancholy, which I used to doodle in the white margins of my textbooks. She was almost always disagreeable and rather cool toward me. Her attitude was perhaps due to the hatred she felt for the nuns or to the discount on the monthly matriculation fees which she

---

*The Spanish word *erizo* has the dual meaning of "hedgehog" and "bur."

granted to my family because of our declining economic status. As a result of certain feelings of inferiority which I sensed in the atmosphere, I was in mortal terror of this teacher and also experienced a pleasant lack of interest in anything that might be beneficial to my intellectual growth. Besides, I felt a certain sad, dull anger which was really a mixture of admiration and envy toward my first cousins, who were also pupils of Doña Concha but were more favored by her because of their large estates and their magnificent carriages with sleek horses that were always at her disposal for afternoon rides, when school was out and the well-pronounced lessons were over.

To get even with that ugly lady, I mentally recited a strange tongue-twister dedicated to her and which I would think of every time I saw her, even when I was in the midst of parroting the rosary. I had chosen this particular ditty from the many I had heard my mother recite, and even today I am convinced that it perfectly and delightfully described Doña Concha:

> Doña Dírriga, Dárriga, Dórriga,
> trompa pitárriga,
> tiene unos guantes
> de pellejo de zírriga, zárriga, zórriga,*
> trompa pitárriga,
> le vienen grandes.

> Doña Dírriga, Dárriga, Dórriga,
> With her wheezing nose,
> Has a pair of gloves
> of zírriga, zárriga, zórriga
> And a wheezing nose
> That are much too big.

Doña Concha probably didn't have any zórriga gloves, or any other kind, for that matter, but those wonderful-sounding names of Dírriga, Dárriga seemed just right for her, particularly when she appeared all decked out in her flowing green smock. In addition, this was the only way my sadness and anger as a secretly offended ex-student of the Carmelite Sisters could be avenged.

*The fabricated words zúrriga, zárriga, zórriga are formed on the Spanish zorro, fox in English.

At least things were more bearable after I got home in the afternoon, when Pepilla, the washerwoman, would take my "little pistol" out of my pants and, tying a string to it, would amuse herself by leading me around the laundry room covered with white soapsuds, among the mounds of recently washed clothes that smelled of bleach.

"Pitárriga! Pistolárriga!" And that strange metallic green I have never forgotten.

It was then that my mother sent me to San Luis Gonzaga, a school run by the Society of Jesus, where I was to continue my religious education.

At that time I was probably no more than ten years old.

CHAPTER II

AS A RESULT of some kind of revolutionary uprising that took place in Spain around the middle of the nineteenth century—my great-uncle Vicente blamed it all on the Masons —the Jesuits in the Puerto had to abandon their recently founded school temporarily, and many of them took refuge in the wealthiest homes of Cádiz or in other towns scattered around the bay. My family had been among the most delighted to welcome a large number of those extremely bright and frightened religious fathers, whose no less acute descendants were later to become my severe and even cruel teachers. In gratitude for that undercover assistance from the rich, the members of the Society of Jesus decided to open a free day school for the children of the Puerto. It was there that my mother took me and it was there that, along with the usual and justified childish horsing-around and skipping of classes, I was to suffer a series of humiliations and bitter resentments which I remember to this day with deep feelings of rancor.

San Luis Gonzaga was a very beautiful school. Due to its huge size and large enrollments, it was known throughout Spain as "*El colegio grande,*" "The Big School," whereas Chamartín de la Rosa in Madrid had attained the distinction of being called "*El gran colegio*"—that is, "The Great School"—because of the aristocratic background of many of the students enrolled there. A very revealing differentiation this, well within the spirit and letter of the Society of Jesus.

The location of San Luis Gonzaga on the outskirts of the city was truly magnificent. It was bordered on one side by the old San Francisco Plaza with its magnolia trees and araucaria pines, situated close to the bullring from which, on those Sunday afternoons in the spring, the sounds of bugle blasts would reach those of us who were being punished by having to be in school that day; on another side of the school there was a long street lined with wine cellars that led to a common pasture ground where cows and young bulls grazed and awakened in me, as well as in other boys of the village, our vivid bullfighting fantasies; on the western side of the school was the beautiful Bay of Cádiz, where we could see the movement of seagulls and boats through the eucalyptus and palm trees as we stared out the windows during study periods.

The first morning I spent in that Jesuit palace is lost forever to my memory; but as every morning was more or less the same as the preceding one, I know I always showed up there half-asleep, since 6:30 in the morning in the dark of winter is not a particularly pleasant hour to attend Mass or go to Confession and then, on an empty stomach, have to open a math book. I can't remember if it was because of timidity or an exaggerated innocence on my part, but during the first year I was practically a model student: conscientious, studious, devout, filled with respect for my fellow students and teachers. In the awarding of prizes at the end of the year I was named second rank-leader.

It is common knowledge that the Jesuit schools are organized along military lines. Ours was made up of four divisions. Each of the top three corresponded to two years of study toward the baccalaureate degree, and in the lower division were the smaller children on the elementary and kindergarten levels. Those of us enrolled in the day school formed a separate division with our own study room. Our contacts with the boarding students took place only during the hours of instruction. The highest honor in the school was to be named Prince; the most modest was to be given the title of second rank-leader. Generally only the son of some local aristocrat, political boss or wealthy landowner could become Prince. The Jesuits always tried in one way or another to favor the people in the upper social strata. Those of us who were in day school, undoubtedly due to our accepted condition as inferior beings, could never aspire to such a post; we were only allowed to attain the rank of Brigadier, Quaestor, Edile, and Rank-Leader. The uniforms worn by those in the boarding school were dark blue with gold stripes sewn on the cap and trousers, but *we* only had our regular street clothes. Just as in the army, the officials wore stars and clusters on their sleeves, but our official ranks were indicated by various medallions, heavy and unsightly things that hung ridiculously from our necks over our democratic jackets. The certificates or diplomas that we fought for, and won either through industriousness or good behavior, were made of inferior cardboard with our names unevenly typed in, while those earned by the boarding students with evident ease were of parchment decorated with beautiful Gothic lettering. These major and minor differences were a source of pain to us, and as we grew more sensitive and our ability to reason became more highly developed, feelings of resentment began to ferment within us, an attitude to my mind not unlike what workers today feel toward their employers—that is, class hatred.

During this first year I also belonged—another honor—to the congregation of San Estanislao de Kostka, a little Jesuit saint who was probably pretty stupid, to judge by his appearance in the religious stamps and sculptured carvings of him I have seen. He, together with San Luis Gonzaga and San Juan Bergman, comprised the young angelical trinity of the Society. In every talk or sermon delivered to us, we were incited to follow the example of these three pale adolescents. Many of us felt closer to San Luis. An extremely chaste lily, the slim figure of Gonzaga, the patron saint of the school, awakened in us a certain mixture of admiration and obscure feelings which were very understandable in children of our age suffering from precocious as well as ambiguous desires. I see them now, each one of these three virtuous and sensitive creatures, framed in their respective and equally hideous chapels, the ogival Gothic arches highly varnished, the ridges resplendently covered by a coating of poor-grade gold leaf, the kind that in time turns a greenish-brown color and flakes, the pieces finally falling to the ground.

My religious education does not coincide with that great period of golden altars and cornucopia when gilt was applied under fire, but belongs instead to the decadent and lamentable era of false gold, of deceptive splendor, of mass-produced Sacred Hearts, and those ridiculous, highly "productive" miracles performed by Our Lady of Lourdes or the Christ of Limpias.

I offer below a list of examples which form a tragic, descending scale or ladder that reveals the decline of the creative Christian and later Catholic spirit whose bottom rung, the Jesuits, I reached on foot before my escape:

From the simple Beatitudes and "Glory to God in the highest, and peace on earth to men of good will," to the arrogant and partisan "I will reign on Spanish soil even more than in the rest of the world."

From the anguished, stately and celestial Gregorian chant to the idiotic lyrics of the Spanish Royal March, a typical product of the Society of Jesus's most recent poetic outburst.

> La virgen María
> es nuestra salvadora,
> nuestra bienhechora.
> No hay nada que temer.
> ¡Guerra al mundo,
> demonio y carne;
> guerra, guerra, guerra
> contra Lucifer!

> The Virgin Mary
> Is our savior,
> Our benefactor.
> There is nothing to fear.
> War to the world,
> Flesh and the Devil;
> War, war, war
> Against Lucifer!

From the Autos Sacramentales of Calderón to the "Divino Impaciente" of Pemán by way of the mystical-economic opportunism of Eduardo Marquina.

From the Escorial Monastery to the grotesque and unfinished Church of the Almudena in Madrid, or any of the recent Jesuit temples in Spain.

From the garnets, amethysts, emeralds, topaz and pearls on the Holy Robes to vulgar, dime-store costume jewelry made of dull, lifeless bottle-glass!

From the inspired, dedicated Spanish sculptures of religious imagery to the bourgeois mass-produced products—the ornate, "standard" Sacré Coeur with its violently red heart stamped on an undershirt.

From a glorious faith filled with thunder and lightning to the lowest form of hypocrisy and the most miserable kind of exploitation. In sum, from the purest gold of the stars to the purest of dry turds.

The very soul of the Society of Jesus was overflowing with this form of human matter when I entered their school in the Puerto. I suffered, I raged, I hated, I loved, I had fun, and I learned practically nothing during my four years there.

Who were my teachers, my initiators into the study of mathematics, Latin, history, etc.? I would like to leave behind a catalogue, not only of those Fathers and Brothers who were involved in my education, but also of those who occupied other positions at the school and with whom I had very little contact but would see occasionally in the corridors or strolling under the trees of the orchard.

Father Márquez, Professor of Religion, whom we called Balaam's Ass, undoubtedly because of his wisdom.

Father Salaverri, Professor of Latin, a Peruvian with the face of an Indian idol, who, because of his colorful complexion, had received the insulting nickname of Henrietta Redface, a popular prostitute in the Triana section of Sevilla. It was the Sevillian student Jorge Parladé who had originally invented the name.

Father Madrid, Professor of The Principles of Arithmetic and Geometry, pale-complexioned and completely overwhelmed by the love of his students.

Father Risco, Professor of Spanish Geography, an insipid poet and also author of nonsensical "educational" stories.

Father Romero, Professor of Spanish History, also deeply in love with his students. (This Father gave me such a whack once that if I were to meet him today I would return the favor with pleasure.)

Father Aguilar, the brother of a Count of Aguilar, Andalusian, a kind and understanding Jesuit, a man of the world who was gentle in his punishment and reprimands.

Father La Torre, Professor of Algebra and Trigonometry, graced with the name of "Father Puffed-Cheeks" because of his unpleasant, inflated jowls.

Father Hurtado, Professor of Chemistry, whose bony shoulders rising out of his broomstick frame were always covered with ashen dandruff.

Father Ropero, Professor of Natural History, half mad, whose handkerchief was always filled with miniature, electrified lizards he had collected under the sun in the garden which would jump out every time he blew his nose.

Father Zamarripa, the Rector, the maximum authority, a red-faced Basque, as cutting and frightening as a black sword and always showing up at the most inopportune moments.

Father Lirola, our Spiritual Father, sentimental and innocent, who always pressed the student souls that had gone astray against his distraught heart, holding them a bit more tightly than was absolutely necessary and always consoling them behind the closed doors of his room.

Father Ayala, the Prefect, dirty, his shoulders also covered with layers of dandruff; a dark, vigilant shadow who suddenly appeared on the scene without anyone having heard his approaching flannel-covered footsteps.

Father Fernández, conceited, elegant, flashy, perhaps the only Jesuit I remember who parted his hair. During the two years he had our division under his tutelage, he distinguished himself for his kindness toward me and his surprisingly unexpected delicate handling of our situation as nonpaying students.

Father Andrés, an unhappy martyr who suffered under our atrocious and barbarous behavior; he was the second in command of our division.

Father Lambertini, Italian, refined, sickly, a good man, my confessor, who always smelled of his breakfast coffee whenever I unburdened my sins.

Brother "Vegetables," so-called because he constantly and without any good reason sent us out to eat his nickname. (All of us third-year students knew and secretly talked about the fact that this Brother used to masturbate outside in the sun, alongside a secluded eucalyptus tree in the garden.)

I also remember the sick Brother, the gate-Brother, the gardener-Brother, and others I knew only by sight and to whom I had never spoken.

I can recall very few of my fellow classmates who began their studies when I did and were still there the year I left to move to Madrid with my family. They must not have made much of an impression on me since I can hardly remember their names. However, because of their unpleasantness and provincial vanity, I *do* remember some of the boarding students, like Jorge and Enrique Parladé from Sevilla—their father was a famous breeder of brave bulls—very well liked and flattered by the Jesuits and unjustly favored in class, although they were no brighter than a pair of Andalusian donkeys; there was Galnares Sagastizábal, also from Sevilla, puny and with his hair already plastered down, but very good in arithmetic; Guzmán, a Roman or Carthaginian Emperor in Latin class; Claudio Gómez from Córdoba, sour and dark, with his Riffian face, the son of some political boss from Montoro or Pozoblanco; José Ignacio Merello, my first cousin and my classmate in Doña Concha's school, but who changed quite a bit when he enrolled as a boarding student in San Luis Gonzaga and then made little effort to disguise his haughty attitude toward me, something I found sad and offensive since we had been such good friends, playing games and getting into mischief in the dark patios of the wine cellars; Eduardo Llosent, always with his brightly colored shirts and blinding ties; Sánchez Dalp, Ponce de León, Pemartín, Osborne, Estrada, all of them sons of rich wine merchants or landholders, the future owners of endless fields of vineyards and olive groves.

From among the day students, the proletarian student body, I remember the Bootello brothers, somewhat better treated than the rest of us because their father was the stationmaster in town—the Jesuits could obtain through him as an employee of the railroad some kind of discount during the June examination period, when the students of San Luis Gonzaga daily occupied the trains to Jérez where our yearly examinations were held; I remember José Murciano, who died one afternoon in March—we all went together with Father Fernández to bury him in a cemetery outside of town, on the road to San Lúcar; there was Gutiérrez, a rough, mean-tempered gypsy type who was not particularly proud of his father's profession as a veterinarian and horseshoer; and also Cantillo, small and always freezing, with his round starched collar and pink silk cravat, the son of a lieutenant in the Civil Guard; Porreyro, whose mother was said to be a prostitute on Jardines street; Juan Guilloto, the son of a slender and refined lady whose name was Milagros, and who I think was at one time a seamstress in our house. This Guilloto was slightly younger than I and he became, some twenty years later, the most worthy and extraordinary school friend I ever had, blotting out the memory and feelings I might have had for all the others who mean nothing to me now—merely a name, a physical characteristic, or some unimportant anecdote.

It happened in Madrid during the great heroic days of November

1936. The Fifth Regiment had asked me one rainy, bomb-dropping afternoon to recite some ballads and poems of mine on the defense of the capital, for a program to be broadcast over their radio station. In the hallway of that requisitioned mansion an officer in the Militia, a young major, stopped me suddenly as I was leaving.

"I know you very well," he said with an Andalusian accent as he placed a heavy hand on my shoulder. "My name is Modesto."

"Modesto! Who doesn't know you by reputation? But this is the first time I have ever actually seen you."

"I'm Jūan Guilloto, from the Puerto; we were together in the Jesuit school."

I embraced him, proudly. "If Father Andrés only knew! I'm sure no one in the Puerto suspects anything."

"Not even my parents know about it. The rebel press is always criticizing me: they have been calling me a party chief, an outlaw and even a Russian. What they don't know is that I am a barrelmaker from Cádiz!"

We went into a small sitting-room where we were served brandy. How wonderfully happy I was as a result of this unexpected surprise! I felt a kind of justified vanity, the pride of someone who has just discovered that something he knows will sooner or later bring him prestige; that young Andalusian was a hero, and yet at that moment I saw him only as a boy, a childhood friend of mine—the distant past suddenly took shape, becoming a lovely, pleasant reality filled with illuminated scenes of our forgotten youth.

What true Andalusian youngster has never dreamed of becoming a bullfighter? Behind the school building was a huge communal pasture where my Uncle José Luis de la Cuesta's cows and bulls used to graze. At the age of eleven, when a boy nourishes his dreams of becoming a *torero*, there is no such thing as fear. During math or Latin a few of us—Luis Bootello, José Antonio Benvenuti, Aranda, second- and third-year students at school—would go into the fields all set to separate one of the young bulls from the herd or take on the first animal that decided to charge. Although slightly younger than the rest of us, Juan Guilloto would sometimes join the group. Occasionally we were also accompanied by a slightly older gypsy boy who was called Blackie. We admired Blackie tremendously, since he had once jumped into the ring during a bullfight and had ended up in jail.

The moment arrived when we had to get the beast away from the herd. But the cowhands were watching over the animals and we had to distract them from their vigilance. A dangerous moment. The intrepid bullfighters approached the cattle individually, our pockets fiilled with stones and with a reserve supply of ammunition which Juan Guilloto was gathering up in his cap and storing away behind the conveniently placed clumps of broom. A whistle was the sign of attack. And before the guardians could defend themselves, the stones rained down on their unprepared heads, forcing them to run or throw themselves down on the ground to avoid being stoned to death. This maneuver also made it impossible for them to reply by aiming their slingshots at us. During the battle, whoever could manage it tried to separate a young bull from the herd, but at times the bull turned out to be a hideous cow, a horned locomotive who made us scatter to the winds, our frantic retreat blocked by the terrified herd as well as by a torrent of stones and insults.

Whenever we did manage to have a bullfight, it consisted of some awkward passes with a suit jacket, various spins and tumbles and a few well-placed kicks that were later transformed into painful aches and black bruises. In spite of the ensuing pain, those blows and contusions were like a badge of honor to us. We would think about the terrible gorings suffered by famous bullfighters which they had received in a delirium of fluttering fans and applause in the immense bullrings throughout Spain. And then there followed the illusory conversations and enthusiastic commentary. Such conversations were filled with words and expressions like "the bullring's dim, dark emergency room; iodine; the intestinal mass; gangrene; a fractured femur or instant death from shock(!)": a vocabulary we had picked up from reading bullfighting magazines and uttered at times with more fear than valor because of the mysterious connotation such expressions still had for the uninitiated and uninformed students that we were.

"We used to hold those bull sessions," recalled Modesto, "while we stuffed ourselves with prickly pears or green almonds stolen from the orchards, particularly those owned by your Uncle José Luis, that poor uncle of yours who always ended up being robbed the most."

"Like the day we practiced on a pregnant cow who finally aborted, sending Uncle José Luis racing furiously to complain to my mother, who then reported it to Father Ayala—all of which really endangered my bullfighting vocation."

"And also," continued Modesto, "the time Blackie stole a whole pile of onions and tomatoes from your uncle . . ."

". . . which he then smeared on my shoulder blades, making them look like a salad, in order to lessen the pain from that angry kick I got from a brown baby bull."

What a marvelous period in our lives, when we innocently and seriously dreamed of a future filled with glorious afternoons, our pictures appearing in magazines and our handsome faces displayed on matchboxes!

"But perhaps you don't know, Modesto, how my bullfighting pretensions finally turned out. You remember Manolillo, the barber on Luna Street, a real *aficionado* of the bulls. One day while he was shearing me, he had the bright idea that I ought to have a *coleta*. So that day I left his shop with a tuft of hair protruding from under the top' of my head like the budding shoot of a garbanzo bean. At first nobody noticed and I only told Benvenuti about it, showing it off to him proudly since of all of us he was the most serious about his future as a bullfighter. Two months later that growth had really sprouted so that I could hardly ever take off my cap. In class I covered it up with my hand and in that way I acquired the look of an extremely pensive student, a posture that awakened all kinds of suspicion. But the day finally arrived when my secret was out in the open. I was denounced in my French class, accused by one of the boarding students who sat behind me. I had been careless—an indiscretion on the part of the hand I had been using as a cover. The accusing student couldn't help but notice. That indecent thing hanging there was already quite a sight, but how embarrassing it was to hear his loud guffaw."

"'What's the meaning of that noise?'

"'Look, Father Aguilar!'

"Father Aguilar stood up, with a severe questioning expression on his face, but he didn't come down off the podium."

"'Explain, this instant, the reason for your laughter!'

"'Alberti's *coleta*! Look, look!'

"Tremendous confusion. The whole class up on its feet. And Father Aguilar's stare, hard as a bullfighter's sword, penetrated to my very soul. The embarrassment I felt made me blush to the roots of that threatened taurine symbol which I still kept trying to hide behind my trembling fingers."

"'Silence!' commanded the French professor."

"Then Benvenuti, who was sitting next to me, took out a dull, rusty penknife that had *Domecq Brandy* written across the face of it and cut my braid with a terrible, unforgivable tug, throwing the trophy onto Father Aguilar's desk. The latter, with an uncontrollable gesture of disgust, tossed it into the wastepaper basket. Without my *coleta* I felt defeated and old, like some tragic fifty-year-old *torero* who has outlived his triumphs."

"I didn't know anything about that," said Modesto, laughing noisily. "I was only with the Jesuits for a year. My parents were poor; they needed my help. I got a job in the wine cellars of Don Edmundo Grant, where I was fired six months later. I then went to work at Lucuy's drugstore on the corner of Larga and Palacios, remember? There I learned how to make flu capsules. But they also kicked me out of there for playing games with those glass funnels pharmacists use. I would toss coins at them from a distance and I finally broke a few. Lucuy tossed *me* out on my ear."

Modesto, without even realizing it himself, began to relate the story of his life, which he told in the style of a *Lazarillo de Tormes* or some other picaresque character: the amusing and bittersweet life of a Spanish child of the people, always the hero of anonymous poverty and legendary acts of prowess.

"I changed my career from pharmacist to barrel-maker, working as an apprentice in the mill that belonged to Don José María Pastor. I worked there until I was called to military service, and then went to Cádiz where I enlisted in the first Coastal Artillery Regiment. Because I ran off to the Puerto without leave one day, I was punished by six months of imprisonment. But since my situation was awkward after that incident, I and a few other companions requested and received permission to go to Africa, and I even earned my corporal's stripes in the Fourth Group of the Larache National Guard. But I got drunk once and lost these stripes soon afterwards. My period of service was running out anyhow, and I was supposed to be discharged before too long, but under the pretext of my drunkenness and a stupid argument with a civil guard I was exiled to a forced work camp instead of returning home. One day, bored and fed up, I escaped—naturally without papers of any kind; my usual bad luck stayed with me, however, because as soon as the ship reached Cádiz I was grabbed and thrown into jail at infantry headquarters. After a few months, having earned the trust of some of the guards, I asked for permission to eat outside—granted. And quick as a bird I grabbed the first train for the Puerto, taking my final leave from the armed forces."

In Paris I continue to write these memoirs, the beloved memories of my early years in this world, in the sweet, sad and happy lost grove of my childhood. It is now 4:05 in the morning, October 6. War again. Good Lord, how short the vacation was! When I had barely begun to understand again what it was like to walk calmly through a city of lights, all of France is suddenly blacked out, the sirens screaming in Paris and the sound of cannons booming along the Maginot Line. I have been living here since March 12. On March 6 I left Spain, my precious and unfortunate Spain, headed for Orán ("I served the King in Orán . . ."*). I took the heavenly route, traveling by plane through the skies. In the town of Elda, the last official stop for the government of the Republic, I saw Modesto; I also saw Dr. Negrín. It was the last time we were to see Modesto. In the small garden adjoining the house of Generals Hidalgo de Cisneros and Cordón where María Teresa and I were staying, Modesto performed for us on that deceptively peaceful and tranquil night some flamenco dance steps—"bulerías"—in the magnificent style of the very best gypsy dancer. He laughed. "One day, when we are alone, we will dance. But we will have to be alone," he repeated looking around him. Early the next morning the Fort at Cartagena rebelled and raised the flag of the Monarchy on its ramparts. Hours later, in Madrid, Colonel Segismundo Casado rose up against the government of Negrín, making a gift to Franco of our strong, beloved, invincible and heroic capital that was to be a constant source of amazement to the world for more than two years. On the way to Orán we got lost and our plane almost came down in Melilla. Minutes after we had landed in Orán, another plane taxied into the same airport carrying La Pasionaria. The heart of Spain had been sold—betrayed once again.

With my soul filled with the memory of so much noble blood and my ears ringing from the explosions they had heard, I walked the streets of Paris and lived with the truly great and human Pablo Neruda, a veritable guardian angel of the Spaniards, in his house on the banks of the Seine: 31 Quai de l'Horloge. Toward the middle of August, in order to

---

*"Servía en Orán al rey" is the first line of a ballad or *romance* by Luis de Góngora y Argote (1561–1627), which recounts the story of a soldier who suffers a conflict between his loyalty to the king and his desire to remain in bed with his mistress when, in the middle of the night, the call to battle is sounded.

keep from dying of hunger as well as to avoid being any further burden to the fearful and not overly generous French, María Teresa and I accepted an offer from the Paris-Mondial radio station to translate their broadcasts to Latin America into Spanish. We obtained the job through the auspices and on the recommendation of Pablo Picasso. What did I actually accomplish during all these months? What did I produce? Hardly anything at all. I only saw many good Spaniards die of starvation and persecution, and I witnessed the departure from Europe of many close friends. But some day I will talk about all this. The present is too harsh, too sad to write about now. I wish to go back to those other days of my childhood, on the shores of the Gulf of Cádiz, letting the undulating pine trees along the coast clear my mind and feel my shoes fill with sand, the blonde sand of the burning dunes shaded here and there by clumps of Spanish broom.

The dunes! In my third year I decided to find out what it would be like to enjoy myself by playing hooky from my classes. The dunes, with their golden, shifting sands, became my fiery place of refuge during math period and those dull afternoon Rosary sessions. We sat beneath trees shaped like huge green bowls and known locally as "transparents," probably due to the shape of their long, widely-spaced branches only sparsely covered by leaves. To us these trees were our tents or cabañas, and after burying our clothes and books we would run stark naked down to the shore—totally free of theorems and equations. The Gulf of Cádiz! What a sense of harmony and dazzling light is awakened by the sound of those words! Blinding, too, is Lope's Sonnet:

> *Esparcido el cabello por la espalda,*
> *que fué del sol desprecio y maravilla,*
> *Silvia cogía por la verde orilla*
> *del mar de Cádiz conchas en su falda.*

> Her hair a marvel that scorned the sun,
> Spread out across her shoulders,
> Sylvia gathered shells in her skirt
> Along the green banks of the Cádiz Sea.

Only the very good, the very foolish or the very blind children of the school never knew those radiant hours filled with wind and salt, vibrant with the whiteness of the salt flats out there in Puerto Real and La Isla, sufficient to bathe an entire life in an infinite blue light which one's eyes would never forget. *When I die—that is, if some European bomb doesn't send my body flying into oblivion—let them open my eyes gently; they will see their fingers and nails become whitened by sea spray and fine sand, and in my pupils, like two tiny crystal coves, they will find the round and perfect bay dotted with sailboats and encircled by my beautiful cities with their shimmering masts and chimneys.*

"Look, he's already got hair."

"Well, he's older than you are."

"That's right; I'm twelve."

"I've got something else to show; you want to see it?"

With a mixture of curiosity and embarrassment, because we already knew what was going to happen, we said yes. All of us, nude as we were, sat in a circle at the door of our tree shelter. The student who had spoken sat in the center of the circle. No one else made a sound. Sitting down, the boy had said very slowly: "I'm in my fifth year and I'm taking a course in physiology." No one understood why he had chosen that day to join our group of second- and third-year students in our illicit leave of absence from classes nor why he had so proudly mentioned that fifth-year course.

Physiology! A strange word, with its suggestions of forbidden fruit. Wasn't that all about nude women? And if that were true, how could they allow it to be taught in a Christian school? We didn't remember where, but we all thought we had once gotten a glimpse of some large pink charts depicting dissected female bodies with captions that read: Physiology I, Physiology II . . .

We all looked on silently as this student, with a sad expression on his face and his eyes looking off into the distance, began to move his fist up and down in the darkened regions of his crotch, his fingers still covered with wet, warm sand. Gently pulsating, the "lion's nail" licked his thighs. Oh, how long would it be before that miracle also emerged from us? We were only in our second or third year, students of history and Latin; we wouldn't be studying physiology for at least another two or three years—but then! . . .

We all returned home that afternoon sad and pensive. No one said anything along the way. After that, the physiology student was very reserved toward us and he never joined us again on the dunes.

One day, after we had spent the previous one cutting classes and playing on the beach as usual with our clothes off, trying at times to reproduce the miracle we had seen performed by the fifth-year student, the Spiritual Father of the school unexpectedly asked to see me in his room.

"My child," he murmured, after he had locked the door and made me rest my head against his chest, "I am very annoyed with you. If your poor Uncle Vicente, saintly man that he is, should ever find out! What you and those other little devils are doing is one of the worst sins a child can commit. Do you think I don't know about it?"

"Know about what, Father?" I dared to ask him, terrified, and suddenly remembering the physiology student.

"Nothing at all. I am ashamed to mention it."

And he pressed me more firmly against his cassock, kissing me on the forehead.

"Father!" I whispered, frightened to death.

"God has seen you all. He has seen *you* in particular."

There was a sad silence filled with the buzzing of flies. The Spiritual Father continued. He had one of my ears pressed against the buttons of his cassock and with his arm he had unwittingly covered up the other, so his voice reached me from far away, as if he were standing behind a padded wall.

"What do you hope to gain from that, my child? You are only displeasing Him and me. But it isn't only a question of damaging your soul, but also of doing something that is very bad for your body. Do you promise you won't do it again? The Prefect doesn't know anything about it. You would be expelled from school if I were to tell him. You promise? If your poor Uncle Vicente should ever find out!"

That very night a sixth-year student told my brother Agustín everything, and Agustín later had a very serious talk with me about it, although he was probably biting his tongue to keep from laughing the whole time he spoke: "Father Hurtado saw all of you through his spyglass from the window of the physics lab."

The news spread among the accused, causing great panic and fear. It was true: pointing in the direction of Cádiz, a large, long-range telescope could be seen peering out of one of the windows overlooking the orchard.

From that moment on, our vacations from class were spent at a different spot on the dunes where we couldn't even see the lighting-rods on the school roof. Although, as I have said, I used to cut many classes, I generally never missed my Spanish history class. We were studying a work written in a very florid and pleasant style by a professor of the Instituto in Cádiz, Moreno Espinosa. My particular specialty was dates. There was no battle whose date I didn't know. And without realizing it, I was instrumental in forcing the other students to learn them as well.

"Anyone who doesn't know the dates by heart on the final exams will fail the course," threatened Father Romero, our history professor. One day when I had been locked in his classroom for a few hours because I had done something wrong—although I can't remember what it was—in captivity I wrote on the blackboard the place and date of every battle that had ever taken place in the entire history of Spain.

My classmates hated me. There were many failing grades on the exam, but I got an A and a recommendation for Honorary Mention.

I still remember entire rhetorical and sonorous paragraphs from that metaphoric book, and I have always successfully quoted them during those frequent and amusing conversations we used to have about the stupidity or the ingenuousness of the textbooks assigned to us in our youth. Moreno Espinosa was roundly sententious when he wrote about the Phoenicians: ". . . and all this happened in the time of the immoral and corrupt Sardanapalus and the lustful Semíramis." In the same lesson was this final rhythmic sentence that the whole class loved to sing: ". . . because they brought to us the alphabet on their tongues, brought money on their fingers, and in the sails of their ships brought civilizing breezes from the Orient."

Lines and entire pages from other textbooks, even those that go way back to my early childhood, dance in my memory, and I still enjoy reciting them to myself. I remember an excerpt from *Juanito*, a book which dates from the period I spent in the Carmelite school: "No, no. I must not sleep. My Cecilia is very sick; she has been bitten by a snake. . . . I would be a bad mother if I went to sleep. . . . No, no. . . ."

And also another selection from this same incomparable, archangelical book. Juanito, who was a very bad boy, one day climbed over a wall and stole the most beautiful pear in the orchard. But when he was strolling away, having hidden the stolen object, he heard a mysterious voice that shouted to him: "God has seen you, *picaruelo!*"*

Picaruelo is the diminutive form of *pícaro*, the name given to the protagonist of the Spanish picaresque novel and more or less synonymous in meaning with the English

Of all the little phrases that continue to spin around in my mind, this last one is my favorite, particularly the delightful diminutive: *picaruelo.*

There are other words I learned then that make me happy every time I come across them. Does anything more delightful and ridiculous exist in our language than the descriptive nouns *badaluque,* and *mentecato,* or even the exclamation *cáspita?* * Like all authors I have my preferences and my dislikes. From a very tender age I have felt a special antipathy and strong aversion toward the noun "voluptuousness" and particularly toward its adjectival form, "voluptuous." How disgusting! My whole mouth fills with saliva and my toenails curl every time I hear the word or see it written. Even in French it's enough to make you sick. Only Baudelaire has been able to make the word acceptable to me, in one of his verses from the "Invitation au Voyage":

> *Là, tout n'est qu'ordre et beauté,*
> *Luxe, calme et volupté.*

I also detest the noun *terruño.** You'll never find these odious words in anything I have ever written, either in my poetry or my plays. And I swear never to defile any future page of mine with their presence. But I did defile my soul very frequently while attending the Jesuit school of San Luis Gonzaga, as I have already mentioned —with examples—by sinning against chastity, a sin necessarily related to that of lying. My second spiritual counselor was the Italian Father Lambertini. How many times, after squeezing from me the confession of my sins, did he reprimand me in his harsh and rhetorical fashion!

"If you could only see your soul, you would die of horror. Yours is filthy, just like a Bishop's stole all splattered with mud. Because if the soul is darkened by lustful behavior, lying makes it even blacker. You sin and you refuse to admit your error. You are thus committing a double sin."

Paquillo, the coachman's son, was then my companion in sin. The setting always had the form of a window, a type of open skylight in a

---

word "rogue"; *badaluque* is a colloquial synonym for "fool"; *mentecato* is another synonym for "simpleton"; ¡*cáspita!* is an exclamation of admiration; *terruño* is a clump of earth and, by extension, one's native soil.

greenish roof. We used to climb up to it mysteriously, late in the afternoon, and we would crouch alongside that piece of glass as though sitting on the edge of a puddle. We did this on Sundays during vacation, at my Uncle Vicente's house. We would hold our breath and wait, almost suffocating with excitement. Sometimes nothing happened. The glass would get darker and darker, paralleling the night and reflecting the light of the first star. But when what we were waiting for finally happened—ah! Then the illumination rose from below, sending up a glow like a candle submerged at the bottom of a pool. And there, beneath us, framed against the pale yellow glow of a rattan mat, was my Aunt Josefita, still young, changing her clothes and revealing herself to us for a few short seconds, dressed in a slip—a long, sad slip. Overwhelmed and mute, the coachman's son and I stayed up there on the roof until suppertime.

Chastity! Chastity! In that atmosphere of insane Catholicism and exaggerated bigotry, how was it possible not to always have before one's eyes, filled with fear and sweetness at the same time, the fleeting image of one's sister or mother undressing, or that of a cousin and a sister suddenly discovered urinating together, a broad smile on their faces, behind the rockroses in the Pinar del Obispo or half-hidden by the clumps of broom along the beach?

God, how sinful! Impossible to mention it to Father Lambertini the next day without trembling. How were we to answer his insistent question which we were always afraid to hear: "Have you sinned against chastity, and how often?" Horrors! Horrors!

"No, Father, no. I haven't done that for a long time. That's the truth."

Lying, then, was our only defense, the only way to soothe our confessor's anger and to be able to approach the confessional, terrified and with a sense of sacrilege.

In Andalusia, masturbating is called "tossing a straw" (hacerse la paja). There are straws everywhere—on the rooftops, along the seashore and on the stones of every castle. Now that I am free of remorse, I salute you, oh first straws of childhood; I salute you for your elementary beauty in the sunlight of the bay, while at the same time I see framed against the sky the first images of those young girls and women which fate, or enterprise, had placed before my eyes.

During this period of the straws, the Great War of 1914 broke out. I know nothing about the first year of this war and I only remember one word I must have heard at that time: "ultimatum." I wasn't very interested or even curious about the struggle until two years after it had started. In the meantime . . .

My father continued to travel in the north of Spain, and the rest of our family, Mama, her six children and Paca Moy, had moved. We now lived on Neverías Street, the street in town where they made and sold ice cream and cold drinks on summer nights.

My older brother Vicente had graduated from high school and he was soon sent to Cádiz to study engineering—the "career of engineering," as the old servant proudly stressed. He was a tall, blonde, handsome fellow with blue eyes. Along the Atlantic coast of Andalusia, there are many people with sea-colored eyes and hair almost the color of bright green. Blonde gypsies from Cádiz with Germanic last names, I have seen them camping under the bridges of the Guadalete River, as well as on the plains of Jerez and in San Lúcar de Barrameda along the estuaries of the Guadalquivir. My own family is full of lovely dark-haired girls with white complexions, Mediterranean and Nordic at the same time.

When the wines of Jerez and from the Puerto became internationalized and my great-grandfather, Don Vicente Alberti, made his business trips, he was one of the principal kings and ambassadors of the juice from our vines as it flowed toward the north of Europe. The Kings of Sweden, Norway and Denmark and the Czars of Russia named him Purveyor of their royal tables. England also became addicted to the aromatic vineyards in that corner of Cádiz. Scandinavians, like the ducks from their fjords that migrate to the flatlands of France or the plains and mountains of Spain to spend the winter in the warm swamplands of the Guadalquivir, also reached the docks of Cádiz and settled in those rich and extraordinary villages. The *soleras*, the abundant wines, the toasted, almost black muscatel, the clear wines from the *majuelo* vine of Jerez and the *amontillado* sherry became Europeanized, even universalized. Italians, Englishmen and Germans also began to arrive. The Domecqs from France, the Burdons, the Gordons, the Osbornes, the Pemartins, the Iversons, the Byasses, the Bolins and later the Terrys, the Ahupols and the Grants are names that began to be heard from Puerta Tierra to San Lúcar. Most of them came attracted by the smell of wine, but they arrived with empty purses. I always heard my mother tell how the first Osborne was a poverty-stricken Englishman with patched pants who could be found in the squares and streets of the Puerto selling religious stamps, rosaries and other holy trinkets.

They are the blue eyes, they are the blonde hair, and they are also that romantic and refined Andalusia that extends from Cádiz, skirts Gibraltar, and reaches as far as the lemon groves, the fields of carnations and the sacred vineyards of Málaga. My great-uncle Don Vicente Alberti married a Merello, the daughter of another Italian originally from Genoa, and he and his wife had five sons: Agustín, Vicente, Julio, Ernesto and Eduardo, who promised on their knees at the deathbed of their father that they would never split up but would continue to cultivate together that marvelous vinic inheritance. But what with Agustín's ostentatious way of life, Vicente's unhappy business ventures, Ernesto's incompetence, Eduardo's loafing and Julio's indifference, all this going hand in hand with the most perfect and obsessive religious hypocrisy, the inheritance dwindled away and the creditors began, little by little, to take over the crammed and humid wine cellars.

Among the principal creditors were the Osbornes who, after only a few years, held a monopoly of the coastal region's rich wine-producing industry. Although the sons of my great-uncles and others continued for a period of time to have their small business firms, the Osbornes in the Puerto and the Domecqs in Jerez de la Frontera were the ones who grew powerful in the kingdom of Bacchus, putting all the lesser vineyards out of business. One victim of this empire was my father, whom Osborne had named general agent for Spain in order to sell within the country wines which before had only been exported to England. My father was sent to the Galician and Cantabric coasts first as ambassador of their "Fino Quinta" and "Fino Coquinero" and, later, of a brandy which had been developed exclusively to compete with one produced by Domecq. And so entire years passed without my seeing him, not knowing what he looked like and not remembering even his voice. I know my father was an honest man and a very hard worker. I often heard it said in secret that he was also a great lover and a great drinker of the liquids he represented, thus upholding an old, alcoholic family tradition.

Who hasn't seen the streets of the Puerto literally tremble with aristocratic gentlemen, completely soused, late in the afternoon, between the light of day and the dark of night? Some of them were serious and dignified as they walked to the Chapel of Our Lady of Miracles to offer her on their knees a devout Hail Mary, at times sobbing in the dark—their souls overflowing with guilt; others, sad and melancholy, would be walking along the river bank in the direction of the eucalyptus trees that grew on the beach; some seemed lost in thought, seated on the benches which lined the main street and talking to their shadows; there were still others who shouted and carried on violently in the doorways of the bars, making remarks to the women who strolled by, ruining these ladies' evening stroll; and in the less affluent parts of town, the workers employed in the wine cellars were reeling from one side of the street to the other, accompanied by a deafening noise from gangs of young delinquents who seemed to explode from the entrance halls or deep patios of the houses in the neighborhood.

Violent alcoholic afternoons—the fragrance of sweet basil and night-blooming jasmine mixed with the putrid, acid smell of vomit. Some of the drunks would go down to the sea where the lights of Cádiz flickered in the distance like a band of fireflies, and rest their flaming foreheads filled with blue thoughts against the sand that was cooled by the fleeting, lacy edges of the waves. Those who found themselves alone in some abandoned square or strolling down a nocturnal path when they felt the wine go to their hearts and make them dizzily sentimental, would burst into mournful song whose echoes shredded the air with anguished cries of "Aye, aye, aye . . ."

My uncle Guillermo sits alone on any convenient stoop in front of a closed door. As a young man he wanted to be a priest. From that time on, all of us in the family—children and adults alike—as well as his friends and enemies, called him Guillermo the priest. He returned to town after having studied at some seminary in Cádiz or Sevilla. And now he gets drunk, all by himself, and cries about an unfortunate love affair with a first cousin of his. At times when he comes by the house, Paca Moy mockingly sings the following song under her breath:

> *Estudiante de día,*
> *galán de noche,*
> *malas pintas te veo*
> *de sacerdote.*

> *Student by day,*
> *Playboy by night,*

Your being a priest
Is quite a sight.

Uncle Guillermo doesn't work at anything. He has earned for himself a great reputation as a bum, as a man displaced by life. Every day he usually eats at the house of some relative or other, and he visits us very often. We love him. We drive him half crazy by making fun of his tonsure: "Come on Guillermo, show us the top of your head."

He smiles goodnaturedly, and bends down to show us his totally bald, pink scalp.

We knew that the Jesuits were after him all the time, trying to convince him to return to the fold. For a long time he resisted; he was in love. But suddenly one day he mysteriously disappeared. A year and a half later we learned that Uncle Guillermo had just offered his first Mass in Málaga. He returned to the Puerto and all of us wanted to have him as our confessor. Only one of my mother's sisters, Aunt Pepa, a delightful and amusing lady, was lucky enough to have her way.

After a few months that fresh, well-fed face, that round and ample physique, had disappeared—"a great decline" was the way Paca Moy sadly described it. The pink color of his cheeks and even of his bald spot began to fade in such a way that his skin began to look like the old yellowish covers of a prayerbook. Everyone began to take him seriously, to respect him. Now we all agreed: "Uncle Guillermo has the face of a saint."

The Bishop of Málaga, a former fellow student of his at the seminary, became his best friend and often invited him to his palatial residence. Among the religiously devout old ladies and the young girls of the best families in Málaga he became famous as a confessor. It was fashionable to be absolved by Uncle Guillermo. But he continued to look more and more like a saint until one day, after a long illness that he suffered with great patience, he commended his soul to God, leaving behind on earth a pleasant fragrance of muscatel—the mysterious aroma of fermenting grape.

My Uncle Ignacio was also immersed in a high tide of alcohol. It wasn't waves of wine that overcame him and sent him into orbit, but brandy. He was a district court judge. Both at home and in the Hall of Justice he would always be seated behind a tall glass of Martel into which he would dip his cigars as if they were paint brushes. The sleeves of his jacket and his baggy, Solomonic pants would be covered with chalky dust from the whitewashed walls in town. I remember him surrounded by his children, leading the afternoon Rosary at top speed and—another family tradition in which Uncle Vicente was still the undisputed champion—farting in unison with each litany: "Sancta María (poom, poom!), Sancta Dei Genitrix (poom, poom, poom!), Sancta Virgo Virginum (poom, poom, poom!)."

A genial and pleasant man whom I never saw again in my life.

In the absence of my father, our aunts and uncles counseled my mother about the kind of education we should be given, laying down to her the rules and regulations that were to govern our behavior. Since I was the youngest, I was probably also their favorite target. I know, for example, that Aunt Tití was always accusing me of something: "That child is very clever, but he is almost always late for Mass."

That poor and angelical lady, one of my father's sisters, was the right person to gauge my punctuality with great precision, since from early dawn each day she could be found all huddled up and sitting alone in the depths of St. Francis, the school church where we day students were forced to hear Mass at seven every morning.

Our hooky-playing sessions were becoming very dangerous, due to the mania my aunts and uncles had for strolling in the strangest places. The Lost Grove itself and the Mazzantini Road were now off limits to us. My Aunts Josefa and María Luis had decided that these places were perfect spots for their romantic twilight rosaries, which they recited aloud among the Spanish broom and the rows of prickly-pear cactus.

The road to Jerez was no less risky. All those uncles of mine who were involved in the wine business would race back and forth along that thoroughfare at all hours of the day. The road to Puerto Real that crossed the salt flats and pine forests in the direction of the San Pedro bridge was no longer to be recommended as an open-air retreat during Latin class. My small cousins used to ride along there in a beautiful two-horse carriage driven by Uncle Jesús.

In the spring that avenue along the beach next to the gas factory, bordered by eucalyptus trees, became as dangerous as all the others. Uncle José Luis and Aunt Milagros, elegant, silent, and melancholy would ride by in their *barouche* pulled by English horses that seemed to move in slow motion as the passengers watched the sun go down over the golden domes of the Cádiz Cathedral. So, as it turned out, the only ideal time to cut class was in the morning when we could perch on the humps of the undulating dunes.

Although those zealous advisers denounced me to my mother very often and were the cause of my having to suffer the most severe punishments, they didn't forget about my brothers and sisters either.

One day, looking through the cool opening of a keyhole, I witnessed the arrival—one by one—of all these relatives and saw them silently sit down in the downstairs dining-room that opened out onto the garden. Something serious must have come up for Mama to have requested the presence of all those irritable relations in the house. All of them, seated around the table at which she presided, listened very seriously to the terrible reasons that had made her convene this urgent family council. I held my breath and squeezed the tiny hand of Pipi, who was too small to reach the keyhole or even understand what was going on. As I watched the proceedings with an inexpressible mixture of tenderness and fear for my mother, I fixed my trembling gaze on her, convinced that she was going to break down in tears in front of all of them or faint dead away on the table, since she looked so pale and disturbed.

"I have received a letter from Cádiz, from Uncle Julio," she announced finally. And unfolding a small sheet of paper with trembling hands, she read its content in an almost watery voice: "'Your son Vicentito, who is basically a good boy and a good student, seems lately to have gone astray. The company he keeps will be his ruin. Imagine, just the other night, someone who has been duly authorized to go to such places found him in a theatre with his gang of pals watching a performance, believe it or not!, of *The Pharaoh's Court!*'"

My poor mother, who had intended to continue reading, suddenly remained silent, interrupted as she was by the mumbling sounds of that strange tribunal, sounds that soon developed into exaggerated and repetitive exclamations:

"*The Pharaoh's Court!*"
"Christ!"
"How indecent!"
"Christ!"
"Vicentito at *The Pharaoh's Court!*"
"Christ!"

"*The Pharaoh's Court!*"

"Well, well, well, well!"

And together they drew up a frightening letter to be signed by my mother and addressed to Uncle Julio in which they reminded Vicentito of the torments of Hell, threatening him with the possibility of continuous and painful tortures for all eternity.

Uncles, aunts, auntuncles! I still love and admire you and I even enjoy speaking tenderly about you all. What more do you want from me! Look. It's now five o'clock in the morning. The German planes have bombarded the bridges over the inland bays of Scotland, searching for the British Navy. While I, in the meantime, remember you and relive your obsessions and your religious manias, from this radio station in Paris where I earn a salary of 60 francs a night, minus 12—war tax—for staying awake all night long and sleeping only a few hours a day.

But the one who enjoyed the greatest position of authority over my mother and the rest of us was her brother Jesús.

Uncle Jesús had about fourteen or fifteen children at that time. (I think he ended up having seventeen.) The oldest boy, José Ignacio, studied at the San Luis Gonzaga school with me, although he was among the boarders. Uncle Jesús had truly inherited the family spirit. In him one could clearly see the capriciousness and obstinate religious oddities of old Uncle Vicente, combined with the charm and temperament of our other great-uncles. But although on this cold, rainy Parisian night I remember him kindly, I could never have the same sense of confidence in him that I had in the others, as much my uncles as he. During those school years his face always represented to me an image of terror, of obligatory respect and forced gratitude. He had become my mother's main source of consolation and support. Those bad months when Papa could not send money home, Uncle Jesús would "help us along," supplying Mama not only with money but also with somewhat threadbare suits belonging to him or his children that could be altered and fixed up for us. Although I couldn't put it into words then, all this vaguely depressed me and caused me such pain at times that I used to go from roof to roof or from terrace to terrace crying all by myself.

That indefinable feeling of well-being that I had, for example, when I was with old Uncle Vicente, turned into one of distrust and a lack of spontaneity in the presence of Uncle Jesús. My relationship with his children also produced in me a mixture of envy and sadness. Although I spent the best vacations of my childhood with them, I could never look at those luxurious carriages pulled by Blackie and Sorrel, those deep wine cellars and country retreats that I could enjoy only as a guest, without having feelings of discomfort which at times turned to hatred. I remember that right after I had enrolled in the Jesuit school as a day student, my cousin José Ignacio—marching along with the boarding students on the way to seven o'clock Mass —practically turned his head in the opposite direction so as not to greet me. And if at times he did acknowledge my presence, it was done in such a cold way that for me it darkened the light of many future days. Nevertheless, I never said anything to him about it and only at this moment, almost thirty years later, do I risk confessing these sad and petty transcendental tragedies which now perhaps seem ridiculous even to mention.

José Ignacio was generally surly and strange. As an adolescent he always went horseback riding alone along the beach or down the road that led to Puerto Real, quickening his gallop as if in fear whenever he glimpsed someone coming toward him, even if the person happened to be a member of his own family. Now I remember that at home they used to call him "the odd one."

His little brother Agustín was different. Witty and clever, he also had an admirable gift: he could fart as many times as requested; that is, he could do it to order.

"Agustinillo," they used to say to him at times, even in front of guests, "make three long ones."

Agustinillo, with his eyes open like two saucers, raised his leg and obeyed.

"Now, five: but three long ones and one short one and the last one has to be really long until we tell you to stop."

Agustinillo would then ask with a horse-like expression on his face, his jaw all askew: "Do you want me to do them on all fours, like Blackie?" When he was little, Agustinillo had wanted to be a horse. He used to spend the whole morning in the stable studying the gestures and stance of Blackie and Sorrel. Whenever we went out walking he would always lead the way, trotting or rhythmically moving his head like a proud mare. If he came upon a puddle or a pool of water he used to bend over immediately and, stretching out his neck and lips, he would noisily suck up the water until one of his brothers came up behind him and gave him an affectionate kick in his pointed buttocks. A little further on, he would roll in the grass with his legs in the air and neigh so perfectly that the horses which were tethered and grazing in the area would reply immediately, in disconsolate tones.

He was always funny; a poor student but a good guy. When I last saw him, some ten years ago, his large bulging eyes and the straight line of his cheekbones oddly enough brought to mind the memory of Sorrel and Blackie, his equine models from that happy time when his ideal had been to disappear in a galloping burst, long mane and ears to match, along the banks of the Guadalete River.

Who hasn't at one time or another in his life wanted to be a four-legged creature or a bird? One aunt of mine dreamed of becoming a bird, just an ordinary bird, so that she could fly through some open window. This desire on her part was merely something that had unconsciously stuck in her mind, left over from the lyrics of some popular ballad she had once heard. With the passing years and her extended spinsterhood, she ended up by going insane. She insisted that her bedroom was a cage, and since she had now become an imprisoned bird, it would be impossible for her to get out. Besides, she claimed, her wings had been cut. Finally, pale from so much darkness and lack of fresh air, she died in a small village in Sevilla.

Andrés the Blessed, one of the poor unfortunates my family had taken under its wing and a great admirer of my mother, was convinced he was a flea and that he had fought against Palomo, the pharmacist, who had lost the battle in spite of the fact that he had attacked Andrés in the form of a white elephant.

My Uncle Javier wanted to be a wild turkey or a grouse so as to meet death by a rifle fired from a small boat in the lagoon. He could barely spell or write his own name. To keep him out of trouble, the family put him in charge of a sporting-goods shop which they called—as evidenced by the sign in great white letters painted on a red background—The Port's Sports. One day when my brother Agustín was walking by the store, Uncle Javier whistled to him.

"Look, Agustín," he begged with the look of someone in a deep quandary over an insoluble problem, "since you know English, would you write 'English gunpowder' on this label?"

Trying out a rifle on one occasion, he caught his eyelid in the hammer and almost lost an eye. Instead of "edifice" he would say "orifice," and every time he tried to decipher the word "maritime" it unfailingly came out as "marital." He kept chickens on the roof of his house, and in a notebook he would record the number of eggs they laid each day. Since he was absolutely convinced that zeros to the right represented the same value as zeros to the left, he came down from the roof one night both elated and stupefied to announce that his generous hens had produced 10,000 eggs on that single day.

One of my mother's uncles by marriage, Don Manuel Docavo, upon returning home from the priory after vespers would leap immediately into bed, removing only his socks, which he then placed on his hands like gloves while he continued with his devout readings. We never knew if this measure was meant to ward off the cold or the mosquitoes, or simply just a strange personal mania of his. When he finished with his prayers, he would jump out of bed, run to the empty kitchen armed with a fork and, on the first try, spear the single piece of bacon that appeared and disappeared on the surface of the bubbling stew cooking on the stove for dinner. Then, like a sudden lightning-bolt, he would race out in search of a bar on the outskirts of town where he spent his alcoholic evenings drinking and gossiping with other uncles of mine until it was time to return home.

Holy and adored family! How nostalgic I feel as I think about you, poetic aunts and uncles of my life! I would like to meet you all here, in Paris, on this rainy war-torn night so different from those nights in the heartland of Spain, as I sit alone in this immense building on L'Avenue Segur performing my tiring nocturnal duties.

Come in, come in. Have a seat. It's a bit cold; your shoes must be sopping wet. And although you're brown and toasted from the suns of Cádiz, your umbrellas are taking a sad Parisian leak all over the new parquet floor of this radio station where each night I translate the insipid joint communiqués from the French High Command.

What news do you bring from Spain? How are her seas and mountains? Her olive trees and orange groves? Her sky, her wild bulls nostalgic for death as they move through the fields and swamplands?

Blood. Blood. Blood.

I will not criticize you nor do I hold any grudge, distant aunts and uncles, because I remember your admirable virtues, your ignorance, your charm and obsessions. This poor nephew of yours has let you down. "Remember how we said he would go too far!" You surround me in a circle of silence that I know is filled with disapproval, with Christian con-

demnation. But that doesn't bother me, my aunts and uncles. You were
excessive and generous like the wine in our cellars. What news do you
bring of our Spanish wines? Of the Jerez vineyards and the grapes of
Valdepeñas? What about our land that was turned into battlefields? And
our true friends, our true brothers?

Blood. Blood. Blood.

Uncles, aunts, auntuncles! Leave this place. Go away. This rheumatic
French climate will penetrate deeply into the marrow of your bones. I
cannot go there, where I wish to be, floating through the air. My head
rolls along the ground, bouncing three times. Flashes of lightning dart
from my eyes that finally close against those of my dead companions. So be
it. All is well now.

Goodnight, dear uncles and aunts.

At this moment the street corners, papered with blue posters from
the Compañía Trasatlántica, call out to me: the *Balvanera*, the
Patricio Satrústegui, and the *Infanta Isabel.*

On the *Balvanera* my grandmother set sail for Buenos Aires with
three of her sons—Pepe, Agustín and Miguel—never to return or
fall asleep again in the garden at the foot of her favorite jasmine bush
while reciting her prayers.

I see myself now, hanging onto the grating and afraid of being
caught, as I tear off that painted boat from which I always imagined
my young grandmother Josefa peering sadly and longingly through a
porthole, disappearing from wave to wave on her way to America.

I began to draw the ocean liner, copying it in the same dimensions
as in the poster. The *Balvanera* defines a particular period in my life.
I was becoming less and less interested in books and studying as the
days went by. I spent several weeks in class filling the white margins
of my textbooks with *Balvaneras* sadly pursued by flocks of seagulls
in open "V" formation. I even played hooky more often. At home,
after having supposedly spent the day at school, I devoted myself to
making exact copies of this ship. On the beach and along the banks of
the Guadalete, I covered the pages of a notebook with sketches and
watercolors of maritime scenes, generally placing in the background
of each one the sparkling salt flats where the salt was piled up in
frozen pyramids, the castles of Santa Catalina and La Pólvora, and
always Cádiz, lightly traced there among the masts and the wisps of
smoke from its chimneys.

After long afternoons of hard work, my version of the *Balvanera*
seemed to be an exact reproduction. I proudly wrote my name in one

of the corners of the page in large, well-formed letters. When I had finished, I ran to show it off first to María the cook and then to my Aunt Lola.

The cook was a myopic old lady from Algeciras who believed in witches and seemed to have great admiration for me; Aunt Lola from Granada was my grandmother's sister, a gardener and painter in her free time. The opinions of these two ladies were for me the only respectable ones available at that time.

María, cupping her hand over her eyes like a visor, reacted very concisely to my drawing: "Very realistic."

And Aunt Lola, examining it intently: "It's just fine, Cuco." (The whole family always called me Cuco, the name both of a bird and of a famous *banderillero*.)

Aunt Lola, who suffered from a heart condition since childhood and had spent most of her life sitting on a balcony that faced the street, immediately sent for her daughter Gloria. "I am going to give Cuco my paints. Get me the box from the middle drawer of my bureau."

That afternoon I learned of the existence of a color called burnt Sienna and others as well: Veronese green, Spanish white, cadmium, Sevillian earth . . .

"Now I want to give you something of mine for you to copy. But you'll have to do it here in the house, because it could break."

And Gloria, following her mother's instructions, placed before me a large painter's palette round in shape and covered with landscapes and figures.

"These are all pictures of Granada," explained Aunt Lola proudly. "At the bottom are the Catholic Sovereigns, Don Fernando and Doña Isabel. On this side are Boabdil and Aixa, his mother, who is scolding him: 'Cry as a woman for what you have not been able to defend as a man.' In the center is a scene from *The Surrender of Granada*, copied from the famous painting by Pradilla; above that is a villa on the banks of the Darro River. I want you to begin with the simplest thing, the villa. It is a painting I did of a house where we used to live. I want you to copy it on a board I will also give to you. Since I haven't painted for a long time, I've run out of oil of turpentine—you can buy some at the pharmacy or the corner hardware store, it will only cost you a few pennies."

Oil of turpentine! Oil of turpentine! What kind of strange oil could that be? I had never heard of it before.

The next morning I left the house early to buy some, anxious to

Buenos días

Buenos días

primavera al plano de María

La lira de mi balcón

    te canta esta melodía

He aquí a esclava de la flor

Y el Sí y el No de los pañuelos

Rosa de los cariños

Tu corazón natal es el cielo

Banquera del relente

La luna cuelga de tus trenzas

    melocotón azul

Caracola de mar el viento

discover what this mysterious oil recommended by my aunt would be like. And under Aunt Lola's demanding but helpful gaze, in a few hours I had painted the villa along the banks of the Darro, completely overwhelmed by the magical powers of this oil of turpentine that cleaned brushes and gently spread the oil paints over the board. It was also at Aunt Lola's house that I discovered *La Esfera*, the weekly magazine from Madrid with its color reproductions of the famous paintings hanging in the Prado Museum.

Of all the Spanish artists, the one that had always impressed me the most as a child was Murillo, a truly popular painter, particularly in Andalusia. I had seen his *Immaculate Conception,* and his versions of *St. John the Child* reproduced in those religious stamps we had as children, but I don't think I knew any of his other paintings. As for Velázquez, he was only a name to me then and one that wasn't mentioned as often as this other painter from Sevilla.

While I had been copying the villa, Aunt Lola prophesied with great conviction: "This child will be another Murillo."

This was a prediction also made by others members of my family, but without the slightest enthusiasm. "He'll just be another Murillo."

But it never occurred to any of them to think that I might be another Velázquez. I don't think anyone even knew who he was.

Murillo!

"If you don't fail your June examinations, we'll take you to Cádiz to see some of his paintings there."

And it was Aunt Lola who told me one afternoon that the gentle and tender Bartolomé Esteban had fallen to his death from a scaffold in Cádiz while painting church frescoes.

Perhaps it was because Velázquez was a less familiar name to me, and I knew nothing at all about his paintings, that I was so overwhelmed by the reproductions of his work which appeared in *La Esfera.* I can never forget my feelings of wonder and joy when I first saw the equestrian portrait of Prince Baltasar Carlos. This immense, impossible, hulking animal with that elegant golden child seated on its back opened a window to me that looked out on some indescribable place.

"Will you let me borrow this issue of *La Esfera*, Aunt Lola?"

"But, child, that's very difficult. I wouldn't even dare copy it myself."

At dawn of the following day and in an upstairs laundry room of our house that was no longer in use, I began to make a copy of that equestrian prince.

I made many changes in my first version, did some retouching and then waited until the paint had dried to add the finishing touches. After little more than a week, when it was done and completely dry, I brightened it up with an aromatic transparent varnish I had bought at the neighborhood drug store.

I raced downstairs in search of the old cook.

"Look, María, look!"

María, with her severe myopia, shielded her eyes with her visored hand in order to concentrate her poor overworked vision on the object I so violently shoved in front of her nose.

"Very good, child, very good," she commented after a brief silence that seemed painfully interminable to me.

"What is it supposed to be?" I asked her angelically, convinced that she would describe the painting in minute detail.

María became absorbed in thought, shading her eyes again with her hand and after another, even more anguished silence, she calmly replied:

"What do you mean, what is it supposed to be, child? It's a little English girl riding a small mountain pony."

I was furious. I turned my back to her and my exact words at the time were: "Go shit in your hat."

I then ran, panting all the way, to Aunt Lola's house where I enjoyed a resounding success, and swore from that moment on never again to consult old María on any pictorial matters.

As I have already mentioned, the war in Europe had broken out and Germany had presented an ultimatum to France. Shortly after the outbreak of hostilities, *La Esfera* began to publish in every issue a two-page spread covered with horrendous war sketches signed by someone named Matania. These drawings depicted the most contorted attacks imaginable launched by the Germans against French barbed-wire defenses in which decapitated bodies flew through the air accompanied by flying helmets, splintered rifles and leather harnesses. There were horses up on their hind legs pulling cannons, and wagons packed with assault troops that were running over and crushing the cadavers strewn all over the ground; a whole range of cruelties which stirred my imagination and served as an invitation for me to make copies of those blood-curdling scenes.

Such an idea was repugnant to Aunt Lola, and she was opposed to my spending hours on end filling pages and pages with scenes of such frightful slaughter, an activity which had the ultimate effect of awakening in me the stupid desire to play war games.

As an easily defeatable enemy I chose my sister Josefa, better known to us as Pipi. In one of the interior patios of our house I drew some maps of France and Germany with a piece of coal, arbitrarily separating these two countries with my version of the English Channel. I began to buy a collection of paper soldiers which at night I would paste on a piece of cardboard and then cut out. In this way I managed to recruit a respectable army of more than one thousand infantrymen which I shared—unequally, I might add—with my sister. I was Germany—the Kaiser; and she France—M. Poincaré. Flattened caps from my father's wine bottles served as ammunition, almost like the real thing, and we threw them at each other during the fighting. The fleet was composed of tin cans stuffed with straw, which we reduced to ashes in our great naval battles by bombarding them with lighted matches and firecrackers.

Our passion for that stupid game sometimes had the effect of causing us to fight in earnest, slamming each other around to the point where we were finally forced to suspend hostilities for a few days, until we had calmed down.

We would send urgent messages to Papa, who was still traveling in the north, asking him to send us reinforcements so that we could continue the war. Our armies increased in size until the beginning of the year 1917 we had, between the two of us, some five thousand troops. Our war, which took place under the brilliant sun that shone through the skylight of the patio, became so famous among our cousins and the rest of the family that not one day passed without someone coming to witness the reenactment of a battle we had read about in the newspapers the night before. A detestable game, and my memory of it has become transformed over the years until I see it today as a black stain of real blood; a sad, dark pool lying there in the midst of my bright Andalusian childhood! It always comes back to haunt me and weigh on my conscience, demanding exoneration. An example of this is the following poem which I had happened to find among the few original works I had salvaged, along with my own neck, from the Spanish Civil War:

¡Qué sabíamos nosotros,
hijos con una infancia de azoteas,
de jardines ociosos y largas vacaciones por el río!

Las revistas llegaban por la noche,
ilustradas de muertos,
de trincheras voladas
y barcos que al hundirse se volvían
altas trombas de sangre.
¡Qué sabíamos!
Ayer diez aviones se hundieron en el mar
y un submarino herido invadió aguas neutrales.
Mira.
A la luz de la lámpara,
tranquilos y lejanos,
era la guerra un juego que abría en la almohada,
        heroicos sueños turbios.

What did we know,
Children with a childhood of rooftops,
Of leisurely gardens and long vacations by the river?
The magazines arrived at night
With illustrations of the dead,
Of exploding trenches
And sinking ships becoming
Waterspouts of blood.
What did we know?
Ten planes disappeared yesterday in the sea
And a wounded submarine invaded neutral waters.
Look.
By the light of the lamp, distant and calm,
War was a game, casting its shadow on our pillows,
And awakening in us darkly heroic dreams.

Another forced halt in this lost grove which becomes harder and harder to find as it becomes both more distant and yet closer to my Andalusian childhood.

M. Fraisse, the young director of Paris Mondial, reservedly and regretfully advises me that it is Marshal Pétain himself, having recently returned from standing in line like an ordinary sergeant before Generalísimo Franco's door, who has requested that the government of "La France Eternelle" discharge us immediately from "La Radio" since it is urgently essential to find some way to please the Caudillo's Number

74

One Spain. How could anyone tolerate the fact that two formidable reds, two dangerous writers who had one day been received by Stalin in the rooms of the Kremlin, two enemies—who could possibly doubt it?—of France, the nation which had just celebrated the hundred and fiftieth anniversary of its Revolution, were being permitted to ruin their eyesight at the going rate of forty-eight French francs per night by broadcasting to the world over those spiritual Gallic radio waves the "heroic" war bulletins concocted by the splintered French High Command?

"Votre travail comme speaker, mes chers amis, était excellent . . . mais c'est le Maréchal . . . vous comprenez?"

"Oui, M. Fraisse," we respond to him gratefully. "Nous sommes fiers d'être mis à la porte de la France de votre noble Maréchal."

And on a blacked-out Parisian night, filled with the trembling of that immortal panic so characteristic of the French bourgeoisie in the years 1936 to 1940, we departed from the Gare de Lyon heading for Marseilles where, before leaving France, we did honor to the last unenslaved lobsters and bowls of bouillabaisse in that country whose name still signified eternal light, but which a few months later would be sadly and symbolically changed to that of a bottled mineral water: Vichy.

"Je quitte l'Europe"—like Rimbaud, but not to sell horses or wander over hot desert sands. I abandoned Europe, my Europe, to fulfill my destiny as a wandering Spaniard, as an immigrant and pilgrim of hope in America.

Miraculously, and for the third time in four years, I managed to save my life. The Mendoza, in its last crossing to Buenos Aires, liberated me from the hands of the "noble" Marshal who was to turn over to Franco so many good and trusting Spaniards.

En el Mendoza,
todo suena a español
raído, de Orán.

Azul, se retira Ibiza.
Allí fui prisionero
en un bosque de pinos.
Mi vida era una choza
de parasol y vientos marinos.

1936.

Hay áureas del Cuartel de la Montaña
en este viejo barco.
Involuntario, marcha a la Legión
oro puro de España.

On the Mendoza
Are the sounds of threadbare Spanish
From Orán.

Ibiza withdraws in blue.
There I was a prisoner
In a pine forest. My life was a cabin,
Parasols and breezes from the sea.

1936.
There are golden reflections from the Mountain Headquarters
On this old ship. Involuntarily marching off to the Legion,
Purest gold of Spain.

Thus began my poem Diario de a bordo *which I composed on that sad vessel. And the fact is that from the ship's hold, from the depths of its dirty, stinking belly, there arose from under the red feces of Algerian marksmen, and mixed with strange Spanish words, some sad, displaced songs from the Levantine coast of Spain.*

One of those soldiers proudly spoke to us in our language: "The majority of the five hundred men on this ship are from Orán, sons of Spaniards from Alicante. We're returning from the Maginot Line with a month's leave."

From on deck we watched them disembark—a particularly painful scene for us, lucky immigrants on our way to America. Opposite the port of Orán the Foreign Legion volunteers were drilling and parading on a wide terrace bathed in afternoon light: almost all of them pure and wretched Spanish gold—students, teachers, workers, peasants, heroes of our glorious war who, faced with the prospect of slow deterioration in French concentration camps, preferred a hard life of adventure or death in battles fought out of sheer desperation, or perhaps even the possibility of escape.

With tears welling up in me from the very marrow of my bones, I saw them—sad faced and poorly clothed—disappear in formation into the burning heart of Africa, probably never to come out again.

76

The ship set sail ... night opposite the coasts of Almería, Granada, Málaga; moments filled with the frightening and dark presence of our native land.

Still troubled by an anguished insomniac fear, I looked out through the porthole of my stateroom before sunrise. Gibraltar. The Rock: that usurped black tail of the poor Hispanic bull, dawning from the depths of the misty but blood-colored waters. And through the silvery arches of the dolphins that were playing near the beaches above Tarifa, I had a happy vision of schoolyards surrounded by orchards, golden sand dunes, and a picture of myself, roaming freely along the seashore.

Then Casablanca ... the Canary Islands, sensed but not seen ... Dakar ... a long, long voyage, a frightening voyage, when for the first time in my life I felt that the blood of Europe was being drained from my body.

And finally America—Buenos Aires, Argentina, on our way to Chile. Chile? I never got that far, since I decided to stay in Buenos Aires where kind, friendly hands held out nets of hope to me, and where I now live—hard-earned fruits of my labor—in a small apartment not far from the river. It is here that I now try to put my Spanish sorrows in some kind of order, and with them these broken memories of my first, lost grove.

Dolores, María, Gloria: three very beautiful and pale Andalusian women; three strange, mysterious, lonely spinsters from Granada.

As we watched her through the garden gate, scurrying back and forth and reflecting the colors of stained glass, Aunt Lola whispered confidentially in my ear: "Dolorcitas is known in Granada as the *houri* of the Alhambra."

I didn't dare at the time to ask my aunt the meaning of that name —*houri*; but I always imagined this pale and silent Dolorcitas strolling among the myrtle and the trickling fountains of the Generalife dressed in a flowing, colorful but transparent robe, holding up an open green parasol as a playful defense against the birds and butterflies that pursued and surrounded her.

The three sisters were made famous by the whispers and ardent longings of passionate suitors on the banks of the Darro.

Dolores had been courted by a marquis but he had been frightened away by her sister María; María had a boyfriend who had finally been chased off by her sister Gloria; and Gloria had been pursued by several young suitors, but María and Dolores together had never allowed them to come closer than the oleander bushes that grew in the front patio.

So as not to be seen nor admired, the three sisters would race down three different streets to attend early morning Mass in separate churches. And then the rest of the day was like a living death for the three of them as they sat idly on one of the downstairs balconies of their house. Their mother, with her heart condition, would sit on a similar and adjacent balcony trying to forget about her anguished breathing. The three sisters continued to die in the same way during the winter months, the heat of a brazier drying up their beauty; their only consolation was to gaze out at the quiet streets from behind a veil of sheer white curtains. They spoke infrequently, but when they did it was to refer vaguely to some incidents of their life in Granada, confused memories that led nowhere but which the three of them somehow resolved with signs or weak smiles. Those unhappy beauties hardly ever spoke to their two brothers, Tomás and Luis, who supported and protected them. An older brother, Pepe Ignacio, was an atheist and republican—a stain on the family's honor—who had gone off to Madrid as a young man. He had married "beneath his station," and the rest of the family, with their aristocratic pretensions, had never fully accepted his wife. This senseless boy had turned out to be like his father, Uncle Tomás, an old and handsome Garibaldian who used to proudly show off his right hand with its three missing fingers that had been shot off during an attack on the Papal Gardens.

Before I ever knew Uncle Tomás, I had met his lost-sheep of a son. When Pepe Ignacio's imminent arrival in the Puerto was announced, the entire family reacted as if the Devil himself was going to make an appearance. From her screened and doleful corner on the bedroom balcony, Aunt Lola advised the three resplendent and solitary virgins to immediately send word to their confessor. And during that entire afternoon the air vibrated with the slow cadence of numerous Lord's Prayers and Ave Marías offered up especially for "souls gone astray" and repeated in the monotonous tones of a rosary.

Other aunts and older cousins came by to visit, looking grieved and mysterious as if attending a funeral. They stayed for hours on end, sipping hot chocolate, munching on cookies and lamenting the "perdition of such a fine boy." Even Uncle Vicente, taciturn and in very bad humor, also appeared and between glasses of sherry kept mumbling about the Masonic machinations which had robbed him of a nephew.

And finally, one evening, the nephew arrived.

"Here comes our great big republican!" was the way the three sisters affectionately but sternly greeted Pepe.

Pepe Ignacio was a peaceful, gentle and sentimental soul. Very well educated, he was an excellent translator of several theatrical works that had been successfully performed in Madrid. In Granada he had originally wanted to be a painter but his literary aspirations had won out, causing him to abandon his youthful ambitions. He loved his mother very much and was also fond of his sisters, although at times he found them exasperating.

"I hope you won't embarrass us by not going to Mass on Sunday."

"We can't have anyone pointing his finger at *us*."

"There'll be no atheists in *this* house."

With such alternating admonitions, mother and daughters ended up ruining the few days that the poor, wayward Pepe Ignacio had planned to spend peacefully with them in the Puerto. And he returned to Madrid, oppressed by the candles, the advice and the vigils for his salvation. He also left bearing a dark bruise on his forehead caused by the abrasive pressure of a holy medal that the angelically demented Dolorcitas had secretly hidden inside his hat band to hasten his conversion.

What ideas about liberalism and other democratic doctrines were inculcated by the Jesuits in the minds of the poor students who attended their schools? They were considered infernal. And at home, especially in the case of my uncles who had been sprinkled by heraldic juices, such things awakened feelings of horror and hatred that were exacerbated by unadulterated snobbery. It simply wasn't elegant or refined to be a republican. Night-watchmen, coachmen, grocery-storekeepers and even perhaps civil servants at City Hall could afford to be so "common." Naturally, drunks could too. I remember from those days the stumbling figure of a man who had had a bit too much to drink and was wandering that afternoon alone and lost down some alleyway with a confused dream of freedom that made him shout out: "Long live the Republic!"

"Rafaelito, I want you to always remember this piece of advice: don't ever be like your Uncle Pepe Ignacio," Father Lambertini tersely but gently recommended to me after having absolved me in confession on Sunday and while I was kissing his hand before going up to the communion altar, an act I performed with excessive concentration whenever I knew I was being watched by Milagritos Sancho.

Although at that time I was suffering in a state of silent despair because of the love I felt for my Aunt Gloria, I was actually in love with Milagritos, a young girl who lived on Cruces Street not far from school.

Milagritos Sancho, slightly younger than I, was quite pretty, not at all skinny and with very fat legs. Although she never became my official girlfriend, she was the cause and pretext for innumerable class absences, for my poor weekly grades and for my being expelled briefly from this religious center of education.

I shared the news of my budding passion with Treviño, a fifth-year student who was much too tall to be still walking around in short pants. During that school year—1916-1917—the conversation at home insistently revolved around the family's move to Madrid, which gave me even more reason to be thinking constantly about Milagritos as I walked on the beaches and rooftops, far from second-year French and that hateful class in literary theory.

There was an old, dilapidated vacant house on a corner adjacent to the modest little two-story building where Milagritos lived with her mother and sisters. I had actually only been with her once; walking right next to her and half-dead with embarrassment, I had lightly brushed against her hand in a dimly-lit garden on Victoria Boulevard opposite the prison, that sad Puerto Prison which has torn so many mournful "ayes" from the throats of *cante jondo** singers.

"Have you met Milagritos?" shouted a friend of my sisters who was walking with her that evening, turning around suddenly flushed with excitement.

*The *cante jondo* is an Andalusian style of folksinging especially popular among the gypsies of the region. García Lorca, in his lecture on the *cante jondo*, quotes the composer Manuel de Falla, who defined its essential elements as follows:

> Disharmony, as a medium of modulation; the use of a melodic scope so narrow that it rarely exceeds the limits of a sixth, and the almost obsessive repetition of a single note, a method used in certain formulas for enchantment even in those recitations we might call prehistoric. This has led many to suppose that the *cante* precedes the spoken language.

I had been following both of them at a distance all the way from the beach road and there was no way for me to hide or run, faced as I was with the rapidity and unexpectedness of the question. I moved up to them with trembling knees, the blood pounding inside my head, and we then all walked silently down the long avenue. It was already getting dark and the figure of Milagritos at my side began to blend with the nearby wall of the prison, vanishing into the shadowy fragrance of the street. I thought I sensed her ripping off one of the top buttons of her coat (it must have been loose already), and then she shyly placed it in my hand, probably as a romantic souvenir of our first meeting.

More than a month after that silent confrontation, during which time our relationship had consisted solely of casual greetings and an exchange of frightened glances on my way to and from school, I decided I would go with Treviño to pay a visit to the owner of the empty house on the corner, inventing the story that my family needed the key in order to look the place over.

The wall surrounding Milagritos' terrace began at the ground floor of the old empty house, which was only a one-story structure. On an afternoon devoted to spiritual exercises, and already in possession of the immense rusty key, we opened the doors (it seemed to us like the Gates of Paradise) that were to lead us along cracked and flaking hallways, bedrooms and rat-infested laundry rooms, to the eyes, the smile and perhaps even the hand of her who waited on high, a solitary pink and somewhat swollen angel, watching for us to come down her street on our way home from school.

When by means of insistent hissing sounds we succeeded in getting her attention, Milagritos, all red in the face, looked down at us in great surprise. Our fear of being caught there or that Milagritos might be annoyed by our audacity, or even that her mother might appear on the scene—all of it complicated, in my case, by the terrible pounding of blood against my temples—affected our tongues in such a way that the entire adventure concluded in an ecstatic and tripartite silence, broken only by a great shout that surged from somewhere down below ordering our love to come down and eat supper immediately.

Because of the darkness and spookiness of that empty and abandoned place so full of strange creaking noises, we took advantage of Milagritos' absence, which we thought would be temporary, to try to remove ourselves from that big old house—not, however, by way of the door to the street, but rather by jumping from rooftop to rooftop. The first one on our itinerary would be hers, where we would sit and wait in order to surprise her again, and then, before her admiring glance, we planned to continue along the whole block of houses until reaching the house of one of our school friends who lived in the neighborhood, and then we'd jump down to the Plaza of San Francisco.

To reach the starting point of our venture, we had counted on an old ladder that had been left behind in one of the laundry rooms. We would use it to scale the wall that our imagination had already converted into the ramparts of a castle, until arrived at a tower crowned with merlons. I would be the first to ascend, while Treviño held the ladder firmly so that it wouldn't slip on the moss. Then, once on the roof, it would be my turn to support the ladder by holding onto the end so that he could also climb up safely.

After agreeing on this plan, I began my climb upward—some forty rungs—starting to feel my knees shake as the rungs got narrower and narrower and I came closer and closer to the sky. I am not sure today if those tremors I felt were caused by the shakiness of the ladder or by my excitement and fright at the prospect of suddenly coming upon Milagritos or, a most terrible possibility, running into her mother, a massively bulky matron feared by us all. My eagerly anxious hands had already reached the ledge and were holding onto it firmly to pull myself up. As I strained to reach the top, I could see beyond the edge of the wall and through the palm trees and araucaria pines, and my eyes became filled with a hazy vision of the bay with the church domes of Cádiz in the background. I was about to jump onto the roof when a dog, stretched out on the exact place where my feet had intended to make contact, sprang at my face and announced my presence to the whole neighborhood with ear-splitting, highly exaggerated barking. Surprised and terrified and with no available hands to defend myself, my hanging feet searched desperately for the ladder and finally found it. But by that time all the neighbors were shouting and commenting on this scandalous event.

The next day when Treviño and I were passing in front of Milagritos' house very early in the morning, some rough hands suddenly appeared from the doorway and grabbed my friend, who then immediately disappeared within. I later explained to Milagritos what had happened in a letter I wrote at school and which I planned to have delivered to her the next day by using my sisters' friend as messenger. The contents of the letter were more or less as follows:

My unforgettable Milagritos:

When Treviño and I tried yesterday to climb up to your roof to wait for you and be with you, which is what our souls longed for, your little dog jumped on me and started barking and I almost killed myself because of him. When we tried to get away, the people in the neighborhood were bunched up in front of the door to the big old house and the children began to shout that we were not ghosts but just some kids from the Jesuit school. We opened the doors bravely, proudly announcing that that was exactly what we were, and we then ran off with insults and curses ringing in our ears.

This morning when we passed by your door, Toto [the maid] came out and tried to grab us, but I escaped. Treviño wasn't so lucky, and Toto shoved him into a downstairs room of your house where your mother was waiting, furious, to give us a piece of her mind. Treviño told me that she, referring to me, had said it seemed impossible that a boy from such a decent family would dare to compromise her daughter Milagritos by creating a scandal in the neighborhood.

The letter included other innocent details of our frustrated adventure and ended with a declaration of love taken from some mysterious little book that circulated among third- and fourth-year students and contained all the necessary instructions governing various kinds of amorous relationships:

Awaiting your exalted, kind response, which will bring to my soul the respite it yearns for, I take my humble leave.

Yours,
Rafael

For some time my family had been suspicious about my poor academic performance and my equally poor attendance record at San

Luis Gonzaga. Some revealing clues did exist, like often finding my bed in the morning covered with sand from the dunes. Paca Moy, the old servant, mentioned this casually to my mother one day after cleaning my room, but her love for me dictated a certain caution: "You'd think that rascal of a child was studying in a sandpile instead of in a decent school . . ."

I was the only one to blame for Paca Moy's uncovering the secret of my illegal absences, since I used to go to bed almost fully clothed, sometimes with my starched collar still around my neck, and always with my socks on.

That afternoon, after a fiery lecture on the torments of Hell, I was jubilant as I left school with my letter flatly pressed between the pages of my notebook and eagerly awaiting the dawn of a new day to send it off of Milagritos. Hardly eating anything for dinner, I went to bed and fell asleep almost immediately, dreaming of blue rooftops where Milagritos ran and jumped, happily pursued by me to the accompaniment of her barking dog and loud noises from all the neighbors who had even climbed up to the pointed tops of the weathervanes. But the three of us didn't mind. Without Treviño, who had gotten lost in some corner of my dream, we continued to run, to straddle the ledges, getting farther and farther away from those who shouted to us, and we finally faded into the cool darkness of that block of houses whose chimneys sent streams of illuminated smoke out to sea . . .

When the alarm went off at six on the dot, advising me that it was time to go to school, I made my way to the chair where every night I used to hang my jacket and carefully place my two squares of breakfast chocolate. With a feeling of horror that made me jump to the center of the room, I noticed that the notebook in which I had so carefully pressed my letter—my beautiful letter—had flown away while I had been dreaming of rooftops and my pursuit of Milagritos.

After making a long detour down by the docks along the river, I passed in the lingering darkness, more dead than alive, beneath her balconies on the way to seven o'clock Mass. I then marched in formation through the vacant schoolyard that resounded with our footsteps on the way to the study room, my arms crossed like those of a corpse and pressed tightly against my chest where I could feel the empty space left by that letter which had substituted for my heart during most of the previous day. A very sad morning, that, seated before my algebra textbook which I would have liked to understand if for no other reason than to forget my misfortunes, alleviate the pain and drive away that dark wing of future punishment which I felt to be hovering above me.

While I was in the depths of my depression, the Edile had given the signal for us to enter our classroom. My attention was brought back to mathematics only by the cold scraping of the chalk against the blackboard. It was then that a fifth-year student suddenly entered the room and spoke secretly and mysteriously to Father La Torre, the teacher in charge of that class.

"Rafael Alberti, to the visiting room" was the order he crisply communicated to me as soon as the student had turned to leave.

I walked out of the room followed by the open-eyed expectation of the other students in the class. It was very strange for a day student to be called to that room which was generally reserved only for the families of the boarding students during weekly Sunday visits.

I crossed the large and still darkened patio with my eyes looking up at the ribbon of sunlight already hanging from the clock tower. I walked slowly, holding back my steps with the deliberate intention of never getting there. Why the visiting room, I thought to myself, and not the office of the Prefect or the Spiritual Father? Mama! Mama! Could *she* be my visitor? Mama coming here to accuse me with letter in hand? And I felt a throbbing pain like a toothache, an unbearable tugging inside of me that brought tears to my eyes. Finally, there was nothing left for me but to enter the room, since there I was at the door, trembling on shaky legs. When I actually walked in I noticed that I had suddenly recovered from my despondency and I was quite calm, almost happy.

At the other end of this huge chamber was the Prefect, standing next to a rather large lady dressed in mourning who at first did not look at all familiar. But as I approached, she became transformed, much to my great surprise and indignation, into Aunt Tití, my father's unhappy and fanatically religious sister who lived on Cruces Street opposite the house of my beloved.

It was difficult to remain calm as I walked toward those cold, very serious faces that awaited me. Nonetheless, I think that when I reached them I was pretty much in control of myself. But I was alarmed and inwardly frightened half to death by the unexpected presence of my aunt, whom I knew was one of Milagritos' neighbors. I couldn't understand why she, and not my mother, had come to school.

"Rafael" began the Prefect, sourly and somewhat harshly, while Aunt Tití lowered her eyes and nervously pressed her rosary beads against her missal.

There was a brief, anguished pause during which I noticed how a fly had perched on the tortoise-shell frames of the Jesuit's glasses; how, beyond the large window that looked out on the orchard, the Father in charge of the garden with the skirts of his cassock all tucked up, was pushing a wheelbarrow piled high with grass; how the Sacred Heart of Jesus who presided over the room was losing the curl in his beard and no longer had that usual plastered look of someone who has just come from the barber shop. . . . I was about to fix my glance on other things during that short, mortal silence when the Prefect spoke again with authority: "Get your books, your overcoat and your cap."

I remember looking at him in astonishment, my eyes like open mouths straining to shout how excessive, how unfair and unexpected such an order seemed to be.

"Yes," continued the Reverend Father, sharply. "Enough scandals and absences from class! A pupil of San Luis Gonzaga, a day student besides and right in the middle of his spiritual exercises, dragging the Society through the mud! So get moving—don't make me repeat it—your overcoat, your cap, your books. Your aunt has already spoken to me." And as he said this he passed my letter from one sleeve of his cassock to another, so that I would get a glimpse of it. "Now march right off with her, and that's that."

And without even saying goodbye to the confused lady, he was the one who marched right off, covered with dandruff, as unkempt as ever, and with his slippered feet making those flannel-covered noises as he walked across the floor.

I left the school and, standing in the middle of the Plaza of San Francisco with my overcoat, my cap and my books in accordance with the Prefect's orders, I broke into shouts of fury as I tore myself away from Aunt Tití's grasp. "It's your fault! You, you who came here to accuse me because you live across the street from the Sanchos. Mama gave *you* the letter!"

I didn't dare to pronounce the name of Milagritos.

And I dashed away down Sierpe Street, headed for the beach, while my aunt began to whine, completely beside herself: "Child!

Cuco! That's not what I wanted at all. How awful! I can't breathe! When your mother finds out that you've been expelled!"

When I finally reached the dunes and stood there in the nude, looking out to the sea and crying to my heart's content, I not only forgave my mother but also poor Aunt Tití, having at the same time certain thoughts about the Jesuits which I would not put into words until many years later.

At this moment, my memories of the tree trunks and Spanish broom in this lost grove of mine are becoming entangled with the branches of newly planted but intricate liana vines, the color of blood. Forcibly weaving in and out and blending with each other, making it difficult for me to separate them, are my three trips—1932, 1934 and 1937—to the USSR, that country so vilely and desperately attacked by Germany. With tears of anger, of faith, of pride and of hope, my hands reach out to her soldiers and my heart speaks to her great mass of people who are the fertile seeds of the future.

Uncle Tomás appeared one morning before the astonished and questioning eyes of his nephews, at least those of us who had never seen him before.

He was already old then, beautiful rather than handsome with his white, Italian-style sideburns. He was extremely well-groomed and his charming Castilian speech was interspersed with pure Andalusian expressions that had stayed with him since his early days in Granada.

Uncle Tomás was very sick and he had come home to recuperate, to replenish with the salt air and pines of Cádiz the health which he had so badly neglected in his youth. He was a fine example of all those fiery young Garibaldians who had brought about Italian unity. He was a happy man with a fine sense of irony; everything about him, including his way of speaking, retained the spark of the wild young firebrand he had once been.

His glorious past as a soldier could be summed up by those three missing fingers of his right hand, which he would only show to the few discredited liberals in the Puerto while he told them his romantic story. However, because of the insufferable religious severity of his family, whenever they were around Uncle Tomás was careful to hide his hand beneath a fine suede glove, to avoid their snide allusions, their veiled criticism of his "shameful and abominable" past. But neither young nor old had escaped hearing the mysterious rumors

87

that Uncle Tomás had been excommunicated from the Church and that a bullet had neatly sliced off his three fingers as a punishment for his having fought against the Pope.

"Uncle, uncle; we want to see them! Uncle!"—we kept hammering at him whenever the adults were not present.

Uncle Tomás would condescend, in his kind and pleasant way, to remove his glove.

"Can we touch them? Oh, please!"

And with infantile panic, convinced that blue, infernal flames would shoot up from that mutilated and sacrilegious hand, we'd rapidly poke around in those spaces formerly occupied by his thumb, index and middle fingers: "One, two, three! One, two, three!" we shouted in a state of hysteria.

Uncle Tomás was a bit forgetful, either consciously or unconsciously, according to what suited him best. He never remembered his religious obligations or he did a perfect job of pretending not to remember them, although poor Aunt Lola would gladly have served as his constant alarm clock or charioteer: "Tomás, tomorrow is Sunday; don't forget you have to go to Communion at the beginning of the year; there is a *Novena* for our Patron Saint; and don't forget Evening Worship. . . ."

But what he really forgot were not those things at all. He never could remember if he had been born in Genoa or Florence or if he had five or seven brothers and sisters. His lapses of memory were so severe that he would argue violently with one of his brothers about his own mother's name.

"I'm telling you, Agusto, that our mother's name was Rosa."

"You're wrong, Tommaso; mother's name was Catalina."

"And I tell you it wasn't, Agusto; Rosa, Rosa. . . ."

"Catalina, Catalina . . ."

"Rosa!"

"Catalina!"

But since they never could agree, the subject would be put to rest for a short period of time, only to reappear with the same impetus.

And suddenly, when it seemed that the fresh air of the Puerto was making him stronger and lifting up his spirits, Uncle Tomás took to his bed, where he lay stretched out but struggling like a brave soldier against death. His daughters Gloria, María and Dolorcitas became mysterious; Aunt Lola was mysterious, the house was mysterious, and everything surrounding the sick man's bed also became dark and mysterious. Something serious was happening which had to be kept hidden at all costs. No one knew exactly what was being debated, although the incessant whispers, the constant traffic to and from the bedroom of the dying man and the sad presence of a Jesuit priest in the dark sitting-room made it all desperately apparent.

The other uncles appeared one by one, adding rumors and more secrets to Uncle Tomás's last moments. I also arrived with my mother, since I was the favorite nephew, and everyone's grief and sighing restlessness also affected me. Something like the vibration of a taut, invisible string could be sensed in that house, and the moment when it would inevitably break was awaited with fear now that we were all aware of how delicately it was being held together, only temporarily postponing the eventual catastrophe.

The Jesuit priest, his presence diffused from the shadowy corner of the room where he sat, urgently invited all of us to recite the rosary. While the other mourners gathered around the Jesuit, Gloria, María and Dolorcitas fell to their knees and drowned out the five interminable mysteries and the monotonous repetition of the litany with their violent sobbing.

Only Aunt Lola remained at the dying man's bedside, keeping watch over his final struggle.

When, after three *Agnus Dei,* the Jesuit asked Saint Joseph for his divine intercession so that someone, whose name he did not mention, might die well, my aunt's shadow appeared and signalled with a nod to the priest. It seemed that the moment had arrived for the vibrant tautness of the string to give and then remain forever silent. The prayers having been interrupted, an anguished silence hummed through the penumbra of the room which was getting progressively darker as the blackness of the night began to seal up all the openings to the outside world.

"Santa Madonna!" was the long, weak cry suddenly heard coming from the dying man's bedroom.

After a few minutes in which the voice of the Jesuit could be heard reciting Latin prayers simultaneously with the ejaculatory murmurings of Aunt Lola, a contrite moan uttered by the dying man reached our ears: "My Lord Jesus Christ!"

With lighted candles, Gloria, María and Dolorcitas ran toward their father's room, bumping into the priest who loomed like a gigantic shadow in the doorway.

"Now he can calmly receive the Lord," he announced in a voice loud enough to be heard by everyone in the house, as he had intended.

And as he disappeared, victorious and in search of the viaticum, the three daughters entered their father's bedroom joyfully to rekindle the expiring breath of the old, repentant soldier.

The following morning Mama brought me back to Aunt Lola's house. Gloria received us with red, sleepless eyes and she moistened my forehead with a long, tearful kiss. She then let her arm rest on my shoulders and led me slowly through empty rooms and hallways until we reached the one where Uncle Tomás already lay inside his coffin, dressed in the white habit of a Carthusian monk. By the time the roosters began to crow, he had already ceased to exist. A large strand of rosary beads were now wrapped around the roots of those fingers which a Vatican bullet had torn from the patriot's right hand.

"Take the child out of here," Aunt Lola ordered her daughter, after she had first made me kneel down next to her and recite a chain of prayers.

When I entered the sitting-room, I saw the Jesuit priest seated in his corner surrounded by many of my uncles and some other gentlemen whom I knew only from having seen them drunkenly staggering in the streets on my way to school. The women were not there. They were undoubtedly gathered in some other room in the house where Aunt Gloria was now heading, convinced that I was right behind her.

The Jesuit held in his hand a printed sheet of paper framed in black, and he was severely reprimanding Uncle Luis: "There are certain honors that simply cannot appear in the death notice of a man who has died a Christian death, without creating a great scandal."

My uncle's exhausted face was changing its color from yellow to snow-white; the faces of the rest of the group present were, on the contrary, becoming darker with questioning frowns.

"And although we have fortunately discovered this in time to avoid their complete distribution, the few that have already gone out will, by this time, have probably stirred the consciences of some excellent Catholics," he added, pointing to a thick packet of large envelopes also framed in black.

After coughing twice during a brief pause, he continued in the midst of the most remorseful silence: "You must print up other death announcements. The burial will not take place until tomorrow."

And he turned over to Uncle Luis that same piece of paper he had held up before. One of the printed lines had been crossed out with a thick crayon. Someone dared to read this censored item aloud, in a trembling voice: "The Medal of Italian Unity."

"Jesus Christ!" was the only unanimous exclamation to be heard.

Needless to say that in the new announcement, printed and then distributed a few hours later, all reference to the fiendish Italian medal had completely disappeared.

At eleven o'clock the next morning, Don Tomás Alberti y Sanguinetti, holder of the Great Cross of Carlos III, holder of the Cross of Alfonso XII, Knight of the Order of Malta, etc., etc., received a Catholic burial—repentant and confessed of all his sins—in the Municipal Cemetery of the Puerto de Santa María. The old Garibaldian hero, thanks to the militant zeal of the Society of Jesus, was going to rest for eternity divested of the one single honor and decoration with which he would have proudly descended into the earth.

I loved you, Uncle Tommaso, not only because of the fearful admiration which your three missing fingers awakened in me, but because you were one of the few people in the family who had some consideration for Centella, my small and unhappy dog. I remember how you would pet her every time you saw her.

This night in Buenos Aires seems like an endless nightmare. Legions of immense red fleas have mercilessly begun to attack Tusca in the dark. In my semi-conscious state, neither fully awake nor completely asleep, I have been suffering through the constant thumping of her paws against the floor as she defends herself from this aggression in a furious and violent seizure of scratching.

Three dogs bark loudly and come running up to stare at me as they sit in the middle of my life: Centella, of my infancy; Niebla, of my late youth; Tusca, of my American exile.

Centella, accompanying me through the salt flats; along the beaches, among the pine forests and the castles of the Puerto. Niebla, roaming with me in the ruins of Madrid, amidst the explosions and death; one of Franco's prisoners in the surrender of Castellón de la Plana. And Tusca, pure Scotch-Creole, hunter of rats, happy and half-crazy, running freely in the

*wind through the fields of El Totoral de Córdoba, desperately miserable
today in the narrow confinement of a two-room apartment in Buenos
Aires.*

When I was expelled from school and after the death of Uncle
Tomás, my love for Centella entered its most abundant phase. With
one jump she would awaken me before dawn, licking my eyes so that
I had to quickly turn my face away from her wild attacks. After she
had reached the patio she was the first one to race out into the street,
disappearing like a bullet in the direction of the gas works on the
road to the beach, running back and forth to check whether I was
still following her.

Days of freedom with no reason to tell lies when I came home.
Long, naked hours with the tide coming up to my chest and no need
to worry about a spyglass peering from the physics classroom or
about the tortuous visits to the Spiritual Father or the Prefect's
offensive humiliations!

"Go get it, Centella!"

The flat stones, washed by the sea and tossed across its flat surface,
skimmed over the water, bouncing three, five and even seven times
while the delirious dog chased after them.

"You're going to drown, you silly animal."

Still panting and looking like some kind of hollow figure made of
sand, algae and salt, she would crouch alongside my bare feet perking
up her ears to listen intently to the tales of cabin boys—Maine
Reid—or the labyrinthine detective stories of Sherlock Holmes and
Nick Carter which my own enthusiasm induced me to read to her
aloud.

She didn't know the date or place of her birth. She had come into
the world the same day I did, in the corner of a waterless cistern
where an ancient tortoise spent its boring and solitary existence
always remaining in the same place and resigned to the frustrated attacks of ferocious nocturnal rats.

"Centella! We're almost fourteen years old. Soon, I will take you
to Madrid. They have very good oculists there."

In her old age very few people liked her and almost everyone
would apprehensively avoid her. A bluish cloud was progressively in-
vading one of her eyes, pushing her into the darkness of night. But
even in that condition, suffering from old-age infirmities, half blind,
her body dotted with bald spots, she was still spirited and bold

enough to race into the water, roll in the sand and disappear suddenly in unexpected bursts of energy.

Yes, she would soon be cured, since the eventual move to Madrid was now becoming noticeable through the presence of Federico, who served as the master carpenter commissioned to make the crates for our furniture. Our imminent departure was also reflected in the constant excitement of our cousins, riddled with envy over our move to the capital of Spain itself where undoubtedly, according to what they had heard, "we would see King Alfonso XIII and Queen Victoria."

Papa arrived from the north, and his appearance gave a sense of finality to our travel arrangements. Although my fantasy by now had taken me far away from the Puerto, particularly since my expulsion from school, the thought of suddenly being transplanted to an unknown city without beaches, without Milagritos, without Aunt Gloria, and even without all those very aunts and uncles whom I hated as much as I loved, all of this made me feel a sudden sense of anguish mixed with disinterest and indifference toward our departure.

"So you're off to *Los Madriles*?* They have real women there," Paquillo the coachman informed me, winking at me as we drove along the docks of the river.

"Women?"

"I mean! Better-looking and cheaper than the ones in our prison."

My dreams that night were in technicolor, as the city of Madrid wrapped itself around my body like a ripe, red peach or a sweet fresh lemon with pointed nipples.

The following day I ran to say goodbye to the Jesuits, but only the feared Prefect was willing to receive me in his rooms.

"You will finish your studies with us at our great school in Chamartín de la Rosa" were his horrible words as he placed his hand to my lips for me to kiss, an act I was incapable of performing since his suggestion had left me almost totally paralyzed.

And Madrid appeared before me that night in my insomnia with the same towers and sinister windows of the Puerto Prison and with the same chilling, melancholy silence.

"You will write to us as soon as you arrive," said Aunt Gloria, accompanying her request with a kiss and a hug.

Los Madriles is a popular term for Madrid.

After repeated recommendations to me that I always be a good boy, Aunt Lola asked: "Are you going to think of me when you visit the Prado Museum?"

I spent that night, the last night of my childhood in the Puerto, without sleeping at all. I wandered with Centella through the patios and the now empty rooms, and then climbed up to the rooftops to wait for the coming of dawn.

When the first light appeared on the horizon, I raced downstairs to awaken my sister Pepita.

"Pipi, let's burn our soldiers. What are they going to do here by themselves?"

"All of them, Cuco?"

"All of them."

Pipi was impressed and got out of bed. Still not fully awake, she helped me construct a pyre in the center of that interior patio which had served as the scene of so many realistic battles. We then proceeded to make a pile of our cardboard heroes, those soldiers we had so patiently cut out over such a long period of time. The glass panes of the skylight turned pink as our soldiers burned in one single flame, their ashes soon swept away by María the cook.

There was nothing left to do. The time had finally come. Along with our older cousins who had gotten up at dawn to say goodbye, Paca Moy's grandchildren—mourning bands on their sleeves—also showed up. Paca Moy, our old servant, had died "like a saint" only recently, surrounded by the squash, tomatoes and grapevines of her little garden in the town of Rota, at the foot of the bay.

At seven-thirty in the morning we all left for the railroad station in two carriages supplied by Uncle Jesús.

Goodbye, Neverías Street, with your summertime popsicles and ice cream; the gardens on the banks of the river, the San Alejandro Bridge, the inlets and salt marshes! Goodbye childhood, with its freedom, its deep dark patios and wine cellars, and its fishing in the waters of the sea! To me you will always be like a small boat filled with carnations, with sails of sweet basil, bobbing up and down in a sea of lost jasmine . . .

At the station, Carreja the fisherman stood barefoot with his shirtsleeves and trousers rolled up. He greeted Mama: "Doña María . . ."

Carreja, unlike Uncle Tomás, wasn't missing any fingers but had, instead, an extra one, a minuscule little thumb with a barnacle-like nail which we used to touch in horrified fascination.

Mama gave him five *pesetas.*

Quick to tears, like most good drunks, the fisherman's eyes clouded over, and when the train whistle blew he raised his hand up to the window where we were all sadly gathered.

"Well, children," he offered as a sign of gratitude, "before you go away. . . ."

All of us at once and more excited than ever said goodbye to Carreja's little thumb, which left on our fingers the strong odor of blue mackerel and fresh crab from La Isla.

The train began to move.

For a brief instant and as if clinging to the train's trail of smoke, there was Victoria Boulevard, the prison, the rifle range . . .

We had passed the water-wheels in the orchard belonging to Uncle Jesús when I saw the shadowy enameled glow of a small orange grove. At that moment a forgotten riddle I had once heard Federico ask darted before my eyes:

> *Muchas damas en un castillo*
> *Y todas visten de amarillo.*

> *Many ladies in a castle,*
> *All of them dressed in yellow.*

And I silently recited the answer to this riddle in the syncopated rhythm of the train that was making its way up the banks of the Guadalete River to Jerez de la Frontera:

"Oranges, oranges, oranges, oranges. . . ."

END OF BOOK ONE

Cuando tú apareciste,
penaba yo en la entraña más profunda
de una cueva sin aire y sin salida.

MARÍA TERESA LEÓN, 1930

Madrid, 1934. Federico García Lorca,
María Teresa León and Rafael Alberti
on the terrace of a cafe in Cuatro
Caminos.

With María Teresa León.

Madrid, 1936. José Bergamín, Rafael Alberti, Pablo Neruda, Luis Cernuda and Manuel Altolaguirre strolling down Alcalá Street.

Alberti reciting his poetry to a group of soldiers of the Republic during the Spanish Civil War.

A poetry reading during the war.

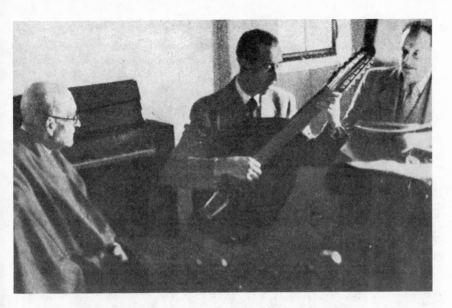

Alta Gracia, 1945. Manuel de Falla, Paco Aguilar and Rafael Alberti.

Buenos Aires, 1949. Alberti with Juan Ramón Jiménez.

Rome, April 1974.

BOOK

two

1917–1931

*It is spring in Buenos Aires, and while rereading the perplexing,
violent, passionate and undoubtedly often false* Life of Benvenuto
Cellini *I feel an uncontrollable desire to continue with my forgotten*
Lost Grove, *whose first small volume describing those blue and
white years of my Andalusian childhood ends with the vision of
golden oranges glimpsed like a lightning flash from the window of
the train that was taking us all to Madrid. And now, on this
warm afternoon—November 18th, 1954—seated in my little
enclosed garden on Las Heras Street under two flowering
poinsettia plants, breathing in the intoxicating aroma of a
neighboring magnolia tree, looking at the four sad rosebushes
suffering a martyrdom by ants, and surrounded by the thick green
clinging vines of ivy, I begin this, my second book of memories.
That distant grove, lost—yes—or asleep and awakening again
today, races to meet me, responding to the eager call of my now no
longer youthful blood! I emerge from my fifty-one years and
passing over so many horrifying events and so much sadness, I fly
toward those other years when humor, joy, transparent faith and
enthusiasm had only been slightly dampened by those pure first
tears which never blind but rather illuminate even more the
beauty, grandeur and profundity of life.*

CHAPTER *I*

... A ND I SEE MYSELF with sleepy eyes that still retained the fleeting but dazzling vision of the Giralda of Sevilla, as we arrived at the Atocha Station in Madrid. May 1917. Disillusionment and sadness! A gray, sunless morning, bathed in that delicate silver light of Madrid I later came to love, but which on the day of our arrival seemed to me to be the most depressing shade of black. How awful it all was! The pupils of my eyes were still dizzy with the whiteness of Andalusia, filled with the blinding white salt from the marshes of La Isla, penetrated by blues and light yellows, by the greens and purples of my river, my sea, my beaches and my pine forests. That brick-red color of the snub-nosed balconies draped with dirty, dripping clothes which welcomed me, was the city—the capital of Spain—which my family had dared to exchange for the Puerto. They brought us here to live in this coal-bin! The place which my father had already rented was not far from the station and was actually on Atocha Street itself. Another cause for disillusionment and protest.

"I won't live here for a minute. Pipi and I are going back to the Puerto," I decided aloud, involving my younger sister without even having consulted her.

What were we going to do, particularly the two of us, in that tiny dark apartment located on that narrow street with its clanging trolley cars? Where were the sunny patios where we could set up our games and fight our dangerous battles? How could we jump from rooftop to rooftop listening to the sounds that came up through the chimneys from the kitchens down below? We would run away, and if my sister couldn't go with me, I at least would escape alone, traveling on foot along the Andalusian highway. To give myself encouragement I wrote a letter to my Aunt Gloria, reviling Madrid, including the Puerta de Sol, and advising her of my plans for escape. But I remember asking several times how to get to the Puerto, and no one seemed to know. Perhaps it was because in my innocence I almost never asked for the road to Andalusia but rather for the road to our town, which many people had never even heard of. Meanwhile, since escape was not easy and my decision, I suspect now, was not all that firm, my Aunt Gloria had time to reply to my letter, begging me to keep calm, a suggestion which besides wounding me deeply contributed greatly to cooling the silent love I still felt for her. Besides trying to convince me to "desist from carrying out my scatterbrained scheme"—those were her exact words—she proceeded to exaggerate the boring aspects of life back home including, among other bits of unpleasant news that I've forgotten, the sad story of Centella, my poor half-blind dog whom we had so barbarously left to her own fate when we moved to Madrid.

What happened was that the unhappy little animal, on finding the door to the house tightly shut, spent days and nights stretched out on the front bench faithfully awaiting our return. During the first week some kindly neighbors brought her food, but she was in such a state of depression that she barely touched it. Half-dead from starvation and pining away, she remained there at the door until one afternoon two charitable Sisters devoted to helping the needy took her away to their shelter where, in spite of her old age and blindness, Centella became the companion of the shepherd in charge of the nuns' herd of animals. On her infrequent sallies into the fields as a watchdog, her awkwardness and torpor made her get closer than she should have to the horns of a skittish brave calf. Undoubtedly disturbed by that black thing that was getting in her way, the calf charged Centella and, impaling her on one of her horns, she sent the little dog flying against the trunk of a tree with her heart torn in two. Such an unexpectedly taurine end for an animal as far gone and decrepit as our Centella deeply affected all of us. From that moment on I considered myself principally responsible for the cruel negligence we had shown toward poor Centella. No one in the house that night closed their eyes without feeling a shadow of remorse weighing heavily on their conscience. In time my family probably forgot all about this sad episode, but not I. It still pains me to remember it and I am quick to tell the story to anyone, perhaps to allay my own sense of guilt, whenever people around me bring up the subject of dogs.

After about two months had passed, during which my nostalgia for the sea and the salt flats had penetrated even more deeply inside of me, although my eagerness to escape had been somewhat placated, I openly declared to my parents that I would not continue with my schoolwork. I told them that if I was to stay in Madrid—I had already, said this to them several times before—it was because I wanted to become a painter.

"You'll die of hunger," predicted both of them, and their opinion was seconded by my older brothers.

"I don't care."

"Paint if you want to, but finish high school first even if you don't take up a career afterwards," begged my mother, always more understanding than the rest.

"No!" I shouted.

"Then you won't get a cent from me for paints and crayons."

"I don't need them."

"That's your business."

Thinking about it some more, and since it was summertime, I changed my mind a few days later and said that I would continue with my fourth year of studies, taking my examinations in June or September of the following year.

This clever decision was immediately worth a few *pesetas* which I promptly used to buy drawing supplies, a small box of oil paints and even a tiny easel for painting outdoors. How marvelous it was! That very morning I felt liberated from my deep melancholy and envisioned myself as a future illustrious painter crowned with glory. I raced breathlessly to the Casón, that precious little palace that had belonged to Felipe IV, located on the street of Alfonso XII opposite the Buen Retiro Gardens. First I wanted to make some sketches, as they teach you to do in the Academies. Somewhat timidly I went up to the desk to register, but they told me this wasn't necessary and that anyone was free to work in that museum. I was informed that the caretaker would even supply me—free of charge!—with a drawing board. I would only have to buy paper and charcoal. The following day by nine o'clock I was already happily ensconced inside the Casón in a state of ecstasy before the Esquiline Venus.

Probably few adolescents have ever been as convinced as I was at the age of fifteen that their true vocation was the art of drawing and painting. In those, my initial days as an incipient artist, I had not yet heard—as I was later to hear so often—the scorn and derision many people felt toward the Academy and the apprenticeship or discipline so essential for the sustenance and development of one's future work. With great dedication in that house of King Felipe IV, beneath the violent allegory that Giordano left hanging from the ceiling of the center room, I made several copies in different dimensions of the white plaster statues, trying to capture the airy clarity of the Winged Victory of Samothrace, the arched outline of the Discobolos of Myron, the supple simplicity of the Apoxyómenos of Lysippus, the infinite torture of Laocoön, the rough anatomy of Hercules, the infantile agility of the Fawn, but without forgetting those famous mothers of love and grace: the Venus de Milo and the Medici Venus. What a superb collection of reproductions were to be found in that museum—fragments, complete statues or heads (including the one of Seneca, the poet, that made him look like a rat)! All of them emerged either in precise outline or diffused chiaroscuro from under the piece of charcoal that my hand had now learned to move skillfully across the tense surface of the sketching paper.

In a few months I knew the Casón collection backwards and forwards. Even today, after so many years, I could probably draw some of those pieces of sculpture without having them in front of me. But what had begun for me as something so incredibly beautiful became in time rather monotonous and dull, particularly once I had learned and mastered the techniques. So without completely abandoning my sketches of these statues, I wanted to try something I imagined would be more difficult: copying paintings in the Prado Museum. I chose as my first project a death portrait of St. Francis, attributed to Zurbarán.

I have yet to mention how surprised I was by our marvelous Museum of Art on my first visits there. Accustomed in my Andalusian town to seeing only poor color reproductions and copies of landscape paintings from the "School of Velázquez" at my grandparents' house, I had thought that the old paintings would be darkly subdued, covered with brownish earth-tones and incapable of the blues, reds, pinks, golds, greens and whites which were suddenly revealed to me by Velázquez, Titian, Tintoretto, Rubens, Zurbarán, Goya ... There in front of me now was the authentic little prince

Baltasar Carlos, standing out against the brightest blue sky and the purest white of the snow that covered the Guadarrama Mountains, a background that had been dead and leaden in that awful reproduction I had copied two years ago, the cause of my break-up with our cook María.

My innocent eyes were opened that first day, and not without causing me to feel a certain blushing discomfort, to the splendiferous, fleshy, mother-of-pearl figures of Rubens. His powerful Graces, flowing Pomonas, Nymphs pursued through the woods, Dianas adorned with dogs and ivory tusks, tall, ungirded Venuses—all those nude goddesses—would later inundate my troubled and sleepless adolescent nights. I knew very little at the time about satyrs, fawns, centaurs, tritons and other sea or forest creatures whose reddish eyes and tense muscles expressed their love for those deities formed from roses and jasmines by Rubens' brush. That confused mass of brute strength created by the Flemish painter awakened in me an awareness of how fertile, desirable and wild life can sometimes be. The golden clarity of Titian, the reclining solidity of his music-loving Venuses, their happy games and gentle smiles under the "tame wind" [el manso viento—quoted from Garcilaso de la Vega] of the trees, instilled in my blood forever a longing for perpetual youth, for a luminous and boundless harmony. In the works of that Venetian painter, as in the spring-colored roofs of Veronese and the warm radiances of Tintoretto, I recognized half unconsciously how much white and blue from the Mediterranean sun and breezes already existed in the Italo-Andalusian marrow of my bones.

There suddenly and in mute amazement I had discovered the full maturity of unadorned beauty, the golden age of color, the indescribable expression of amorous desire, the unfettered passion of the senses. I had thought, remembering the few paintings I had seen in the magazines and books at Aunt Lola's house, that besides having dim colors, the principal subject matter of classical painting was religious and that only devils, angels, virgins, Christs, saints, popes, monks and nuns of all kinds covered the walls of museums. How violently the immense central room of the Prado Museum changed that provincial idea! Not even the Spanish paintings which occupied part of that space were solely dedicated to such themes, although it was true that their melancholic tonal severity contrasted sharply —making the colors look even sadder—with the scintillating madness of Rubens and the melodious joy of the Venetians. I came to

107

realize that in spite of the feathery grays, silvers, blues and pinks of Veláquez, the celestial nebula of Murillo, the incandescent and sulphuric yellows of El Greco, the ivory tones and the whites of Zurbarán and the chromatic range of Goya, in spite of all this tonal richness, my eyes and my blood—my whole being—belonged exclusively in that green and golden pagan world of which Titian more than any other of the great artists—oh Tiépolo—was the undisputed master. Titian with his highly sharpened sense of light was the one painter who convinced me that my roots were definitively and deeply embedded in those civilizations of blue and white. This is what my eyes had seen from early childhood in the façades, the doorframes and windows of those simple houses that stood in the towns scattered around the bay, delicately shaded by the translucent blue from the fresco paintings of Crete which had reached us by way of Italy, projecting their blueness over the entire Mediterranean coast of Spain—in the villages of Cádiz, on the shores of the Atlantic and beyond Huelva to the Portuguese border.

I conveyed my first impressions of the Prado in several letters I wrote to Aunt Lola, whom I still deeply loved for having first introduced me to the world of painting. She died shortly after we left for Madrid, but whenever her health permitted, she would reply with letters of encouragement. One of the last things she requested was a copy of Murillo's *Immaculate Conception* which she wanted to hang in her room. In my own list of preferences I had substituted Zurbarán for Murillo, since even in the company of Velázquez, El Greco and Goya he was the one Spanish painter who astonished me the most.

Ever since I came across them on my first day at the Prado, I have always admired and felt a burning curiosity about copyists in museums, and this admiration later included even forgers of paintings, some of whom were to become good friends of mine. There was one copyist in the Velázquez room who had a "permanent subscription" to *Los Borrachos (The Drunks)*, which he reproduced with great skill and in every imaginable size. I witnessed the height of his success one morning when the museum was jammed with visitors. Having finished a copy of his favorite painting, this time in the same dimensions as the original, he began to wheel his work out of that large room on a movable easel. The people there who had gathered around stepped back to let him pass and broke out in spontaneous applause which this good man—small, odd-looking and bearded—acknowledged with a smile and a nod of his head.

Being very impressionable in those days, I dreamed of reaching perfection in that clever and minor art of copying so that I could hang all my favorite masterpeices on the walls of the apartment. But my restlessness during those years and my growing uneasiness about the latest pictorial techniques were the cause of my never finishing the Zurbarán portrait of St. Francis nor even another copy of Goya's *La gallina ciega (Blind Man's Buff)*, which I had begun somewhat later. What really impressed me was the atmosphere in the museum, the movement of people through its lustrous rooms and corridors that were enveloped in that almost adhesive aroma of varnish and wax, an unforgettable smell that always took me back to the pine forests of the Puerto and the odor of resin in the air.

In winter the temperature at the Prado was delightful; those heated nymphs pursued by satyrs, those Graces and Venuses also bereft of any trace of clothing, calmly offered themselves to my ecstatic gaze in the warmth of those rooms that were sheltered from the penetrating knife-like cold of the Guadarrama Mountains. In summer it was even more pleasant, and the museum could be like a cool bath or a shaded forest since the downstairs rooms—containing the Poussins, the Lorrains and miscellaneous statues—were peacefully tranquil and dark during the *siesta* hour. The shadowy depths of Claude Lorrain's landscapes with their deified twilights, colonnades and temple ruins, filled my Madrid summers with a greater poetic reality than I could possibly have found among the most beautiful trees of Aranjuez or La Granja.

It was summer when I began to copy Goya's *La gallina ciega* which, as I have already said, I eventually left unfinished. Almost all the Goyas were then hanging on the ground floor, and for that reason I always entered the museum through the door presided over by the statue of Velázquez and guarded by the most beautiful cedar trees I have ever seen in Spain. My sister Pepita would come with me almost every morning to watch me copy the delightful Goya cartoon. Under my tutelage she had become very fond of painting and even of poetry, which we used to read together on our walks through the Altos del Hipódromo, the Retiro or the Botanical Gardens. We no longer lived on Atocha Street and had moved to Lagasca, which was quite far from the Prado. As a result I had to get up earlier and always walk great distances. In addition to being extremely timid I was also too proud to ask for money at home, and I was beginning to feel somewhat martyred by all this. I was already aware of my family's disapproval of my artistic vocation, although this attitude had always been latent in them and was generally only expressed through silence. They were also evidently quite suspicious about my never opening a book, since I had not kept my promise to take those examinations a year after our arrival in Madrid. My having been untrustworthy was the main reason I never dared ask them for even ten cents to cover my minimum daily necessities in the streets of Madrid. But during that period of my life I didn't really care one way or the other if I had to walk, not only to the Prado but anywhere in the world.

The Goya rooms, where all the cartoons he did for the Royal Tapestry Factory were hanging, opened my eyes each morning to a kind of celebration, the only real festival to be found among the sad, solemn Spanish paintings in abundance there, and it was all like a refreshing and happily transparent fountain of delight. A popular and colorful street-fair, the authentic and elegant cry of Spain. The play of street breezes, afternoons like a bullfighter's *traje de luces,* avenues resplendent with carriages, airborne kites and fireworks. The most subtle yellows, pinks, greens and blues extended everywhere as if they had been mixed with some miraculous water from a river that Nature had suddenly revealed by making it spring forth from the tip of an artist's brush. Here, finally, was a Spain capable of light, of delicate smiles, of a heart brimming over with a healthy and even boisterous joy. But in cruel contrast to these cooling, fluid tapestries were the drawings and ferocious wall paintings from the Quinta del Sordo which, if I remember correctly, were then also hanging downstairs and only later removed to the rooms on the first floor of the museum. Those works cast a ray of mordant darkness over that other bright arena, and together they defined Goya and the Spain he represented: an enormous bullring violently cut in two, one half black and the other half white: the whiteness of its sun and the lust for life; the deep blackness of its shade and the dark, coagulated blood.

The subtitles which the painter himself had devised and written beneath his drawings amused and even embarrassed me. I was worried about my sister seeing the ones I thought were a bit strong. Goya's spelling in these brief descriptive titles was more than just capricious, and the exact meaning of his language was not to be found in the written word but, rather, in the sketched image. How could a man capable of expressing himself so ingeniously with a drawing pencil be the least bit interested in the rules of grammar? At the time I wasn't too concerned about such things either, but I was still shocked by the discovery of a linguistic audacity and daring whose existence I could not up until then have even suspected. It was probably natural that a child who had only recently left his provincial village would be disturbed by such titles as *Aunt Gila's Queer, A Blind Man in Love with his Mare, They Say Nothing (El maricón de la tía Gila, Ciego enamorado de su potra, Nada dicen)*, or by the obsessive presence of all those greedy, dirty and shameless monks who darkened that museum wall.

My mornings and afternoons during that suffocatingly hot Madrid summer of 1918 were spent looking at the lighthearted *Blind Man's Buff* and the watercolors and drawings of this not overly compassionate portrait painter of the last of the Bourbons. All of it had the effect of awakening in me—although vaguely and innocently at first—the enthusiasm and understanding I was later to feel so strongly for Goya's unfortunate Spain which, sadly enough, still suffers in much the same way today.

Whenever I lost patience with my copying activities at the Prado, I broke the monotony by visiting the Casón where I had met a boy, Servando del Pilar, with whom I became very friendly. He was the most talented of all the young people who practiced their drawing techniques at that particular museum. His father was a garbage collector, a kind and gentle man who would leave his house before sunrise carrying that burlap sack which he filled up with other people's refuse and leftovers. One morning I visited the place where he and his son Servando lived, and I was both astounded and touched by what I saw. A small table and a folding cot were all I could make out in the damp and gloomy darkness of that single dilapidated room that served as their home. That poor, simple and almost saintly man was proud of his son's artistic talent and it was for his sake that he worked at such a menial task from dawn to dusk, dreaming that some day his young painter son would make it possible for him to enjoy a few years of well-deserved rest and comfort. Since I admired Servando, I would sometimes try to console him and make him

111

forget his abject poverty by telling him the golden story of Giotto, the shepherd boy. When my Aunt Lola first told me this story of that marvelous Italian painter, I had listened to her in a state bordering on ecstasy.

When both of us were not engaged in drawing sketches at the Casón or when we tired of the Prado, we would fill the pages of our sketch-pads with drawings taken from real life: landscapes, people sitting at sidewalk cafés, laborers taking their afternoon *siestas* in the shade. Sometimes Servando del Pilar would spend the afternoon at my house, in that bedroom-studio of mine, and we'd pose for each other. The two of us might also just sit daydreaming before the open window, watching the blue of the mountains fade as the sun disappeared behind the peaks and seeing the distant penumbra of Madrid begin to glow with lights as the first stars appeared in the sky.

In spite of the reigning disorder in that room on Lagasca Street—my mother called it a lion's den, but my friends had baptized it "The Triclinium"—it was always the busiest room in the house. Everyone who came to our apartment, even those who for some inexplicable reason were annoyed by my choice of vocation, felt the urge to poke their heads into my room to see what was going on. I was not particularly fond of these inspections, since they usually ended up in scornful laughter or impertinent remarks concerning my paintings and drawings which, although still quite tamely academic, struck them nonetheless as being "crazy and exaggerated."

There were others, however, who were always welcome in The Triclinium. The first of these was my sister Pepita. She was permitted to disturb that beloved disorder of mine and to borrow my books, especially those of particular poets whom we both admired. The other friends who had free access to this inner sanctum were Manuel Gil Cala, Celestino Espinosa and María Luisa, a pretty friend of my sister's who was quite a bit older than I but with whom I considered myself deeply in love. I even did a large portrait drawing of her.

Manuel Gil Cala and Celestino Espinosa were poets; María Luisa wasn't anything at all except tall and dark haired with large, intense eyes. She liked Bécquer's poetry and in those days she was also reading the works of Amado Nervo and Rubén Darío, two poets whose works we had heard about from Gil Cala. That impish María Luisa was responsible for a very serious situation that concerned

Manuel Gil Cala, Celestino and me and which was never openly discussed or fully clarified. When the light began to fade on those afternoons when María Luisa had been posing in my room for several hours, she and I would meet secretly at the small Salamanca Park which was then a mysteriously secluded spot, surrounded by high hedges behind whose deep shadows the benches were practically invisible. The two of us would sit on one of these benches, almost always the same one, sometimes without saying a single word, until about ten o'clock at night when she would suddenly disappear, afraid of being seen. One day Espinosa somehow found out about these clandestine meetings and immediately adopted a strange protective attitude toward me that was filled with whispered warnings and negative remarks about my relationship with María Luisa. He thought it dangerous for us to meet so secretively, suggesting that such an arrangement could easily create a scandal because of the growing friendship between María Luisa's family and my own.

I never knew exactly what happened, but shortly after that María Luisa stopped showing up at our mysterious park and Celestino, in an attempt to console me for my loss, dedicated a poem to me dealing with my "love affair" and containing stanzas that referred to the park bench hidden among the shadows. Gil Cala, whom I never imagined would be aware of anything that was happening, suddenly shocked Espinosa and me by reading us some impassioned verses of his, dedicated to María Luisa. We listened in complete silence without betraying the slightest sign of surprise. After swallowing that bitter pill, I never attempted to find out if María Luisa had deceived me with Celestino or if she had deceived Celestino with Gil Cala. But all during our long and close friendship, the three of us were always conscious of the existence of that dark, unexplored region which we would cleverly and smilingly bypass whenever the subject happened to come up in conversation.

María Luisa never returned to The Triclinium, although that large, full-length charcoal portrait of her remained for a long time hanging on the wall opposite my bed.

I will always remember that "lion's den," my delightful room where I spent so many happy hours and so many anguished, sleepless nights until I finally abandoned it forever at the age of 25. How many dawns entered through its windows, coming to rest on my bloodshot eyes heavy with the fatigue of sleeplessness! But not only gentle sunrises and noisy twilights over the distant mountains spread their pink glow over my pillow, my books, my drawing board and my easel. One day the window was also open to the sounds of death—the rapid sputtering of a machine-gun awakened me brusquely from the stupor of an afternoon nap. The sound was coming from Cuatro Caminos, the working-class district on the west side of Madrid. I knew nothing then about strikes and I understood less about the rights of the so-called proletariat. I didn't have the slightest idea what was happening. It was only later that I found out about the dead, the wounded, the prisoners, and heard for the first time the names of Largo Caballero, Anguiano, Saborit, Besteiro, Fernando de los Ríos . . .

A short time after this incident I also heard about Lenin and the Bolsheviks, but such terms were employed as synonyms for bandits or demons, enemies not only of religion but also of the whole human race. I know now that I lived surrounded by reactionaries, the majority of whom were uninformed and completely blind to what was happening around them, but this was the way they expressed themselves, in words filled with a provincial hatred characteristic of that large class of Spaniards so aptly called "cave-dwellers." Submerged as I was in my vocation and still very young, the meaning of those transcendental events escaped me without leaving any apparent scars, but at least they are recorded in my memory.

Gil Cala was already quite mature and my parents had great faith in his judgment. They thought that being a painter was a career —not a particularly lucrative one, of course—but more or less in the same class as engineering or law, professions that had little in common with my disorganized life as a street artist or my capricious and erratic copying sessions at the Prado Museum. So after consulting Gil Cala, they decided to find me a teacher. I wasn't too happy with the prospect, since I saw it as a threat to the freedom I had enjoyed since my arrival in Madrid. But I offered no serious objections, and thinking that a teacher might after all be helpful to me during this period of apprenticeship, I accepted the one Gil Cala brought to the house. He was a nice, kind person, completely unknown to me and to anyone else, with a long moustache that was pointed at both ends. His name was Emilio Coli. What did I learn from him that I didn't already know during those boring classes devoted exclusively to copying noses, ears, feet, hands, and eyes from a series of illustrated charts? Those hours of instruction were of little use to me, but Coli did get something out of them, since he spent a good part of the time in the apartment flirting with my sister Pepita, who was then beginning to display all the charms of her fifteen years. After awhile Coli became aware of my boredom and recognized the senselessness of my devoting entire afternoons to drawing so many eyes and noses. He recommended that I go back to the Casón and devote myself again to the plaster Venuses and Apollos.

I joyfully resumed my interrupted street existence, racing off early in the morning to Felipe IV's palace to work more seriously at sketching Greek and Roman statues. That change in gallery, from my house to the Casón, didn't cause Professor Emilio Coli any sleepless nights I'm sure, because after that he scarcely bothered to look over my work. Such negligence on his part had the effect of giving me self-confidence in what I was doing on my own. This confidence, however, was shaken from time to time by the embarrassment I felt when I sensed him standing behind me, a smiling expression on his face, and pointing with the tips of his absurd moustache—I was a notorious specialist in Venuses at the time—to the most appetizing parts of the figure I was in the process of sketching. I remember one morning, right after Coli had walked off, when one of the boys who was sketching in the same room and not too far from where I was sitting asked me somewhat maliciously: "Do you have a maestro?" To which I blushingly replied that I didn't, and that the gentleman was a friend of my parents who appreciated painting and had simply dropped by the Casón out of mere curiosity to see what I was up to.

Once Coli disappeared from my life, I somehow managed to get a second teacher, Manuel Mendía, who was even less interested in what I was doing and has not left behind even the amusing memory of a pointed moustache. Completely on my own once again, I threw myself passionately into painting from nature. For the first time I went out into the gardens, fields and country lanes with a box of paints that belonged exclusively to me. I didn't have to worry about the interruptions from the family telling me it was time to eat and, best of all, I didn't have to pretend that I was coming back from school. What a marvelous feeling to be able to sit under the shade of a tree in summer and interpret the reflected ripples of a fountain, the green color of leaves warmed by the sun, the changing violet tones of the mountains—the sharp cutting light of Spain. (How much better this was than later when I had given up painting and would be forced to sit in a room staring at a lifeless sheet of paper or the frightening coldness of a typewriter.) Yes, it was delightful to paint in the open air, innocently mixing colors and taking home the illusion—in the form of brush strokes or little dots—of having had one's eyes fully opened before a landscape! As might be expected of someone my age then living in Madrid, I was at the time a beardless, budding Impressionist or Pointillist, although not too far removed from the other prevailing tendencies in the art world—Cubism as well as several other "isms"—that were to grab hold of young artists all over the world during the postwar period and not let go.

Under the influence of a painting exposition I saw in Madrid, which consisted of some awful landscapes bathed in moonlight, I decided to do something along the same lines. Late one night when there was a full moon and when I imagined my parents were asleep, I silently left the apartment. After roaming up and down several streets and squares in the neighborhood, I chose as a model the Alcalá Gate, whose shaded arches created a special shimmering effect as the blue light of the moon fell across its granite stones. At about three in the morning I considered my version of Carlos III's ample portico finished and I headed homeward, walking happily down Velázquez Street fascinated by the results of my first experiment as a nocturnal painter. But in my ignorance I didn't realize that for devout Catholic Spanish families the opportunity to sin only presents itself under the deep dark cover of night. Not even the brightness of the moon on that particular night could change my father's traditional beliefs. From the beating I received on my arrival home I understood that for him at least the temptations of the Devil do not abandon their corruptive practices even under the brightest rays of that round goddess of lovers. Next morning when I showed my family my moonlit Puerta de Alcalá, I turned to my older brother who was smiling sarcastically and said: "That ought to prove even to you that someone can go out at night without necessarily looking for whores."

His annoying smile had made me realize that he knew what had happened. Later, at lunchtime, my father kissed me as he usually did, so I felt that I was either forgiven or that he perhaps had a guilty conscience because of his earlier unjustly violent behavior toward me. Naturally, that very night I took my box of paints and went out again without permission, going this time to the outskirts of Madrid in search of a new moonscape. That was how I continued educating my family, defending my freedom and gaining respect for my beloved artistic vocation.

During the daytime hours I had many favorite painting sites: the gardens of the Buen Retiro with their ingenuous geometrical paths in the style of Rusiñol and, in autumn, the stately Promenade of Statues; the romantic avenues of the Botanical Garden with its whispering sculpted fountains, green with moss and filled with strange plants and trees that had been classified under names that sounded in my ears like a religious litany—Salix Babylonica, Hanging Sophora, Tree of Heaven . . . Other favorite spots of mine were the green hills of Moncloa with the blue Guadarrama Mountains in the background, the Goyesque banks of the Manzanares River decorated by washerwomen and clotheslines that shimmered in the sun; and to the east, the infinite Castilian plains whose flatness was only broken on the horizon by the Cerro de los Angeles.

I was also strangely attracted to old cemeteries in those days. I would spend horrible Becquerian rainy and windy afternoons painting among the cypress-lined paths and the crumbling, ivy-covered tombstones. The one which fascinated me most was the abandoned cemetery of Santa Engracia. Its children's section moved me deeply, not only because of the nettles and mustard plants covered with snails and the little lizards basking there ecstatically in the sun, but because of the innocent and heart-rending epitaphs which I sometimes copied down in my notebook. There was one whose tender and grotesque use of the diminutive always made me laugh. This small tombstone over the grave of a little child who died in 1870 exclaimed to the world: "Aye, Serapito,* my son, my son!" That was the most tragic of them all.

At the beginning of that year 1919 I returned to the Puerto, a short unexpected trip in the company of my brother Vicente. My father, who in spite of his skepticism and displeasure regarding my cloudy future was actually very fond of me, said to me one night at dinner:

"Although you don't deserve it, since you never did continue with your studies as you promised you would, I am going to let you make the trip with your brother because you're so anxious to go back."

*The diminutive ending *ito* affixed to the Spanish name Serapio creates a slightly vulgar or suggestive connotation. *Pito* is the word for "whistle," but it is also one of the popular terms for "penis."

117

I had never totally abandoned my dream of returning to the Puerto, although I had to confess that Madrid was no longer the hideous city I had found when we first arrived and that the freedom I enjoyed there was something wonderfully new in my young life. I accepted the offer of such a trip with my mind on those seascapes I had sketched and painted a few years ago under the enthusiastic guidance of Aunt Lola. I felt that as a more experienced artist I could now do them justice.

If the Puerto seemed marvelous to me, just as I had always remembered it, I also found it sad without Aunt Lola's presence; sad, too, was San Luis Gonzaga, the Jesuit school where my former schoolmates were finishing up their studies. Sad—sad for so many reasons: because Milagritos was also gone—Milagritos Sancho, that unattainable child with her fat legs who communicated love to me every afternoon from the white rooftop of her house. Whatever was not air, sun, sea, river, houses or pine forests had fallen like yellow dust, creating an aura of melancholy that was like a wilted flower.

I remained in the Puerto for less than a month, staying at the house of my Uncle Fernando Terry, but I spent most of my time with my cousin José Luis de la Cuesta who was somewhat older than I and very enthusiastic about my artistic interests. He was always willing to take me in his magnificent horse-drawn carriage to the most out-of-the-way spots and watch me paint landscapes in that "strange" style of mine. Of all the paintings I did during those few days, the one that most scandalized not only my cousin but all my other friends and relatives as well was of the abandoned cloister in the Carthusian monastery of Jerez, a work done in the Divisionistic style that I later realized was more or less copied from Paul Signac. From the biting commentary directed at my paintings by everyone who saw them, I soon realized that no one in my home town was willing to admire my ability, and that if I didn't leave soon they would end up considering me to be crazy, laughing at me in that vulgarly ostentatious way of people who feel insulted by what they don't understand.

What I felt again upon returning to Madrid was a penetrating nostalgia for the blues and whites of the Puerto, its yellow sands dotted with castles, my happy childhood filled with ocean-going ships and sailboats propelled by the sparkling breezes of the bay.

118

CHAPTER *II*

I continue with my Lost Grove. *This second chapter devoted to my adolescence is also being written among the vines and poinsettia bushes of my small garden in Buenos Aires. My third summer here, far from Punta del Este, from La Gallarda, Aitana's* lovely house situated between the coastal pine forests and the golden-crested acacia, with the voice of the sea nearby. The heat inspires me to work. The fire filtering through the leaves of the few protective trees is like a friendly sword that cuts through the overgrown paths of my memory.*

BACK IN MADRID a terrible epidemic of influenza (for some strange reason called Spanish flu), which became rampant right after the war, began to claim victims in almost every Spanish town. A few days after I had left the Puerto several of my relatives died, including one beautiful young girl, the sister of my cousin José Luis de la Cuesta. The cruel disease also entered our house, affecting my father's lungs and leaving an open wound through which death would make its entrance a year and a half later. Feeling miserable about not having kept my promise, I began to study—not with much enthusiasm, I admit—doing the course work for not only the fourth year but even working on some fifth-year subjects.

Those few days in the Puerto had the effect of making me realize

*Aitana, the daughter of Rafael Alberti and María Teresa León, now lives in Torremolinos, Spain, overlooking the Mediterranean. Her house, like the one in Punta del Este, is called La Gallarda.

how much I already owed to Madrid. I saw myself now as a young man with a goal and a vocation, a far cry from that beach-combing product of the Jesuits dressed in short pants. The ones I was wearing now were long enough, and I even used to occasionally carry a thin bamboo cane which competed somewhat with my own slender physique—that is, my alarmingly pale skinniness. I was quite emaciated-looking then and was beginning to feel the first symptoms of that illness which years later was to partially change the direction of my life. Naturally, I kept all this to myself.

An inexplicable restlessness, an anguished torment filled with insomnia and nightmares had taken possession of me, destroying my sense of well-being and almost obscuring my feelings of happiness. Together with my sleeplessness, I began to suffer from such a severe lack of appetite that I spent entire days without food, except maybe for a cup of coffee which I would gulp down in an old café on Serrano Street. My legs weighed me down, and when I walked it felt as if each of my thighs were holding up a heavy bag of sand. But in spite of all this, a blind and almost delirious impulse kept me going with uncontrollable vehemence. I remember the morning I lost consciousness for the first time in the middle of the street and discovered when I came to that I was being helped by a beautiful lady who was busily dabbing my temples with her perfumed handkerchief while several young girls on their way home from church looked on compassionately. My family knew nothing about these fainting spells until a short time after my father's death. But since my appearance gave them an inkling that I was not in the best of health, and as my father by this time was quite sick, they sent me to the San Rafael Mountains with him that summer. There the mountain sun and the pine-scented air filled my lungs with new life and I was reborn after only a few days spent wandering down the poplar-lined paths and touching the blue of the windy peaks. There I sketched shadowy glens and cascades, watching the water in the mountain streams as it splashed among the rocks. There I committed to paper the ancient pine trees that grow in solitude at those heights, and on the first page of my sketch-pad I baptized them with a literary dedication: "To the sad gentlemen of the air." If I could only be there now enjoying the same bright innocence, in those remote, murmuring places or along the warm shores of Málaga where my father and I went when winter came!

Málaga filled my papers and drawing tablets with rough sketches of shimmering sea spray, of boats and castles, of gardens growing alongside fishing nets, of lemon trees and blinding whitewashed walls. In the mornings I used to go to The Cove to watch them bring in the copo,* a rough and happy celebration filled with the vibration of shouts and the flashing mirrored silver of the anchovies. At night I strolled through the park, but avoided the dark and mysterious corners that were always filled with brash queers who were waiting there for the incredibly muscular men who came off the ships in search of pleasures which in those Mediterranean ports almost no one would consider the least bit perverse.

In spite of my efforts to avoid people, and especially boys of my own age, during that winter I did make some friends and met Luis Altolaguirre, the brother of Manolito, then still a student in the Jesuit school of El Palo but who was to become years later a great poet of our generation.

With that group of friends, who are not totally erased from my memory—unbearable spoiled brats from Málaga's "high society"—I paid a visit one warm night to a lovely bordello near the sea. I was a bit scared—it was my first time—when I entered that Mediterranean house of Venus, but once inside I got over my fear almost immediately. It was an authentic garden where the goddess' dark-haired Andalusian daughters, hardly wearing even veils, stood out against the pots of geraniums and the violently colored carnations, surrounded by an overwhelming fragrance of sweet basil, magnolia and jasmine. A grapevine formed a green awning halfway up the walls that covered the colorfully curtained entrances to their mysterious bedrooms. In the center of that garden patio was an arbor spilling over with cascades of red and yellow roses. Beneath it, a guitarist hunched over his guitar and strummed softly for his audience of sailors who were hanging from the necks and bronzed torsos of their chosen female partners.

Little by little we approached this intimate group with our own partners and finally organized a happy love-fest in which song, the strumming of a guitar, the joyful laughter and shouts that became progressively inflamed by the heat of the wine, all blended with the murmur of the sea that floated on the breeze coming in over the low rooftops. When I arrived home with the sun I was not scolded by my

*Copo is a fisherman's term used to describe a form of fishing with specially designed nets, and also the fish brought in by this method.

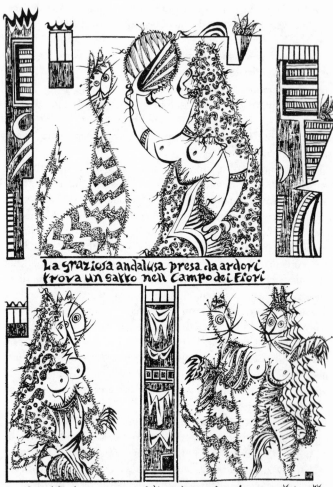

La graziosa andalusa presa da ardori
trova un gatto nell Campo dei Fiori

con el gatto fa una passeggiata   e la graziosa si converte in gatta

father, and this time I wasn't coming back from having painted a moonscape as on that famous night in Madrid.

In spite of the marvelous world opened to me then by my adventure and the revelation of that Pompeyan bordello in Málaga, I went back to my solitary walks and to my sketching of the Cove, the lemon groves, and the distant landscapes and seascapes that could be seen from the heights of the Gibralfaro Castle. And since with each passing day I became more fed up with those Andalusian *señoritos*, those spoiled, rich brats who considered themselves extremely amusing, I tried to avoid the company of these occasional friends who were already contaminated by the worst traditions of the "best people" in that provincial city. I once heard them tell a terrifying story, punctuated by obscene comments and loud guffaws, in which some of them had been protagonists.

It seems that another gang of *señoritos*, also from the "best" families, were exploiting the ephebic tendencies of a rich German who had appeared one winter in that warm coastal area. In this amphibological game these boys allowed themselves to be loved, taking money from the German and then racing off to spend it freely in bars and on prostitutes. One afternoon those who were waiting in a car for the boy whose turn it was to satisfy the German's particular tastes became impatient with the length of the visit and they hurried to the house where the German lived, breaking down the door. The following night the local newspapers screamed out the news of the hideous crime: the discovery of a foreigner who had been crucified, nailed to one of the walls of his residence. The preliminary investigation uncovered the names of some of the better-known members of Málaga's high society. And since one of them on the list was the Governor's son, the matter was quickly buried and thus the perpetrators of this ghastly and repugnant murder were left to roam freely through the city streets.

Having separated myself from that provincially aristocratic scum and once again on my own, I was walking down Larios Street one afternoon when I came upon a picture of Salvador Rueda, the forgotten poet of those wonderful landscapes and maritime scenes. I saw him first on the cover of a book behind the glass panes of a bookstore window. There he was—laurel wreath and long twisted moustache—looking very pensive. Overcoming the sudden flashes of shyness I suffered often then, I decided to pay him a visit. I found him, curator of the Municipal Library, complaining about his in-

creasing blindness and how he had been so unjustly forgotten. In a
gentle voice filled with emotion he told me about himself: a humble
shepherd from his native village of Benaque, he had arrived in
Málaga "with his head filled with beehives." He was well aware of
his role as precursor of poetic modernism, a fact which had been so
generously recognized by Rubén Darío who at the turn of the century had dedicated two magnificent, sparkling poems to him. He
told me that the voice of today's Parnassus was a woman's voice.
Nervo? Villaespesa? Jiménez? Purely feminine poetry.

We left the library together that sunny morning, and I walked
with him down several streets and avenues on the way to his house. I
later found out that his place of residence consisted of an extremely
modest room in a house of prostitution located in Perchel, a working-class district. There lived the unhappy and luminous lyric poet of
those southern coasts, nostalgically contemplating the many laurel
wreaths that had decorated his forehead during the glorious years of
his travels through Spain and America, which were now hanging on
the wall above his miserable bed.

The country had been unjust in their treatment of this authentic poet who still suffered from the wounds of neglect. Deeply
depressed, he complained of never having been able to obtain a
sufficient following to figure among the immortals in the Royal
Academy of the Spanish Language. Apropos of Rueda's attempts to
become a member of this august body, I later heard the following
amusing anecdote that was told to me one afternoon in Madrid:

Salvador Rueda considered that having been a shepherd and
goatherd in the fields of his native village constituted one of his principal assets. He repeated this fact to every moth-eaten member of the
Academy he saw. When he came face to face with the most wrinkled
and crotchety of them all, the old man had said to him with sad sarcasm: "Look, Rueda, don't insist. Unfortunately here in the Academy we don't need any shepherds or goatherds. We're so old we have
no time to kid around."

Poor Salvador Rueda! Many years later I tried here in Buenos
Aires to bring about a renaissance of your past glories by publishing
an anthology of your best poems in the Mirto Series, of which I was
then editor. At the time you were remembered fondly by some of the
literary critics, but that was all. Your poetry, so American in many
ways, never did awaken the echoes that we had expected. This isn't

so surprising, since today not even Rubén Darío touches the hearts of the new generations as he should. A great pity!

Back in Madrid and still being urged by my family to continue with my high school studies as I had promised, I returned to the textbooks with a little more enthusiasm. I was disturbed by my father's declining health and it saddened me to think he might die without my ever having given him that small pleasure. Without abandoning my trips to the Casón and the Prado, my long strolls or the nocturnal poetry sessions with Gil Cala and Celestino Espinosa, I half-heartedly prepared myself during the summer for the examinations in Universal History, Literary Theory and Literary History. In September I appeared in a state of near panic at the Instituto del Cardenal Cisneros where these examinations were held. Horrible afternoons, even worse than those back in Jerez when I had been examined in Arithmetic and Geometry. I managed to get a passing grade in Universal History, but Literary Theory—oh, God! The textbook they used in Madrid was even more mysterious and incomprehensible than the one the Jesuits had forced us to read in the Puerto. The examiners asked me questions about didactic verse and I heard them vaguely mention paragoges, hemistiches, hyperbatons and metonyms. And when, toward the end of the session, in a desperate attempt to give me a passing grade, the professor explained my anguished silence by stating that "the emotion of the collectivity gave rise to epenthesis," I realized more than ever how beautiful and peaceful it was to be able to go out into the fields and gardens with a box of paints tucked under your arm—with your eyes clear and your brain free of that gibberish which was apparently so necessary to anyone who hoped to be a good poet.

Since I failed Literary Theory, I wasn't permitted to take the examination in Literary History. With a drop of bleach I managed to erase the word *fail* which I replaced with *good;* and a blank grade sheet that had been stolen by a friend of mine was just right for falsifying a *pass* in Literary History. And so with the three grades in hand I calmly walked into my father's room (I was actually overcome with sadness) and read off my grades to him from a safe distance. He then barely glanced at them, but a gentle smile brightened up his emaciated face. After such an ugly but basically innocent deceit, I considered myself on vacation and I happily returned to my own pursuits which, in fact, consisted only of entering the virgin woods and seas of life. With Espinosa and Gil Cala I read poetry, and at times this activity lasted until dawn. They were my guides, the ones who awakened in me the tremor of poetry. They introduced me to *Platero y yo*, the magical Andalusian elegy by Juan Ramón Jiménez, in a beautiful edition that had been published especially for children. My first impressions of this book have remained with me over the years. With my sister Pepita I would recite verses from it as we walked in the Botanical Gardens, under the trees of the Retiro and on the slopes of Moncloa. I began to frequent used bookstores and recklessly bought whatever my meager resources would allow. Along with the Italian *novellieri*, whose spicy stories I really enjoyed, I also discovered the Greek classics in editions published by Prometeo, the publishing house in Valencia that was under the direction of Blasco Ibáñez. I was enthusiastic about Aristophanes, particularly his *Lysistrata* which I read and reread, blushing and laughing out loud at the same time. The greatness of Aeschylus kept me awake; the warring gods of the *Iliad* and the blue adventures of Odysseus filled me with heroic illusions; the *Idylls* of Theocritus changed me into a shepherd of roses and cypress trees, and as a result of those readings I began to vaguely feel the anguished desire for precision and clarity that today dominates my work above all else.

With Celestino Espinosa, who was the most musically inclined of the three of us, I attended my first concert. It was held at the Circo Price, under the baton of Maestro Bartolomé Pérez Casas, director of the Philharmonic. I only remember today one piece of music that was on that program, a work which was so much in keeping with my spiritual state at the time that it had a powerful emotional effect on me. Ever since then, whenever I hear Gluck's *Ifigenia in Aulis* I feel as if I am in a state of grace, totally enveloped by the purest of harmonies.

Claude Debussy died that year (1919), and in a concert dedicated to his memory I heard the first performance in Spain of his *Iberia*, a reflection by the most transparent composer in France on the exotic aroma of an imagined Andalusia. In spite of the strange sensation caused by the mysteriously vague sounds that began to flow from the orchestra, those syncopated dance rhythms and muted castanets, I began to feel captivated and as if caught in the undertow of a gentle current that ended by exploding in a tidal wave of applause, catcalls and physical violence as most of the audience erupted in a violently noisy and "taurine" protest. As a result, the orchestra stopped play-ing while people shouted insults at Debussy and at poor Maestro Pérez Casas who, undaunted, made every effort to continue with the performance. But during the orchestra's second season—and this is something I have seen repeated so many times in my life—that same *Iberia* which had been received with such hostility and such savage demonstrations became one of the symphonic works of the repertory most in demand by audiences in Madrid.

That year I also attended my first operas. I was frequently invited by a beautiful Italian lady, the wife of the Teatro Real's architect, who lived on the third floor of our apartment house and had a box at the opera for the entire season. *Tosca* and *La Bohème* by Puccini were very popular then, and Anselmi was the fashionable tenor of the mo-ment with whom many young ladies of the musical world were deeply in love. I remember seeing a photograph of him on the dress-ing table in the apartment of one of my cousins who at the time was already past her prime. I have never in my life seen a more ridiculous and affected face with a rounder dimple in the middle of its chin, nor a more sickening expression of a forty-year-old woman on any man. It has always been very difficult for me not to think of that picture whenever I hear a tenor's voice, making me feel the same repugnance I have for those uneatable, mushy chocolates filled with a white li-quid that looks like the substance that oozes from a squashed cockroach.

From that same box seat I witnessed the first performance of Manuel de Falla's *The Three-Cornered Hat.* Even though Nijinsky had already gone mad, Diaghilev's Russian Ballet continued to astound the world, causing a great stir in artistic circles wherever they performed. At that opening performance, in addition to dis-covering Falla's passionate rhythms and deep *jonda** soul, I was also introduced to the wit and creative force of Pablo Picasso.

That marvelous blue curtain hanging above the little bridge covered with painted dark eyes, those brilliantly whitewashed walls and well, and that simple, warm geometry embraced the dancers and blended with their colorful movements! Nothing I saw performed by the same company surprised and impressed me as much, even though their *La Boutique Fantasque* by Rossini–Respighi, with sets designed by Derain, their *Scheherazade* and *Tamar* by Rimsky-

Jonda derives from *cante jondo.* See footnote on page 80.

127

Korsakov, with the superb fantasy of León Bask's scenography, together with Diaghilev's other spectacular productions, constituted a new language—the most daring expression of the new musical, pictorial and dance rhythms, which in fact served to inaugurate the twentieth century.

Those years, my nineteenth and twentieth, were filled with a restlessness and the delirium of tortured insomnia. I was fascinated by literature and jotted down my fleeting impressions and infatuations in a form of hieroglyphics that I had invented by using Arabic-looking letters—a kind of *aljamiado**—which I found impossible to decipher almost immediately after writing it down.

I was obsessed by a desire to be out of the house. I would race up the back stairway and eat alone in the kitchen, sometimes without even sitting down. If I had some extra money, my dinner would consist of a ham sandwich that I picked up in a downtown bar, and if I didn't run off to Gil Cala's house, I spent my time walking aimlessly through the more lower-class neighborhoods and then, after walking the length of La Castellana, I would return to my room totally exhausted. The visions I had, and my nights of insomnia punctuated by nightmares, left me at dawn with deep rings under my bloodshot eyes. I had sudden attacks of uncontrollable fear. There were many nights when with the pretext of feeling ill I would ask the *sereno** on our block to walk with me up to our apartment; such was the terror I felt at the possibility of finding myself suddenly in the dark silence of the stairway. I remember once returning home one terrifying morning in January when my blood became paralyzed as I stood only a few feet from the door of our apartment building. I couldn't move. Guarding the front door to the building I saw some monks wearing yellowish-white hoods and holding black rifles in their hands. Since I didn't dare approach them and the night watchman did not appear in spite of my frantic clapping, I backed away in horror and wandered through the neighborhood until the first rays of light swept these visions away from the door and I could finally cross the threshold.

Even more than the museums, the streets were my school. When I wasn't repeatedly drawing scenes of workmen stretched out or

Aljamiado refers to Spanish written with Arabic characters, a fairly common practice from the thirteenth to sixteenth centuries in Andalusia. The *sereno* is the night watchman in the large cities of Spain, who patrols the streets and opens the apartment-house doors to residents who return home late at night.

eating lunch beneath the trees, when I wasn't making sketches of workers unloading lumber and bricks at construction sites, I would just stroll through the streets on those spring afternoons observing the city or reciting poetry with my friends Gil Cala and Espinosa. One day they pointed to someone and said: "That's Amado Nervo."

The Mexican poet, who I think at the time was Ambassador to Spain, was walking slowly along Sevilla Street. I had read some of his poetry. I wasn't particularly impressed by his work, although Gil Cala's enthusiasm and insistence were responsible for my having memorized some of his verses:

> ¡Oh Kempis, Kempis, asceta yermo,
> pálido asceta, qué mal me hiciste!
> Ha muchos años que vivo enfermo
> y es por el libro que tú escribiste.

> O Kempis, Kempis, barren ascetic,
> Pale ascetic, what harm you have wrought!
> For years I have wandered sick and pathetic
> Because of your book and what it taught.

We used to repeat this silly poem over and over again. It was probably at the time his most famous work. Many girlfriends of mine used to carry it around stuck in the pages of their missal, and they would recite it devoutly at church. Amado Nervo was considered to be a kind of mystic, and another of his poems in which he compared his beloved to the Ave María brought tears to legions of Catholic ladies of all ages. At any rate, Nervo's poetry clearly showed that he was an extremely good man and not as bad a poet as people consider him to be nowadays when he has been almost completely forgotten.

Another time when we were walking along Alcalá Street, Gil Cala called to a dark, thin young man with piercing eyes set in a truly beautiful face. He was the sculptor Julio Antonio who at the time was putting the finishing touches to his most famous monument as well as to his own life. I knew absolutely nothing about his work, although the name was familiar to me since Gil Cala was very proud of being a friend of his and mentioned him constantly to me. It was Gil who told me that Antonio's downfall had been brought about by women—something which made me see them in my imagination as crawling, blood-sucking monsters—and these creatures had ruined his promising youth, causing him to contract tuberculosis which had left him in such a feverish state. Pleasant and friendly, he invited me to his workshop. I later went there with Gil, but the sculptor unfortunately was not there. His health had taken a turn for the worse —what ugly things had those women done to him? We were greeted by his partner Salazar, another young sculptor who was also quite ill and was then retouching the beard on the statue of Ruperto Chapí, a work that Julio Antonio had left unfinished. The statue was finally completed by his disciple and today stands as a monument in the Retiro Gardens to the memory of this great composer of zarzuelas.*

Julio Antonio's studio was located not far from my house, at the end of Juan Bravo. At the entrance and perched on top of two posts supporting the small gate were a pair of sad, reclining heads carved in stone, executed in a style very classically sentimental—they were supposedly to form part of a commemorative monument to the events at Tarragona during the War of Independence. As works of sculpture they were far superior to the heads that were ultimately used in this statue. In addition to the Chapí work, there was a huge plaster bust of Wagner that rested on a scaffold inside the studio. This belonged to another monumental project which death was to interrupt. What I most remember from my visit was the freezing cold inside that place and an anguished feeling I had that everything there had been abandoned, even though this wasn't the case at all then. But it did come to pass. Julio Antonio never went back to his workshop and his hands were never again to touch those fragments, the bits and pieces of his luminous but wasted youth. A few days after my visit, the people of Madrid stood in line in front of the door to one of the rooms in the Museum of Modern Art waiting to file by his last piece of sculpture—the funeral monument of the Lemonier family. There behind the mother who kneels and weeps at the death of her beautiful adolescent son we saw Julio Antonio—a distant, sunken, yellowish figure, a fading shadow whose flashing eyes offered the only real sign of life.

Shortly after his death I began to vaguely appreciate his work, which I came to know little by little. Several busts that I managed to see before the Museum opened to the public a special room

*The zarzuela is a popular and peculiarly Spanish form of operetta.

dedicated to him suggested to me that in the midst of the industrial realism which had invaded Spanish sculpture it was still possible to find a style well within the Mediterranean tradition with its clear, spiritual plasticity. And even though this came to me at the same time I was shocked into awareness of the aesthetic adventures that were stirring in Europe and beginning to filter into Spain, I couldn't help but sense that in the series of sculptured busts which Julio Antonio had grouped under the title of *The Race,* an ideal of beauty which had by then completely disappeared from our soil was being reinstated.

More personally significant to me than the brief relationship I had had with this sculptor was my friendship with Daniel Vázquez Díaz, an Andalusian painter who had just returned from Paris and whom I also met through Gil Cala. The close proximity of his studio—he lived at the end of my street and on the ground floor of my friend's house—was undoubtedly the reason we became close friends and saw each other so frequently. What was so surprising then about Vázquez Díaz was his wit, his dynamism and his aggressiveness. He was a kind of gypsy from Huelva, theatrical in the extreme and capable of the most hilariously exaggerated gestures. He was married to Eva Aegerholm, a fine sculptress, cultured and audacious, with eyes the color of pale Nordic lakes. The two of them offered a strange contrast: she with her romantic, dreamy, distant personality, and he with that torrential verbosity and sharp tongue. Together they were like a bullfight held in the middle of a frozen fjord, a contest in which Vázquez Díaz played the role of bull, audience, horse and *torero* all at the same time. How I used to laugh listening to him tell his Parisian stories about the amorous adventures of Modigliani and Juan Gris! Attempting to describe the degree of abstinence Gris had attained prior to his arrival in the Latin Quarter, he said: "Juan Gris arrived in France with thirty years of semen on the tip of his prick!" (!!)

Vázquez Díaz would recount these atrocious stories with a mixture of Andalusian and French expressions. His French was simple and elementary but he always translated for us, assuming undoubtedly that his listener was totally unfamiliar with the beautiful language of Molière: *"Oui, oui (Sí, sí). Ouvrir la porte (Abrid la puerta). Comment allez-vous? (¿Cómo está usted?)."* Etc. His Frenchified manner, both in the way he spoke and behaved, was really picturesque. He moved around from here to there making gestures and bowing in what he thought expressed the most refined Parisian taste, and rarely did he end a letter or the dedication of a book without including an exquisite *amicalmente,* a somewhat rough-hewn Gallic touch which the painter incorporated into his charming Andalusian speech.

In the boring and "Academized" world of painting during those years in Madrid, the appearance of Vázquez Díaz acted as a catalyst, causing a kind of rude awakening among the young artists. And although he wasn't what anyone might call an avant-garde revolutionary, his sketched portraits with their simple lines and suggested planes and his paintings, Cezanne-like in their technique but with a strong Spanish flavor, served to clear the air and open the way to new and more daring experiments.

The works of other painters such as the Uruguayan Barradas, the Polish painters Jhal and Marjan Paskiewictz, the French couple Sonia and Robert Delaunay, who had been forced to flee to Spain because of the war, all greatly contributed by their example to this battle of liberation. The official art galleries, however, were still filled with the more traditional works of Benedito, Sotomayor, Eugenio Hermoso, López Mezquita, Romero de Torres, Anselmo Miguel Nieto, etc. I remember that the gold medal, which constituted the maximum aspiration for every painter, not only because of the financial benefits that accompanied it but because of the artistic prestige it conferred on the recipient, had just been won by Eduardo Chicharro, who was then the Director of the Spanish Academy in Rome. The winning painting, *The Temptations of Buddha,* was a horrifying and almost pornographic canvas filled with twisted nude figures bathed in a venomous green light. I believe it was that same year when a painter from Extremadura, Eugenio Hermoso, won the first prize for his painting of some rosy-pink peasant women carrying pumpkins and chickens and seen against the background of a setting sun. In those days there was a great deal of lively interest in what was picturesquely typical, the pretty picture for the Museum of Ethnography, and in a lot of bad Castilianized literature exemplified by the style of Zuloaga and members of the literary Generation of 1898. Romero de Torres, pleasant and dandyish, also contributed his voluptuous gypsy figures that looked as if they had been taken from a melancholy wall calendar to form part of the art scene existing in Spain at the time. Catalan artists like Viladrich and Basques such as Maeztú, the Zubiaurre brothers, Arteta and a few others completed

132

the total picture. When you are eighteen or nineteen years old and you think with your voice or with eyes in the process of discovering profound differences in things, the critics suddenly seem to rise up everywhere with their cutting profiles, killing for the sake of killing and committing great injustices in order to more firmly establish their own importance. I cannot even imagine today just how much that was permanently worthwhile existed in the works of some of those painters. But at that moment what young artist could find anything useful in that formless conglomeration of Spanish paintings which in most cases had not even been touched by Impressionism? This did not apply to certain other painters like Darío de Regoyos, Nonell, Suñer, Mir, Togores—but except for Mir, Madrid paid absolutely no attention to any of them in those days. And Gutiérrez Solana, living withdrawn way up north in Santander, had not yet brought to the Castilian *meseta* his visionary realism which, it must be said, was at times influenced by the worst kind of provincial literature. But he managed to overcome this through his powerful and brilliant sense of form. It is understandable, then, that the sudden appearance of Vázquez Díaz with his first large exhibit in the Museum of Modern Art had the effect of disrupting the sluggish and conformist rhythms which had dominated the art world in Madrid, and of causing a scandal that reached as far as the Royal Academy of San Fernando where the centenarian shadows of Garnelo, Moreno Carbonero and Cecilio Pla were still moving about.

It was during the same year—1920—that I was encouraged by Vázquez Díaz to have my first show. In October I was to inaugurate the very first Autumn Salon in Madrid. Jhal, Paskiewicz, a young Mexican by the name of Amado de la Cueva, myself and someone else whose name I can't remember were to exhibit our works in a special room which on opening day was immediately dubbed "The Rogues' Gallery." My works on display were all very different from one another: one of them, the most traditional of the lot, had been influenced by Vázquez Díaz and was called *Evocation*. Another painting I exhibited, the weirdest of them all, was entitled *Rhythmic Nocturne of the City*; it consisted of a set of curved angles painted light green and red and superimposed on each other to form a kind of repeated musical theme, but also garnished here and there with black dots. My intention had been to suggest in a more or less innocently decorative form the luminous effect of a modern city as seen from above. The painting elicited loud guffaws on the part of almost everyone who saw it, a unanimous jeering that took shape in the form of an amusing cartoon that appeared in the *Fine Arts Gazette.* At the bottom of an angular and speckled comic rendering of my painting, the cartoonist had included the following comment:

> *Este nocturno rítmico de día,*
> *es una descomposición de la sandía.*
>
> *This rhythmic nocturne, by day,*
> *is a watermelon in a state of decay.*

Instead of being disturbed by all this, I was delighted and flattered by the joke which I immediately hastened to show to my friends, convinced that my reputation as a painter had gotten off to an auspicious and resounding start. After this, my public debut into the "art world," I continued to see Vázquez and to paint with great enthusiasm but without affiliating myself with any of the groups that were beginning to make themselves more sharply visible both in literature and the pictorial arts.

I signed my paintings then as Rafael María de Alberti. Perhaps this had a more euphonic ring to it than just plain Rafael Alberti, but it was a pretty stupid thing to do just the same.

CHAPTER III

A horse, without seeing me, is looking fixedly in my direction from the depths of the ravine. Those green waves of other summers have become transformed today into an immense emerald pasture, a calm sea of land where the cattle become petrified in summer by the sun and the wind. One wide river girds the field and another smaller, deeper river running toward this larger body of water cuts extensively across the land, leaving part of it between the two watery currents, and thus creates one of those innumerable islands which the Paraná, with its wealthy abundance of arms and hair-like streams, entraps in its path. The island in front of me is called the Two of Diamonds. When the few inhabitants dwelling there wish to cross over to the mainland, they do it by wading through the Baradero at low tide with all their cattle before the "río grande" joins with its smaller companion to transform the fields into an inland sea from which escape would be difficult. The ocean waves of other Uruguayan summers are, I think, gone from my life, and will remain so for as long as I live in Argentina. I have exchanged the summers in La Gallarda, that beautiful house of mine set among the pine forests bordering the sea at Punta del Este, for the more peaceful ranch called Mayor Loco, above the gently moving cliffs of San Pedro and looking out at the solemn Paraná of Las Palmas. Gazing down on this enormous ribbon of water, which this morning has the serene color of pale strawberries, I pick up the forgotten threads of my Lost Grove—abandoned some three years ago—and I begin yet another new chapter.

*W*HAT A JOY to return to those years in Madrid, years not yet poisoned by hate and still far removed from the rivers of blood which the military uprisings of 1936 were to send racing through all of Spain, inundating the entire country!

My memories are still of the year 1920. A year of great happiness and great sorrows. Three deaths, each of which left a deep impression on me and affected me in different ways, occurred during those spring months: In March, my father's death; in May, the famous bull-fighter Joselito died; and the same month brought the death of the great and popular novelist Benito Pérez Galdós.

One night when I returned home I sensed, as I closed the elevator door, that something terrible had happened to my family. The door to the apartment was open wide and the sound of confused voices, moans and cries, could be heard on the landing. Although my father's health had not seemed to be getting any worse at the time, there was no doubt that his final hour was approaching on the almost totally broken clock of his life.

That beautiful Italian lady who lived in the apartment next door to ours, was the first person I saw as I walked into our hallway.

"What a terrible tragedy!" I said to her. And with a mixture of infantile innocence and cynicism, I took advantage of this painful moment to embrace her and give vent to my long-standing desire to kiss the lady, a desire that had been frustrated up until this propitious moment.

After finally disengaging myself from her lovely neck and without daring to investigate the effect of my unexpected outburst, I ran to the bedroom where the sounds of weeping and moaning could be heard and saw my father stretched out on his bed, still wearing the suit he had on at the moment of his death. He had died suddenly, all the blood of his body bubbling out through his mouth as he collapsed in the front room of the apartment, like a bull that had been stabbed through the lungs. My mother and my brothers and sisters, pale, moaning in grief, formed a tight circle around him. When I approached the bed to kiss my father, Agustín, the wittiest but also the most serious of all my brothers, suddenly let loose with a string of ayes and words that sounded like lyrics from the *cante jondo*.

"Oh, how sad! What pain! Gaze at him there, laid out, awaiting the earth! What is to become of us? A moment ago we had a father, but now ... Aye, aye!"

And he repeated this lament from time to time in the same

dolorous tone of an Andalusian blacksmith singing alone in his shop, accompanied only by the funereal rhythm of his hammer striking against the anvil.

That night of the wake seemed to last forever and was constantly interrupted by the mumbling and grieved whispering of the neighbors who came to call. At about three o'clock in the morning my father's body was wrapped in the white habit of the Dominican Order and placed in a simple, mahogany-colored coffin with four candles set at each corner. Someone had placed a bouquet of flowers near his feet. With the hood framing his face, a rosary and crucifix clutched in his pale hands, his chest somewhat puffed out and his whole figure bathed in the yellowish color of the burning wax, he looked like that impressive painting by Zurburán in which the recumbent body of Pope San Buenaventura, bathed in a powerfully chilling light, seems to be moving upward in all its solidity.

As the morning wore on, people began to disappear from the bedroom and my exhausted family, eyes bloodshot from tears and lack of sleep, also left the room to immediately fall asleep on some chair or sofa in the apartment. Only my mother remained at the head of the casket, deeply lost in a semiconscious state that was nonetheless punctuated by tears and prayers. Confused and deeply impressed by the whole scene, I also stayed at my father's side. There he was, mute, lying in almost the same position as when I had deceived him that other morning by showing him from a safe distance my counterfeit examination grades. And it felt as if a stone—or a ferocious nail—were rising up from my heart to my throat. I was overcome with remorse and filled with an infinite sense of guilt for having almost always treated him with a certain coldness or lack of interest—as if I had never loved him at all. When I was a child in Andalusia and he was always away traveling, my affection for him was expressed only in the expectation of receiving a gift from some distant place, something he would have for me when he finally came home after periods of absence that sometimes lasted two years. When we moved to Madrid—by that time I was fifteen years old—and I lived in closer contact with him and even more intimately during his sickness, I was not any more demonstrative toward him. His manifestations of affection for me, which, in fact, were not in the least demanding, were received by me coldly and with an unwarranted indifference which must have seriously disturbed him, although only rarely did he make his feelings known to me. Yes, I

137

was filled with remorse and anxious to talk to him, to fill his deep silence, now the silence of death, with words of affection and pardon, a delayed response to my unpleasant behavior toward him. I didn't cry then and certainly was not capable of doing so in the presence of eyes that were not my own. All that wailing made people appear hideous, and the thought of how my own face might look bathed in tears filled me with shame and annoyance. But I had to do something, show in some way how miserable I felt. That dark nail which seemed to be puncturing my chest was stubbornly and painfully demanding some sign. I then took out a pencil and began to write.

> . . . *tu cuerpo,*
> *largo y abultado*
> *como las estatuas del Renacimiento,*
> *y unas flores mustias*
> *de blancor enfermo.*

> . . . *Your body,*
> *Massively elongated*
> *Like the statues of the Renaissance,*
> *And some faded flowers*
> *Of sickly pallor.*

I can only recall those lines now. But from that night on I continued writing poetry. My poetic vocation had begun in this way, at the feet of death and in an atmosphere that was romantically lugubrious.

For a long time after that I suffered from constant sadness. They dressed me in black and my whole family became somberly dark. There were rosaries and Masses, a prolonged and unbearable period of mourning replete with afternoon visits from people we knew as well as from those gloomy, crow-like figures who only make their appearance when the smell of dead flesh is in the air. I used to leave the house in search of solitude on the outskirts of the city. The plains with their brooding poplar trees and the blue, distant Guadarrama Mountains were my good friends and companions during those months. I used to stay in the fields until very late in the afternoon, and, miracle of miracles, poems kept gushing from me as if flowing from a mysterious spring that I carried within and could not control.

I also remember now the beginning of another poem that came into being one spring afternoon at sunset:

"*Más bajo, más bajo.*"
No turbéis el silencio
de un ritmo incomparable;
lento,
muy lento,
es el ritmo
de esta luna de oro.
El sol ha muerto.
Y hasta las alegrías son tristezas,
pero del mismo ritmo:
lento,
muy lento.

[*The first line is from a poem by León Felipe.*]

"*Softer, softer,*"
Do not disturb the silence
Of an incomparable rhythm;
Slow,
Very slow,
Is the rhythm
Of this golden moon.

The sun has died.
And even joys are sadness,
But in the same rhythm:
Slow,
Very slow.

There followed other stanzas no less melancholy than this one. It was about that time when a poet arrived from, I think, Fernando Poo, and recited some poems in the Ateneo of Madrid, reading from a small book that had just been published. It was called *Versos y oraciones de caminante (Verses and Orations of a Wanderer)*. The author, unknown at the time, was León Felipe. My own early poetry possessed some of the same delicate accents of his poems, but I didn't realize it then and actually I heard nothing more about León Felipe until I met him fourteen years later in 1934. I want now to let that holy and angry prophet know that his early poetry, uncluttered and serious, made the budding leaves of a still tender lost grove tremble with emotion . . .

One afternoon in May when I was already a bit fed up with my mournful solitude, I took a streetcar and went down to the center of Madrid. On reaching the Carrera de San Jerónimo, I noticed how everyone was racing frantically in the direction of the newsboys who were shouting out the latest news: "Joselito dies in Talavera de la Reina!"

"What's that?"

"What are they saying?"

"It can't be true!"

That afternoon everyone would have accepted as true the most absurd thing in the world, but not the news that was spreading through the streets of Madrid and throughout all of Spain.

"Joselito dies in the bullring at Talavera de la Reina!"

I managed to buy a newspaper, which was probably the first one I had ever bought in my life. It was true. It was there in black and white. A bull called Bailador, the fifth one of the afternoon, had gored Joselito, plunging his horn into the bullfighter's stomach. His brother-in-law, Ignacio Sánchez Mejías, who was fighting that afternoon on the same program, had killed the animal.

"José killed by a bull! That could have happened to Belmonte! But not to José!"

No bull had ever even touched him. His enemies used to say that he hypnotized them or that with a handkerchief dipped in chloroform he was able to weaken them and then perform with all that confidence and playful elegance that seemed to be a mockery of death, something never seen before in the history of bullfighting. Joselito was twenty-five years old. Young and handsome, he died as a god might die. When they brought his broken body to Madrid, an immense and silent crowd gathered and with eyes filled with tears and disbelief they had accompanied him to the railroad station where he was then taken by special train to Sevilla, to be mourned there by the Giralda Tower which had instructed him in the art of wit, grace and luminous joy.

That sudden disappearance of this young Andalusian *torero* left me confused and aimless, and also left a buried current that was to surface again years later, causing me to condense in a few short lines the anguish and sudden sense of tragedy that I had not been able to express then during those days filled with his glorious death.

In that same month of May and in that same Madrid, another soul was carried off—not to Paradise, as was José—but perhaps to Purgatory. This was Benito Pérez Galdós, whose works in those days I had hardly read at all but with whom I was acquainted by having seen him in the Retiro Gardens where he used to go to pose for Victorio Macho. The sculptor, seated beneath the trees, would be chiseling away at his statue and the poor, sad Don Benito, completely blind and weighed down with infinite patience, listened to the scraping sounds of the stone from which his figure was emerging.

Just as with the death of Joselito, the passing of this monstrous novelist also left behind in me hidden wounds which were to open later, revealing to me the greatness of the man and also awakening in me an enthusiasm that I could never have felt in those days when as a narrow-minded youth I was against everything I considered to be "old-fashioned."

1920—three deaths joined forever in my mind when I recall that year: my father, Joselito, Galdós.

Although a few months later the feelings of pain had begun to subside at home, a dark wing of sadness fluttered against my nights that became converted at the coming of dawn into new, somber and anguished poems. Painting, even in spite of my unexpected poetic activities, continued to obsess me. The technique of my wild and rather flashy earlier canvases had changed, and my work was now bathed in earth tones and deep purples, executed in a realistic style similar to the darkest realism of the traditional Spanish school. Then the idea occurred to me to paint a portrait of my sister Pepita, but it would not be a happy and luminous work as might have been more in keeping with her sixteen years, but rather a mortuary portrait with pale features, her body wrapped in a shroud of faded colors. To console my mother I sketched for her two Chopin Nocturnes with their notes flying across the threads of the musical staff like a bevy of dark birds. I began to visit cemeteries again, with the name of Bécquer on my lips and a feeling of oppression in my chest that caused me to lean against the trees from time to time as I walked among the gravestones.

Since my useless vocation—I still kept my new one, poetry, mysteriously hidden—continued to seem very unproductive to the members of my family, one sad day my brother Vicente spoke to me alone, and in a serious voice offered me the following proposition:

"It would be a good idea for you to help me. Papa is dead and you should also become involved in the wine business. You can travel and earn your money according to your talents as a salesman."

I didn't dare refuse. And although I knew nothing about accounting or business matters, I prepared myself to take to the road as a representative of the firm of Osborne to try my hand in the small towns located throughout the provinces of Madrid and Guadalajara. To initiate me into the world of business, my brother thought it wise for me to be accompanied by an expert. His name was Velayos and he was a good man, small in stature and very fond of drinking. He snored at night like a bellows. Besides, at any hour of the day or night he would shatter the air with noisy farts that almost pierced my eardrums. In his company I visited Arganda, a delightful village with excellent natural wines and Alcalá de Henares, where under the pretext of displaying the superb qualities of Osborne brandy we got so soused that the following day we didn't have the slightest idea of how much we had sold nor what stores and bars we had visited. Always in intimate union with his snoring and his flatulence, I journeyed to other, less important villages, finally saying goodbye to him after having convinced him that I now knew the ropes and I took off by myself in a mule-drawn coach that was to carry me to several towns in the Albarracín Mountains.

On my own, I visited the places that have always been associated with the name of the Cid. I was in Atienza, where I sold five cases of wine and two of brandy, and then landed in Sacedón, a village I can never forget. One dark gloomy night when there was a torrential rainstorm, it occurred to me to ask for the bathroom in the extremely primitive establishment where I was spending the night. With a broad smile on his face, someone replied: "There's a backyard —you'll find the umbrella behind the door."

To avoid any further comments, I opened the door without the slightest sign of surprise and walked out into the dripping outdoors. I squatted as best I could next to some wooden planks that had been tied together with a piece of wire that barely missed cutting into my face and, umbrella in hand, I began my simple, human operation. Suddenly I heard a loud noise, a strange fluttering of wings that was accompanied by bird-like noises and—the whole thing didn't last more than a second—my poor buttocks raced out of that place covered with the wounds inflicted on them by the beaks of some twenty assorted barnyard fowl that were crouching there in the shadows. In spite of such a singular experience, worthy of the travels of Quevedo's *Buscón*, I made a few sales. But in the coach that carried me away from Sacedón I had to stand all the way, since I was in no condition to tolerate contact with any type of seat.

Before returning to Madrid I stopped in another town, Colmenar de Oreja. It had a marvelous square that was closed off by immense earthen jugs. I saw a traveling circus there that, instead of amusing me, filled me with sadness. The usual pregnant girl doing acrobatics, the squalid trained dogs, the goat trying to balance itself on all fours on top of a bottle-cap, and a tragic, haggard Gutiérrez Solana to be seen everywhere. That was my afternoon in Colmenar. I sold nothing at all. I wrote a poem, but I can't remember even one line of it. Just the same, when I returned home my brother congratulated me after having gone over the accounts, and he gave me a hundred *pesetas*. That constituted my commission for fifteen days of work.

A little after that experience, and while I was strolling in the Altos del Hipódromo with a girlfriend, I noticed a strange metallic taste in my mouth. I wiped my lips with a handkerchief and found that it was stained with blood. I didn't say a word, but went back home chilled to the bone. Sometime around dawn I awakened my brother Agustín who slept in the same room.

"I'm spitting blood."

"You're an ass," was his reply. "Lie down on your back and don't move."

The following morning was filled with my mother's laments, and there were reprimands from the whole family who were convinced that it was all my own fault. They were probably right. I didn't take care of myself at all and lived like a wild animal. I hardly ever ate and barely slept four hours a night. I really was an ass. They took me to see Doctor Codina, a specialist in lung diseases. After taking a chest x-ray and making an analysis of my saliva, he diagnosed my condition as "Hilar adenopathy that was filtering into the upper lobe of the right lung." I really liked that long description of my illness. I even dedicated a few poems to my poor, suffering chest, calling them *Radiographics*. And I began my period of recuperation by being confined, as I awaited the arrival of summer, between my room—that beloved and disorderly Triclinium—and the adjoining enclosed bal-

143

cony whose wide windows looked out over the trees and houses of the city, with the distant Guadarrama Mountains in the background.

Long months of overeating. Periods of inaction, of boredom, of anxiety, and of almost absolute silence because suddenly the fear of becoming seriously ill and dying once and for all became as overwhelming as my carelessness and indifference had been before. From the very first days of this vigil over my health, I had begun to neglect my friends, even refusing to talk to my family since speaking excited me and raised my temperature by a few tenths of a degree. Besides, they had advised me to have lots of fresh air, and I kept the windows open even though it was fall and the freezing wind from the mountains sharply penetrated my solitude. This not only scared away all unwanted visitors, but also my mother, my brothers, and my sisters, who were not interested in catching pneumonia by walking into the "freezer," the name they gave to that part of the house.

This change of life—I owe almost everything to it—had the effect of calming my nerves and slowly transforming that wild and bucking bronco of the last few years into a calm, tamed creature. I read a lot. I managed to get the *Antología poética* of Juan Ramón Jiménez and the *Soledades y Galerías* of Antonio Machado, as well as the first books that were appearing at that time in the *Colección Universal* published by Calpe. I wrote constantly and passionately, without losing touch with what was happening outside, thanks to my younger sister. I heard the loud literary and artistic echoes from the street as they reached me through *Ultra*, a kind of underground literary broadside that the young so-called *Vanguardistas* were distributing in Madrid to the great consternation of and in the face of protests from not only the old guard but also from people far removed from the literary world. Except for the familiar Ramón Gómez de la Serna, I saw written for the first time the names of Gerardo Diego, Luciano de San-Saor, Humberto and José Rivas Panedas, Ciria Escalante, Ildefonso Pereda Valdés, Jorge Luis Borges, alongside other names of foreigners who were also unknown to me: Ivan Goll, Jules Romains, Apollinaire, Max Jacob . . . Among the disjunctive lines of poetry, the vibrant prose pieces, the tasteless aphorisms and the disconcerting typography on those pages, there were also explosive artistic collaborations—drawings and woodblock prints—by such people as Norah Borges and others who were already known to me: Barradas, Paskiewicz, Jhal, Delaunay, etc.

One name stood out more sharply and noisily than all the others

144

in that wild and directionless *Ultra;* that of Guillermo de Torre, the founder and most daring catalyst of the movement. He had issued a manifesto accompanied by a lineal portrait by Barradas, under the title of *Vertex,* that sounded like a screeching locomotor. This work surprised and pleased me, but I rejected its contents from the start. I do remember still some lines from this manifesto: "Lesbian morphine addicts inject into their endocardia the hyperesthesia of linotype ..." and: "Dark-skinned beauty, unravel before me the film of your carburative eyes...." (Later, someone was to make me realize how similar this last line was to the language spoken by the pimps and dandies of Madrid in the plays of Arniches. I hope this small revelation doesn't offend my good friend Guillermo.) I finally became very enthusiastic about *Ultra,* waiting for the appearance of each issue with real interest and impatience. I myself wanted to publish something in that journal, but since I didn't know any of those new writers, I unabashedly sent one of my poems to them by mail. I don't remember the poem itself now, but I recall the brief accompanying note I forwarded with it. It said: "I attach herewith my contribution. You may do with it the best or worst thing that occurs to you." I suppose it eventually ended up in the wastepaper basket, since I never saw it published in spite of the fact that I strained my eyes looking for it in several subsequent issues. I became disillusioned and saddened, telling myself: "That's what happens to you for sticking your nose where it doesn't belong. Maybe they know me better as a painter, and naturally ... etc."

My tremendous, ferocious and anguished battle to be a poet had begun.

It was becoming more and more obvious to me by the day that painting as a means of expression left me completely dissatisfied and that I couldn't find a way to include in a canvas everything that was seething in my imagination. On the other hand, I could put it down on paper. It was easier for me to write anything I pleased, finding the right form to express sentiments that had little or nothing to do with the plastic arts. My feelings of nostalgia for the seafaring life of the Puerto began to come to me in a different form. I still saw it all in lines and colors, but blending into a multitude of sensations that were impossible to capture with a paintbrush. I resolved to forget all about my first vocation. I only wished to be a poet. It was something I wanted desperately, since I felt that at the age of twenty I was almost too old to start out on a new and extremely difficult road. But

I saw then that, surprisingly enough, I was not at a loss for words, and that I had at my command a certain richness and variety of vocabulary. But I was also aware that my orthography was worse than deficient and that from time to time I had serious syntactical problems. I began to read more carefully, looking at each word and consulting the dictionary often, but I couldn't find any solution to my problems through the study of grammar. Time and hard work helped in some ways but never totally resolved these problems, and even today I am filled with doubts about whatever I write.

I spent that first melancholy winter watching Madrid dissolve in mist, become covered over with snow or bathed in the light from those very special skies above the city, tense with tones of frozen blue. I found some consolation in gazing at a young girl who spent hours and hours behind the windows of a balcony in a house opposite ours, and then spring arrived, making it necessary for me to think about getting ready to leave for the pine forests of San Rafael.

Warm and restful summer days spent stretched out on a comfortable chaise-longue, reading, writing, or absorbed in watching the gentle movement of the clouds. That peaceful silence was only interrupted from time to time by the sound of railroad cars heading toward the summer beaches to the north.

> *Con la nostalgia del mar,*
> *mi novia bebe cerveza*
> *en el coche-restorán.*

> *Nostalgic for the sea,*
> *My sweetheart drinks a beer*
> *In the dining-car.*

I used to read my poems to a person who was older than I and who frequently occupied a chair next to mine. He was French and a student in Madrid, but the state of his health had also made it necessary for him to seek out the healthy mountain air. Eighteen years later, when our civil war was over and I was exiled in Paris, he came to see me, turning out to be Marcel Bataillon, the great French Hispanist. He brought me a copy of his latest book, *Erasmus in Spain*, a true masterpiece and a fundamental work on the ideas prevalent in Spain during the sixteenth century.

Up in the mountains of the Guadarrama, my body absorbed the

146

sun that shed its light on the pine trees and I was virtually reborn. My afternoon fever disappeared, I gained weight—more than a young poet should—and began to stroll again, a half-hour each morning and another half-hour before sundown.

I wrote like a madman. I was almost happy with my poetry which was very different from what was then in vogue among the *Ultraistas*, although naturally it contained some of the same shocking effects. One day a painter friend of mine who came to visit me brought me a volume of poetry. *Libro de Poemas* was its title, a work that was being critically acclaimed in Madrid. My painter friend was Gregorio Prieto, and the author of this book was Federico García Lorca, a young man from Granada who spent his winters in Madrid at the Residencia de Estudiantes. I was very enthusiastic about many of his poems, particularly those that were simple and popular, adorned as they were with charming, song-like refrains. There were other poems of his, however, which I rejected totally. I couldn't understand how anyone could publish a hymn to Doña Juana la Loca and other similar things in the same old tired, academic tone when there was so much innovative activity taking place. There were certain outmoded echoes of Villaespesa and even of Zorrilla—both singers of Granada—which could be heard throughout the book. But in spite of this, it was obvious that a great new poet had appeared on the literary scene, and I was very eager to meet him. That, however, wasn't to occur until three years later.

One day when I was lying near a hidden stream, the one-o'clock train arrived in town and the paths and woods of San Rafael were suddenly filled with a repeated cry that at first was a complete mystery to me. The newsboys were shouting:

"A disaster at Annual! Disaster at Annual! General Navarro taken prisoner!"

This constituted a great military and political disaster in Morocco—thousands of our soldiers killed by Moorish troops—and as a consequence it was to bring about the military dictatorship of Primo de Rivera two years later. I couldn't possibly know then that our generation would grow to maturity under that banner. Another literary generation, the Generation of 1898, had also come into being during another national catastrophe: the total collapse of the Spanish Monarchy. These events left a well-defined imprint on the writers of both generations. But our group was not aware until the coming of the Republic in 1931 that we were going to reach our poetic maturity during those dictatorial years. But I will tell more about all that later.

Toward the end of October, already well into the fall season, I returned to my "freezer." I was sad at having to leave San Rafael, which had become solemn and melancholy now that its summer residents had gone. The poplars were bare and their yellow leaves were being swept up by gusts of wind along the roads. The arrival of autumn in the mountains was beautiful. The sun and the hissing of the wind among the pine trees seemed to belong more exclusively to me. With the first biting cold and clear blue days, the mountains seemed to stand out even more, and those that faced Segovia forming the configuration of "the dead woman" offered an extensive and impressive profile. I returned to Madrid that year accompanied by a delicate prelude of snow and the early howling of wolves in the nocturnal forests. I prepared myself for another endless winter. Although my need for rest and silence was not so pressing, the fear I still had about my illness induced me to be prudent and not very eager to receive uninvited guests. It was fortunate for me and for my isolation that the girl across the street reappeared behind the windows of her balcony, remaining there for hours on end. We exchanged mutual glances until dusk.

I continued writing. A slow, cold month without my seeing anyone. Then suddenly one afternoon the first visitor of the season appeared, unannounced, in my room. He was a young writer whom I had met years before at some art exhibit, at a Salón de Otoño, I think. His name was Juan Chabás. Originally from Valencia, he was dark-complexioned with large eyes and almost larger eyelashes and a mellifluous, even pompous way of speaking. He wore a gray suit with a narrow collar and a black bow tie. A real Levantine type, undeniably handsome, pleasant enough, but also at times a bit tiresome. He brought me a little book of poems—*Ondas (Waves)*—the first one he had published. I read the dedication: "To the painter Rafael Alberti." And I couldn't help showing some signs of annoyance.

"You may not know this, but I have given up painting. The doctor has forbidden me to be on my feet too long—and besides, the smell of paint is not good for my health," I said to him, exaggerating a bit. "I'm a writer now."

"That's fine—you can sketch sitting down, and go back to painting when you're completely cured."

"I won't have time for both things. I would like to be forgotten as

a painter. I prefer poetry. I'm going to read something to you. You
don't mind, do you?"

And without waiting for his reply I quickly recited three poems by
heart. One of them—the only one I can remember right now—went
as follows:

> *La noche ajusticiada*
> *en el patíbulo de un árbol.*
>
> *Alegrías arrodilladas*
> *le besan y ungen las sandalias.*
>
> *Vena*
> *suavemente lejana*
> *—cinturón del Globo.*
>
> *Arterias infinitas,*
> *mares del corazón que se desangra.*
>
> *The night was condemned to death*
> *On the scaffold of a tree.*
>
> *Joys on bended knee*
> *Kiss and anoint its sandals.*
>
> *A gently distant vein*
> *Encircles the Globe.*
>
> *Infinite arteries,*
> *The heart's bleeding seas.*

"You know, that's very good," he said after a deliberate silence.
"Do you have more?"

"Many more. A whole book."

Another silence.

"I came here on a different matter. I thought you might like to
prepare a showing of your paintings in the gallery of the Ateneo. I'm
on the Board of Directors and I can arrange it for you . . ."

"Why would I want to do that? That wouldn't help me in my
new career."

"Don't be foolish. You will always be a painter even if you do write."

"That doesn't interest me any more."

I was deeply disappointed. He hadn't liked my poems, I was sure of it. It wasn't too difficult to pretend about such things.

"You could get together your best works—a collection of oil paintings and drawings . . ."

"No."

"I'll take charge of everything; it would be your farewell appearance as a painter. What do you think of the idea?"

I hesitated. I was already convinced of my failure, certain that no one would take my writing seriously. From now on I would write only for myself. My sister Pepita would be the sole judge and critic of my poems.

"All right. If you arrange the whole thing. It will be my farewell to painting, as you say. I never go out . . . What are the dates?"

"Sometime around the beginning of the year."

"I will show up at the Ateneo on opening day."

We shook hands and he left.

Lying there in my bed I almost wept with anger, but on the following morning I had gotten over it. I began to write again, although I felt the battle had been lost.

A little more than a week later Chabás appeared again. He wasn't alone.

"Dámaso Alonso . . ."

That name was not completely unfamiliar to me.

"He also has a book for you."

I looked at the title of the book which this new author was presenting to me: *Poemas puros: Poemillas de la ciudad. (Pure Poems: Little Poems of the City.)*

"It's a formidable piece of work," commented Chabás with his usual pompousness.

Dámaso Alonso reacted with an expression on his face that conveyed both annoyance and irony. When Dámaso and I later became good friends, I was able to confirm that his reaction to the Valencian's praise had been sincere. Dámaso Alonso, very young at that time but precociously mature and extraordinarily talented, was suffering from a sense of disillusionment or what really was an incomprehensible lack of self-confidence which at times bordered on the tragic. He had a complex about his own appearance: short,

150

pudgy and crowned by a bald spot that was visibly spreading. His second surname—Redondas (Rounded)—which I soon discovered and not from his own lips, caused him a great deal of suffering. He drank more than he should, something which greatly annoyed his mother, and he spent much of his time with prostitutes. People were already speaking about him as a minor phenomenon of wisdom and erudition. He had a tremendous memory—even better than the one I am plagued with—and during the period of our enthusiasm for Góngora he had learned to recite that poet's difficult *Soledades* and *Polifemo* without a single mistake. He had all the makings of a great poet, although he wrote infrequently because of his exaggerated sense of self-criticism and those feelings of disillusionment and insecurity which weighed so heavily upon him.

I became very fond of him, and I am deeply indebted to him for many things—one fundamental thing in particular: he introduced me to Gil Vicente, a poet who still contributes a sense of freshness to my most recent works of poetry. The book he had left with me that afternoon was very good and a far cry from that "ultraistic" agitation. It was a kind of harbinger of the tranquil and very traditional Spanish poetic style that was to distinguish our generation. Closer to the poetry of Antonio Machado than to that of Juan Ramón Jiménez, *Poemas puros: Poemillas de la ciudad,* because of its human vibrations and extreme economy and simplicity of expression, opened the way to the great poetry of that decade. There are many, perhaps, including Dámaso himself, who might not remember this work, but I do. I recall it so well that even now I can recite by heart some of the sonnets and refrains which I memorized on that very wintry afternoon in 1921 after his first visit to me.

I think he liked those poems of mine which I read to him, although not as much as the ones I was to write later. But since I was aware that my own sense of insecurity as a beginning poet was at its most dramatic stage and that he was not unaware of my artistic vocation, I tried not to let his expressions of approval influence me too much or create illusions about my poetic talents.

In January or February of 1922 I attended the opening of my exhibit at the Ateneo. The kindly Juan Chabás had faithfully kept his promise and taken care of every detail: the placing of the canvases and the drawings, the preparation of catalogs, the pricing of each work, etc. I wasn't displeased to see my work of that period, exemplifying the most varied tendencies, gathered together and displayed with a certain flair. There were figures and landscapes influenced by Vázquez Díaz, explosions of color presented with dynamic rhythms reminiscent of the works of Delaunay placed next to the most innocent geometric exercises that were purely Cubist in inspiration. There were also some schematic drawings of dancing figures, lineal reminders of the Russian Ballet mixed together with visions of prehistoric caves. Looking at that grouping of my works, I was tempted to renew my already waning artistic vocation. But I could not do that. It was too late to turn back. The road was now blocked, and my having walked along the new path of poetry convinced me that turning back would have been a serious error.

The exhibit attracted more attention among the young writers than among painters. I wasn't particularly happy about this, nor was I in the least embittered. Among the friends of our "guild" who visited the exhibit I remember Gregorio Prieto, who was then rather well known, and Francisco Bores, on the eve of his departure for France where he would almost immediately become one of the most individualistic and distinguished members of the Spanish Group in the "Ecole de Paris" which was then beginning to form. One of the surprises of the exhibit was that I sold a painting for three hundred *pesetas* to a member of the Peruvian Embassy who with some enthusiasm carried the work off with him even before the show's closing date. The person whose works were scheduled to be shown in that little gallery of the Ateneo after my exhibit closed was Francisco Cossío, who shortly thereafter was to become an integral part of the Parisian group of Spanish artists. I was a friend of his but nonetheless refused to greet him years later, when upon his return to Spain he showed a great lack of talent by becoming a member of the Fascist Falange.

I was immensely relieved when my paintings were back at the apartment. I felt that I had made a public confession of all my sins, purifying my conscience and finding it now without feelings of remorse, in a state of grace and prepared for the worst of my struggle to achieve what for so long had been the cause of many sleepless nights. Would victory be far off? It was difficult to know at the time. But after that exhibit in the Ateneo I somehow saw the way more illuminated and open to me for the first time (even though some resistance to my achieving success on the part of the young writers of the period was to be a serious barrier).

I must admit in all justice that Juan Chabás, in spite of his obvious interest in my painting, was perhaps among all the writers the one who most helped me to abandon this area of activity. In those days a new magazine, *Horizonte (Horizon)*, had just come out. It was more subdued and restrained in its approach, like a rainbow appearing after the ultraistic downpour. Its director was a new poet by the name of Pedro Garfias, from the town of Osuña, and he was considered together with Gerardo Diego to be one of the most promising poets of the day. (I learned later that Garfias was not overly flattered by being compared with the poet from Santander.) As was becoming the usual case, it was Juan Chabás who was responsible for the visit of this Andalusian poet whom I received in my "freezing compartment" (less frigid now that the spring breezes had begun to enter through the open windows). Garfias listened attentively to the poems I read to him without any introduction and in response to Chabás' insistence. His reaction was to have a pronounced effect on my life:

"Let me have the three which you like the best for the next issue of *Horizonte*."

I didn't sleep that night, and I was in a state of anxiety for several weeks after that until this issue of the magazine was due to appear. Would Garfias publish my poems? Would he change his mind when he reread them and found them not to be so good after all? None of this finally happened, though, and my name appeared in this eagerly awaited issue alongside the "Baladilla de los tres ríos" of García Lorca, some poems by Garfias himself and several short songs by Antonio Machado. *Horizonte* lived up to its title. In its clear and ample firmament poets who had been deliberately and temporarily excluded from *Ultra* appeared again side by side. Juan Ramón was placed again beside Machado. Very few members of the primitive vanguardist ship had succeeded in swimming to shore. They had almost all sunk to the bottom except for the invincible Gerardo Diego as a poet and, as critic and captain of the vessel, Guillermo de Torre.

There was another journal I was familiar with that had been in existence for about two years and was published in La Coruña under the delightful name of *Alfar*. It had a very broad critical base, and in its harmonious and spacious pages there was room for the most diverse authors representing different artistic tendencies. In the area of Spanish literature it ran the gamut from Azorín, Unamuno or

Miró to the latest ultraistic cry; and from Latin America there were Lugones, Sanín Cano, Alfonso Reyes and even the most extreme *Martinfierristas.*

The dedicated editor and manager of *Alfar* was a sincere and ardent Uruguayan poet, Julio J. Casal, who was also his country's consul in that Galician city. He and his compatriot, the painter Barradas, a true budding genius far ahead of his time, left behind in Spain the memory of their indelible presence and the deeply planted seed of their abundantly generous work. Although at the time I had some contact with the painter, I did not become a friend of the poet's until 1940 when I was living in exile in Argentina. Daniel Vázquez Díaz was responsible for my having made contact with him, since it was Daniel who had sent him an article I had written about painting which Casal published and illustrated with some of the best paintings by several Andalusian artists. My eagerness to be known was becoming obsessive, and after some time I suddenly remembered *Alfar* and sent them several poems, feeling, nonetheless, intimidated by my own daring. A few months later I received an issue together with a brief but affectionate letter from the editor. And there were my poems, prominently included. They were similar in tone to the ones that had been published in *Horizonte,* and I have never included them in any of my books since I had completely forgotten about them. But now that Robert Marrast, a young French Hispanist who has translated some of my plays, has been kind enough to send me a copy of this issue of *Alfar,* I would like to include them here since they may be of interest to the reader of this short prehistory of my poetry.

BALCONES

1

Te saludan los ángeles, Sofía,
luciérnaga del valle.
La estrella del Señor
vuela de su cabaña
a tu alquería.
Ora por el lucero perdido,

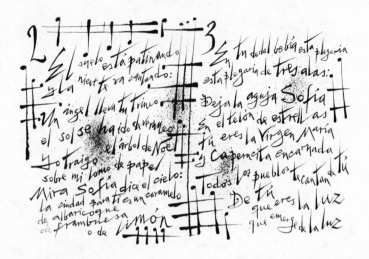

linterna de los llanos:
por que lo libre el sol

de la manzana picada,
de los erizos del castaño.
Mariposa en el túnel,
sirenita del mar, Sofía:
para que el cofrecillo de una nuez
sea siempre en ensueños nuestro barco.

2

El suelo está patinando
y la nieve te va cantando:

Un ángel lleva tu trineo,
el sol se ha ido de veraneo.

Yo traigo el árbol de Noel
sobre mi lomo de papel.

Mira, Sofía, dice el cielo:

la ciudad para ti es un caramelo
de albaricoque,
de frambuesa
o de limón.

3

En tu dedal bebía esta plegaria,
esta plegaria de tres alas:
Deja la aguja, Sofía.
En el telón de estrellas;
tu eres la Virgen María
y Caperucita encarnada.
Todos los pueblos te cantan de tú.
De tú,
        que eres la luz
        que emerge de la luz.

BALCONIES

1

The angels greet you, Sophia,
Firefly of the valley.
The Lord's star
Flies from its bower
To your rustic dwelling.
Pray for the lost star,
Lantern of the plains:
So that it may be freed by the sun

From the half-eaten apple,
From the burs of the chestnut tree.
Butterfly in the tunnel,
Little siren of the sea, Sophia:
May the little coffer of a nutshell
Always in dreams be our sailing ship.

The ground is skating
And the snow sings to you:

An angel pulls your sleigh,
The sun has left on summer vacation.

I bring you a Christmas tree
On my shoulders of paper.

Look, Sophia, says the sky:
For you the city is made of candy
Of apricot,
Of raspberry
Or of lemon.

From your thimble I drank this prayer,
This three-winged prayer:
Leave your needle, Sophia,
In the curtain of stars;
You are the Virgin Mary incarnate
And Little Red Riding Hood.
All the nations sing your name,
You,
> *Who are the light*
> *That springs from light.*

This Sofía was a twelve- or thirteen-year-old girl whom I used to gaze at during the first long months of my illness as she sat alone behind the sparkling windows of her room, studying the pages of an atlas. From my room, which was just one storey higher than hers, I used to see how her finger slowly moved along the blue seas, the capes, the bays and the solid patches of earth imprisoned on those maps between the thin network of meridians and parallel lines. Sofía also embroidered flowers and initials on filmy cambric or heavy burlap, a task obviously assigned to her in school and which she pursued with the same concentration as her travels. She was my silent consolation during many afternoons. She hardly ever looked at me, and if on rare occasions she did dare to glance in my direction it was done in a strange way without the slightest change in the expression on her face. This pure and primitive image of Sofía at her window remained with me for a long time and even found its way into the songs I later included in my book of poems *Marinero en tierra (Sailor on Land)*, by which time she had already exchanged the blue of her atlas and the embroidery needle for a Sunday morning flirt as she came out of church. If, at the age of thirteen, Sofía had been stingy about offering me a simple look out of the corner of her eyes, now, at the height of her fifteenth year, she would blush to the roots of her hair every time we saw each other in the street, turning away and becoming so obviously uncomfortable that I ended up being even more embarrassed and always let her pass by with feigned indifference as if she were completely unknown to me. From that time on, even though I continued living in the same house until 1930, Sofía's presence was totally erased from my memory as if she had actually died, and what remained was only a beautiful name which became woven into the threads of my poems.

In a long series of poems written in the same style as those I had dedicated to Sofía, I began to compose a book which I had already given a title very much in keeping with the taste of the times but which almost nobody liked: *Giróscopo (Gyroscope)*. I thought that this word perfectly described my poems with their multiple images, works that might bring to mind that musical top with its colorful striations that so delighted children. Juan Chabás sent some of these poems off to the novelist Gabriel Miró who at the time had retired to his beloved Levantine countryside. I soon received a letter from Miró in which, together with generous and polite comments, he wrote that "In your *Giróscopo*—the title troubles me [he didn't like it either]—there are expressions of sharp beauty." Miró was right, of course, since my obsession with the beauty of the word had reached a state of almost violent convulsions during the year in which the literary world was celebrating the tricentennial of Luis de Góngora's death, and when in my *Cal y canto (Whitewash and Stonesong)* an interest in formal beauty had taken such a strong hold on me that it had left my emotional senses in a state of paralysis.

CHAPTER *IV*

*Now in Castelar some thirty kilometers from Buenos Aires—and
at the home of my dear friends, the Dujovnes—I look for the
necessary tranquility and peace of mind to conclude—is it possible?
—this second book of my* Lost Grove *which has been interrupted
so many times. But between the previous chapter and the one I
begin now, what a long parenthesis there has been, what an unusually full two years have passed in my life in which that chain of
monotonous inactivity had been broken and I was able to free
myself from that unwanted anchor that had made me feel as if I
were living through a period of sterilizing drought! What torrential rains, what beneficial irrigation fed my plants and my thirsty
roots, making me flourish again, turning me once more into a tall
tree capable of opening its branches and its leaves to the singing of
the birds and the wind!*

*I tell you, poplars, oaks, cypresses, cedars and eucalyptus trees of
these woods, the wondrous frost of the Polish forests, the muted
snow-covered sounds of the bells in Cracow, the pastoral echo of
flutes in the valleys of Rumania, the German forests of birch and
pine, the sun circling the gold stars of the Kremlin, the proud and
clear look in the eyes of the pure people of those nations, you can be
seen, now that my heart is at peace. To you, roses of autumn,
brilliantly colored paper-like zinnias, dahlias as round as shields,
jasmines like snowflakes, to you I confess the secrets of the flowers of
China. I will tell you about the complexion of her women, softer*

and more beautiful than your own petals; of the open sails of the Chinese junks, enormous butterflies, as they move along the silken ribbons of their rivers. I have traveled, I have seen different faces, skies and countrysides. Distant maps have spread out before me their previously unknown colors. And now, so many thousands of kilometers removed from these places, the blood passes through my heart filled with millions of eyes, millions of voices, millions of fraternal hands which touch and warm this heart of mine giving it a new beat and bathing it in words that will continue to stir the remembered breezes of this, my Lost Grove.

In TIME my adenopathy with its "infiltration into the upper lobe of my left lung," improved, so much that I had never felt stronger. I no longer had to rest all day long. I would only stretch out in bed for an hour after meals, keeping awake by reading a book. Nevertheless, I didn't go out very much, and those exhausting hikes during my early years in Madrid were now reduced to short walks in the open fields surrounding our neighborhood, through the Retiro Gardens and Moncloa or in visits to the few friends I had made. Among the latter was Luis Alberti—the son of Aunt Lola, my first painting teacher, and the brother of José Ignacio, the anarchist and Republican translator, and also a friend of the novelist Pío Baroja during his Bohemian years.

Luis was a gentle soul who led a rather solitary existence in Madrid accompanying those three Granada beauties—Dolores, María and Gloria—who, like him, also lived in a withdrawn and unhappy spinsterhood. Extremely affectionate towards me, Luis would receive me in his office at the Casa Calpe, the publishing firm where he worked. I owed to him the growth of my literary culture, since because of his generosity I rarely left his office without a pile of books under my arm. That series known as the *Colección Universal*, with its yellowish covers, introduced all of us to the great Russian authors who had been virtually unknown before Calpe had begun publishing them. Gogol, Goncharov, Korolenko, Dostoyevsky, Chekhov, Andreiev—darkened and disturbed my days and nights. There was one novel amongst them all that deeply impressed the young Spanish intellectuals in whom there already existed strong and violent inclinations toward anarchism: *Sacha Yegulev* by Andreiev, an author who had recently died in Finland far removed from Lenin's revolution, which he had never truly understood. I was among those young people who were kept awake by the adventuresome and heroic youth of Sacha. Dostoyevsky's *The Idiot* baffled rather than impressed me; that entire world of madmen who behaved so naturally, and in which abnormality seemed to be the correct form of behavior, left me perplexed and pensive. As a result of that book I began to realize that Spain, particularly in its villages and even more so in those of the South, was filled with similar types of possessed individuals, a group which included more than a few members of my own family. From the strange madness of Dostoyevsky's characters I moved on to the captivating wit and melancholy of those created by Chekhov. With my sister Pepita I read and reread, to the point of tears, the short stories of his poor coachmen, peasants, modest employees and teachers. The first thing I read by Gorki was *Malva*, a marvelous story whose final cry—"Who has carried off my knife?"—somehow strangely ended up in one of my songs in *Marinero en tierra*. Perhaps we Spaniards have not yet fully admitted how much we owe to that surprising revelation that was opened to us by the appearance of all those Russian novels during those years.

At that period of my life I was always penniless and scarcely had enough money for the street car. My illness had been very expensive: medicines, injections, x-rays, long periods of recuperation up in the mountains. I could hardly ask for money at home, and therefore I could only buy very few books. To my Uncle Luis, who gave me so many books when I visited him, I am in debt for most of the reading I did in my youth, and the prerevolutionary Russian authors then occupied a preferential place in my personal library. My Uncle Luis was a delightful man and was also touched by his own brand of madness. During this gift-giving period of his, he was lonelier than ever. He had just broken off relations with his mistress—she had been getting too fat. Several times he had warned her: "When you reach 175 pounds, I'll leave you." One afternoon he weighed her on a subway scale; that was the fatal moment. The marker, without any hesitation, indicated that the lady had gone somewhat beyond the limit. And right then and there, on the subway platform, Luis left her, never to see her again.

I no longer saw Gil Cala and Celestino Espinosa, those two

friends of my early years in Madrid. Gil Cala was working some-where in Sevilla, I think, and Espinosa was doing his military ser-vice in Africa. On the other hand, I saw Vásquez Díaz more than ever. He was still as amusing as he always had been, repeating his stories about Paris and having nasty things to say about painters —and everybody else for that matter! How well we got along together! What an extraordinary wit and sense of humor he had! I still laugh when I remember him.

But a new friendship had begun in my life, a friendship that at the beginning one could have called highly mobile, since we always met on the platform of the Number Three streetcar on our way to the Puerta del Sol. My new friend was Vicente Aleixandre who resided, as I did, in the Salamanca district. It wasn't in the Ateneo at the time of my painting exhibition that we first saw each other, even though Vicente today is convinced that we met there. Where could it have been? I can't remember now. Perhaps it was through Juan Chabás, Dámaso Alonso or some of Vicente's own cousins who lived on the second floor of our apartment building. Many vivid memories of this poet have remained with me and will surface often throughout this diary of mine. His first book, *Ámbito (Perimeter)*, was to clearly mark him as one of the most important poets of our generation, a genera-tion which the civil war violently tore apart and dispersed, even caus-ing the death of one of its most talented voices. I remember many things about him but the image that will always stand out above the rest is a tall, thin, blonde Aleixandre—before his illness and the mountain air of Miraflores had given him that pinkish complex-ion—perched on the platform of that nocturnal streetcar that was taking him to his box at the Royal Theater, where I would only go from time to time as the guest of Consuelo Flores, that beautiful Italian lady who lived in our building.

Since taking care of my health had become a comfortable habit, no sooner had spring come and gone than I suggested to my family the possibility of my going to the mountains to escape the summer heat which would be so harmful to my still not totally calcified lung. And off I went, alternating between total rest, obsessively taking my temperature—I would break innumerable thermometers each year—more or less durable infatuations and, particularly, working on a new book of poems that was taking form and already had a title:

Mar y tierra (Sea and Land). Not long before that, Dámaso Alonso had introduced me to the poetry of Gil Vicente and to Barbieri's *Cancionero musical de los siglos XV y XVI (Anthology of Musical Ballads of the Fifteenth and Sixteenth Centuries)*. Among the pine trees of San Rafael I composed my first ballad in the traditional style: "La corza blanca" ("The White Deer"), in which I imitated almost the same melodic rhythm of one of the shortest, most mysterious of the anonymous ballads in that anthology, the one beginning with the words "En Avila, mis ojos ..."

As its title suggested, *Mar y tierra* was divided into two parts. The first contained the poems directly inspired by the Guadarrama Mountains and others of various thematic content, and the second part, which I called "Marinero en tierra," consisted of those poems born of my nostalgia for the Bay of Cádiz with its inlets, little boats and salt-flats. Dámaso would come to visit me and I would read my poems to him receiving, at times, his enthusiastic approval. I was far removed then from all ultraistic ingenuity or confusion and was seeking extreme simplicity, a clear and precise melodic line similar to what Federico García Lorca had already fully achieved in his "Baladilla de los tres ríos," but my new lyrical style was not nourished only by song. I was also immersed in the works of Garcilaso and Pedro Espinosa (Góngora would come later). I was equally attracted by sonnets and tercets, but not so much by the royal octaves so beautifully wrought by both these poets, which were too limiting, slow and boring for my purposes and impatience in those days.

For the ultraists who represented a violent and almost armed reaction against classical and romantic forms, writing a sonnet would have seemed worse than committing some hideous crime, but I composed them anyhow since I was after all younger and freer than most of them. Besides, I was almost completely unknown. I wrote one poem in alexandrine verse—"A Juan Antonio Espinosa, capitán de navío" ("To Juan Antonio Espinosa, Ship's Captain")—with a motto taken from Baudelaire. This Juan Antonio, Celestino's brother and now a practicing novelist, was probably not a captain at the time and certainly not of a large ship, but I admired him greatly simply because I had heard he belonged to a fishing fleet that regularly sailed the waters of the Bay of Biscay. I even tried my hand at stringing together tercets, grouping them under the title "Sueño del marinero" ("The Sailor's Dream") in which I expressed all my longings to travel and my growing melancholy as a child of the sea anchored to the land. Both these poems were eventually included in my book, and in the final version the second one served as a prologue. Was I therefore a deserter or traitor to the poetry which was then considered to be very "avant-garde," by my having reverted to the cultivation of more traditional poetic forms? That is not the way I see it. The authentic and really new vanguard was to be formed by us, by those poets whose work was on the verge of becoming known, although with the exception of Dámaso, Lorca and Gerardo Diego, most of it was still unpublished. Nevertheless, some of our poems had appeared in the journal *Indice* which Juan Ramón Jiménez was editing in conjunction with the publishing firm of the same name. That earlier vanguard, the ultraists, was in retreat. The number of casualties, heroes if you prefer, left strewn on the battlefield was high; only a few had survived.

Although Juan Ramón in a moment of justifiable anger toward me was later to categorize me as an "ist"—that is to say, as a poet who had actively cultivated the "isms" of the day—I must express here my sense of horror of all classifications and my love, on the contrary, for the most absolute independence, for the variety and permanent adventure of unexplored forests and uncharted seas. It was inevitable and natural that I would brush up against these "isms," that I would even at times be infected by them to the point where it might seem that I was caught in their nets. Such "isms" infiltrated everywhere, appearing in sudden waves like seismic tremors, and it was almost impossible to emerge completely unscathed from this incessant tidal movement. But now that I am so far removed from all that, I can in effect ask myself to what particular "ism" does my work belong today, or for that matter to which one do all the Spanish poets of my generation belong? I think I can safely affirm that they belonged to none and that our poetry at its best was above all fads and was rarely bogged down in sterile activity. Thus it constituted the true vanguard of a lyrical movement which, in spite of all the ensuing sadness that was to follow, continues in a certain way—and I don't think it immodest or exaggerated to say so—to prevail in Spain today.

Gregorio Prieto, who at the time admired me much more as a poet than as a painter, came to see me during that summer in San Rafael. His own prestige was on the upswing. I think he had even won a medal in the National Exhibit for a painting with an extremely long and literary title: *Soledad, Encarnación y Asunción Recolectando Manzanas.* Upon my return from the mountains, well into autumn, he suggested that I sit for a portrait, and I went to his house, on one of the more typical streets of Madrid, to pose for him. Not so long ago Prieto himself sent to me, in Buenos Aires, a photo of that very painting. There I am from the waist up, still dressed in mourning for the death of my father, wearing a thin white collar but no tie, drawn, my head held high but with a distant expression in my eyes and an open book between my fingers. This was a youthful work, but over the years it still seems to retain some of its original charm and warmth.

In order to show it to a well-known author and at the same time offer me a chance to read some of my poems, one afternoon Prieto invited Enrique Díez-Canedo to his studio. I had never seen him before. His name was not unfamiliar to me, but his works were. I knew he was a very important drama and literary critic whose reviews appeared in several journals and newspapers, and I was aware that he also wrote poetry. At that moment of my life the only contemporary but older Spanish authors known to me were Antonio Machado (more than Manuel, his brother) and Juan Ramón Jiménez. I knew Gabriel Miró only through having read some of his short stories and his *Humo dormido (Slumbering Smoke)*, a delightful novel which dealt with education in a Jesuit school and therefore had attracted and moved me deeply, causing me to recall my own school days in the Puerto at San Luis Gonzaga. I had begun to read Azorín's *Clásicos y modernos (Classics and Moderns)*, and I liked it. But there were also Unamuno, Baroja, Valle-Inclán, Pérez de Ayala, D'Ors, Ortega y Gasset—so many of them! I was almost still a painter and only a nebulous poet who was nonetheless killing himself for the sake of poetry, often waking up in the morning with eyes all bloodshot from not having slept enough because of poetry. The Spanish novel interested me only slightly or, to put it another way, something existed in me that prevented my seeking it out. Philosophical essays bored me, even though I only knew them from a distance. Perhaps such brutishness during that period of my life was necessary to allow me to concentrate exclusively on what I wanted, on what I was about to demand with great insistence: that I be considered exclusively as a poet. Everything else was to come later.

There would be plenty of time to fill the huge wells of my ignorance.

At first I was shocked by Díez-Canedo's girlish voice, which came out in little puffs like a broken whistle, and by his silky mannerisms and perpetual noncommital smile composed of widely spaced, yellow teeth. He praised the portrait and couldn't conceal his surprise when Prieto asked me to read my poems, a reaction that I had unhappily anticipated.

"I thought you were only a painter," he ventured to say somewhat timidly.

I was on the verge of saying something quite nasty to him, but fortunately I controlled myself, realizing how unjust and impolite it would have been. I was a bit nervous as I took out my manuscript and for the first time read some of my songs and sonnets to an "important person." Canedo's comments were positive but sparse. He especially smiled on hearing my sea verses. Like Juan Ramón and García Lorca, I was also Andalusian, and this fact was apparent in the particular tonality of my incipient poetry.

The few words he spoke were not in the least displeasing to me. For an illustrious critic they were sufficient, particularly if one is aware how carefully such critics usually express themselves so as to avoid the risk of being mistaken. A short time later I heard from Gregorio Prieto that Díez-Canedo had gone even further in his praise of my poems and this filled me with new enthusiasm and inspiration.

The months passed. Another winter with fewer worries about my health but spent in voluntary retirement in my "freezer," where I was only rarely interrupted. *Mar y tierra,* that great obsession of mine, grew and stretched while the fluttering ribbon worn by my little sailor floated on the imaginary breezes of my bedroom. That sweetheart of mine, only vaguely glimpsed from a roof terrace in my distant maritime childhood, was becoming transformed into a gardening siren, a beloved caretaker of underwater flowerbeds and orchards. I decorated the delicate masts of my songs with ribbons and banners of the most diverse colors. My book was beginning to be like a festival, a sparkling regatta propelled by the southern sun. I composed a Triduum of Dawn—three sonnets—to the Virgen del Carmen, the smiling patron saint of the sea, which I dedicated to my mother. She was deeply touched, assuming that those lyrical prayers signified a rebirth of my religious faith. I saw myself as a pirate plundering the Aurora Borealis and sailing uncharted seas. I glimpsed a blue bull—taken from classical mythology—racing along the perfect arch of the Bay of Cádiz, on whose white shores I had spent one distant night in my childhood, combing the luminous tail of the Halley Comet. I saw, dreamed or invented many other small things that were all drawn from that nostalgic well which was getting deeper by the day as I moved further away and further inland from my earlier life. In this way I succeeded in gathering together a group of poems which possessed a great variety of "color, perfume, music and essence," without resorting to the "facile trappings" of the picturesque, as Juan Ramón Jiménez was to say later while comparing my poetry to that of García Lorca.

Everything was now ready for me to meet Federico. The hour had finally come. It happened one early autumn afternoon. And it was also Gregorio Prieto, as he has pointed out to me recently in a letter, who introduced me to the poet of Granada. We were in the gardens of the Residencia de Estudiantes where García Lorca, then studying to be a lawyer, had lived for several years. Since it was October, the poet had just arrived from his Granada. He was dark, olive-skinned, with a tuft of hair plastered across his broad forehead. His eyes sparkled and his open smile could, at any moment, become quickly transformed into a burst of laughter: he looked less like a gypsy than a peasant, with that mixture of refinement and coarseness that seems to spring from the Andalusian soil. (This was how I saw him on that afternoon and how I see him still whenever he comes to mind.) He received me joyfully with embraces, laughter and exaggerated gestures. He insisted he knew me very well and that he was equally well acquainted with the Granada branch of the family. Among other things, he told me that years ago he had seen my exhibit at the Ateneo, that I was his cousin and he wished to commission me to do a painting of him sleeping on the banks of a stream while up in the top branches of an olive tree the image of the Virgin would appear holding a banner with the following inscription: "Apparition of Our Lady of Beautiful Love to the poet Federico García Lorca." I was flattered by this commission, although I warned him that it would be the last painting I would ever do, since I had abandoned this activity some time ago and was now only interested in being a poet. He didn't seem to consider this to be of any particular importance.

That night he invited me to dine at the Residencia together with some other friends of his, among whom were Luis Buñuel, not yet the famous film director he was to become, the poet José Moreno Villa from Málaga, and a slim young man with a blonde, absurd and funny little moustache, whose name was Pepín Bello and whom I liked tremendously right from the start. After dinner we went back to the garden, that beautiful enclosure guarded by poplar trees, with its arterial stream from the Canalillo, dotted with oleander and covered with jasmine bushes that grew in waves against the student pavilions. I had never heard Federico recite, but he had the reputation of reading extremely well. And in that darkness, distantly lit by the illuminated windows of the student rooms, I discovered that his reputation was well deserved. García Lorca recited his latest gypsy ballad which he had just brought back from Granada:

"*Verde, que te quiero, verde . . .*"

"*Green, how I love you, green . . .*"

How unforgettable, that night of our first meeting! There was magic, *duende,** something irresistible in everything Federico did. How could anyone forget him after having seen him or heard him just once? He was a truly fascinating human being: singing, alone or at the piano, reciting, telling jokes and even talking nonsense. He was already a celebrity and would repeat his poems, his phrases, his thousands of anecdotes from Granada—some true, others invented—at all the literary gatherings held at various cafés in town or when he found himself surrounded by groups of students. His most fundamental works written during those years were as yet unpublished. Up until that moment only two books by him had been published: one, barely known—*Impresiones y Paisajes* (Impressions and Landscapes) (1918)—dedicated to his music teacher, and another—*Libro de poemas* (1921)—well received by the critics and which I had already enjoyed reading up in the Guadarrama Mountains. Federico did not speak much about these works, although I did hear him recite ballads from the last one. What the poet was shouting to the four winds at the time were his gypsy ballads, which he alternated with individual little songs or poems he had gathered

*In his lecture on the *duende* or daimon, García Lorca defined it as "a power, not a construct" and "a creation made act."

together under the title *Poema del cante jondo*. Among his friends, two theatrical works were also mentioned: *Títeres de cachiporra* and *Mariana Pineda*. I later heard him read both these plays. But from that first night of our friendship I will only and always remember his "Romance sonámbulo" ("Ballad of the Sleepwalker"), with its mysterious dramatic quality which seemed even more chilling in the semi-darkness of the Residencia garden, recited to the accompaniment of the rustling poplar trees.

"Goodbye, cousin," he said to me sometime after midnight when we were alone.

It had begun to rain. A sudden flash of lightning signaled an approaching storm. And although I reached home dripping wet, I was happy in the knowledge that one page of my life had been stamped with an indelible date. A few days later I brought García Lorca what he had commissioned me to do and something else besides: a sonnet that I had dedicated to him (the other two sonnets, which I also included in my *Marinero en tierra*, were written somewhat later that same year). He greeted my painting with the most hyperbolic words and gestures, and immediately hung it above his bed. Promising me that he would also hang it in the same spot at his country home in Fuente Vaqueros, I was invited on the spot to spend the summer there "so that I could see for myself." As for the sonnet—he liked it and asked me to repeat it for those friends of his who always invaded his room. I took advantage of the occasion to read him some of my ballads. He listened to them attentively. When we said goodbye in the garden I remember what he told me: "You have two fine qualities for a poet—a good memory and Andalusian blood. But don't give up painting."

In spite of the ambiguity of his remarks, I returned home in a happy frame of mind.

Since it was October and the academic year had begun, a thin young man with a beautiful, finely chiseled, sunburned face and a strong Catalan accent appeared one day at the Residencia. During one of my occasional visits, Federico introduced me to him:

"This is Salvador Dalí, who says he has come to study painting in Madrid."

(Dalí! Everyone knew him except me, although I did know something about his talent from Daniel Vázquez Díaz as well as from reproductions of his paintings that had appeared in the journal *Alfar*.)

"To study painting! Is that true?" I asked in astonishment.

"Yes, it's true," answered Federico in all seriousness. "He wants to get his degree as a painter, from the Royal Academy of San Fernando. He still has two years to go before he can graduate."

What seemed at first to be a typical Lorca joke was the absolute truth. Dalí's father, a distinguished notary public from Figueras, wanted his son to do things correctly and by steps. Painting was a career like any other, like being a notary, for example, and one had to take examinations for four or five years in order to obtain an official title. Nothing could be better than to receive one's degree from such a competent authority as the Madrid Academy. Maybe he was basically right. (It could also be that part of the prim and lifeless academism of Dalí's recent works dates from that period. But this will be treated later in the third or fourth volume of these memoirs.)

Salvador Dalí seemed to me then to be very timid and a man of few words. They told me he used to work all day, sometimes forgetting to eat or arriving at the Residencia long after dinnertime. When I visited his room, a simple cell similar to the one occupied by Federico, I almost couldn't get inside because I didn't know where to put my feet. The floor was covered with drawings. Dalí had a formidable vocation and, in spite of being only twenty-one, was already an astonishing draughtsman. He drew whatever he felt like drawing, real or imagined: a pure classical line, perfect calligraphy which, although it brought to mind the Hellenistic period of Picasso, was nonetheless admirable; or complex webs that were like hairy moles, blots and spaltterings of ink slightly diluted with water which were clear precursors of the great surrealistic Dalí of those early years in Paris.

With a certain typically Catalan seriousness that nonetheless contained a hidden sense of humor which was not at all betrayed by his facial expressions, Dalí always explained what was happening in every one of his drawings, and in this way he displayed his undeniable literary talents.

"Here is the 'Bestie,' vomiting." (It was actually a dog, but it seemed more like a ball of straw.) "Here are two civil guards making love, with their moustaches and all." (In effect, two bundles of hair wearing three-cornered hats could be seen embracing on top of something that suggested a bed.) "This is a piece of putrefaction

170

sitting in a café." (The drawing was a simple vertical line with a thin little moustache on top and split by a horizontal line which was supposed to be a table.) "And here again is the 'Bestie,' still vomiting . . ."

Dalí's "putrefactions" at times recalled the schematic figure of Pepín Bello, that amusing and likable resident whom I had met through Federico. I even think they were invented by Pepín and then transformed by Dalí with his usual wit. These putrefactions, as one would imagine from the name, constituted a kind of summing up of all that was decrepit, dead and anachronistic in various people and objects. Dalí hunted down these putrified creatures and painted them in different ways. There were some with scarfs, riddled with coughs, sitting alone on benches along the boulevards. There were others with walking canes, elegant, a flower in their buttonhole and accompanied by a "Bestie." There was an academic putrefaction who was in a putrified state without even realizing it. All the sexes were represented—masculine, feminine, neuter and epicene—as well as all ages. The term was eventually used to refer to everything: literature, painting, style of dress, houses, the most disparate objects and anything that smelled rotten or might hinder or prevent unobstructed progress. For example, Azorín in those days was considered by us to be among the putrefactions. It goes without saying that included in this category were Ricardo León, Emilio Carrere, or such painters as Benedito, Eugenio Hermoso, Sotomayor . . . His Majesty Alfonso XIII was also a putrefaction, as was the Pope. Many of the French lecturers who passed through the Residencia were also classified as putrefactions, as were so many other individuals and things which I no longer remember. Those were enjoyable and amusing days, days of our lives that were also productive and fertile when works were conceived which were to bear fruit in subsequent years.

Another of Pepín Bello's inventions was the *carnuzo*,* which at times was closely related to putrefactions but with different nuances and seen with greater precision and perception by Pepín himself, who was always brimming over with wit and imagination which he

---

Carnuzo derives from the Spanish word *carne* or "meat"; the ending *uzo* suggests something like a "lump of meat."

Ratoncillo mecánico

Este ratoncito Pérez
rasguña
todos los días mi madriguera
siempre blanco
lleno de ojos azules

cuando ni lo veo
ni lo oigo
duerme quietecito
siempre blanco
lleno de ojos rojos

generously shared with his group of fellow residents. One of the members of this circle was Luis Buñuel, who years later, in collaboration with Dalí on the film *El perro andaluz (The Andalusian Dog)*— the most extraordinary surrealistic film ever made—was able to take full advantage of many of Pepín's brilliant and amusing ideas. I will come back later to the subject of my friendship with Pepín Bello and his other graceful talents, filled as they were with freshness and poetry.

I wish to mention two other people who were of great help to me along the difficult and painful poetic path I had chosen to follow; one was José María Chacón y Calvo, a Cuban diplomat and writer, and the other was Claudio de la Torre, also a writer but from the Canary Islands. I think I met José María Chacón through Federico, and that it was Juan Chabás who introduced me to Claudio.

José María was a good person who had that certain softness commonly found in tropical fruit, and he was a great admirer of mountain snows, where he spent most of the winter skiing. Up until that time he had published only one book, *El hermano menor (The Younger Brother)*, and I believe he was preparing a Spanish edition of the complete works of Martí, that delicate poet and apostle of freedom for his country. He was an enthusiastic admirer of my sea ballads and my early tercets. Whenever I felt like breaking out of my self-imposed retirement, he would invite me to dinner at his apartment on Pardiñas Street. He would also ask me to read some of my poems to him and to the frequently large number of guests who often congregated there.

One night he introduced me to a huge and pompous gentleman with an enormous head, combed eyebrows and rounded stomach, who was wearing a black jacket and pinstripe trousers. His name was Eugenio D'Ors, "Xenius," the Catalan philosopher and author of the *Glosario (Glossary)* and *La bien plantada (The Girl with her Feet on the Ground)*, a delightful work that I had just finished reading. After dessert and coffee, José María, always anxious to have someone new listen to my poetry, asked me to recite to D'Ors some of my ballads which I knew by heart and which in that period of enthusiasm and passion I would gladly recite to anyone at all with only the slightest encouragement. Eugenio D'Ors listened to me attentively with his eyes almost disappearing beneath his bushy eyebrows and a pleasant smile on his fleshy lips. He made only one comment which he let fall gently, almost like a whisper, when I had finished my performance:

173

"They make one feel like writing poetry *a la manière de* . . ."

At the time I didn't quite understand what he meant, but after a few moments I did realize the importance of his praise. The proof is that now, at the age of fifty-five, I have not forgotten it.

Nor have I forgotten Claudio de la Torre, whose memory stays in my heart in spite of the difficult and confusing years that followed the Spanish Civil War. He played an important role in my life in those early days. What gentle affection and natural interest he displayed toward me and my poetry from that first afternoon we met in some hotel on the Gran Vía where he was staying! What a good friend in those early and complicated days in which I was embarking on a literary career. Perhaps my admiration for Claudio was based somewhat on the premise that opposites attract, for he was a man of extreme neatness, restrained, absolutely refined, and possessed of a gentle voice with its charming accent of the Canary Islands that was so pleasing to my Andalusian ears. Yes, I admired him for all these reasons, but even more for having been born on some islands whose ancient name—Las Afortunadas (The Fortunate Ones)—had made me dream about them ever since I was a child living alongside my Bay of Cádiz. I dedicated a sonnet, my second in alexandrine verse, to Claudio a few weeks after I had met him. It was an homage from the land-locked sailor to his new friend who had arrived from afar and with the added prestige of being an inhabitant of green shores encircled by oceanic waves.

One night in his hotel room, after I had read him my most recently composed series of ballads, Claudio de la Torre said to me: "Why don't you try for the national literary prize this year? The group of judges is excellent. It includes Antonio Machado, Gabriel Miró, Menéndez Pidal, Arniches, Gabriel Maura and Morena Villa."

I honestly thought that Claudio, so formal and so little given to jokes, had gone mad and was even making fun of me.

"You may even win the prize," he added. I didn't reply to him immediately. What he had suggested was unheard of.

"What are you saying?"

"I'm telling you to submit your work and that you might just win first prize," he repeated without any sign of sarcasm.

He had won the National Literary Award the year before for one of his novels, *En la vida del señor Alegre*, which I still had not read. But Claudio was a professional author. Mature. Serious. Very organized. In other words, the ideal person to receive such an award. On the other hand, who was I? Where had I come from? What did I have to do with literature? What would an Antonio Machado think of my poor ballads? And someone like Menéndez Pidal? Moreno Villa was the only one who knew something about me, but only as a painter . . .

"How can you suggest such a thing? I can't believe you're serious," I said in a burst of anxiety.

"You could win. Why not try?"

I stood up to leave.

"Do what I tell you," he insisted as I stood in the doorway of his room.

I then asked him for a few cents for streetcar fare. He gave me five *pesetas*. I remember that very well. (The amount of the prize was five thousand.)

A few days after this last visit to Claudio de la Torre, and hearing in my mind his insistent phrase, "You might win first prize," I took a train south without saying goodbye to anyone. I headed for Rute, a small village hidden in the mountains of Córdoba, where my sister María had lived since her marriage to Ignacio Docavo, a pleasant, lively and witty notary who was very intelligent and also happened to be distantly related to our family. I spent a period of time there with them, always thinking about my health, which was now perfectly fine but was constantly on my mind and had become a pleasant habit after so many years of rest and recuperation. I was very grateful to my right lung, as a matter of fact, since I was deeply indebted to it for helping me to abandon my early vocation and making it possible for me to advance steadily along a new road.

It was almost dark when I reached Rute, my soul filled with olive groves and strangely affected by the vision of Lucena, an ancient city walled in by huge earthen pitchers used to hold olive oil; I had been impressed by Martos with its sharp peak and by the blinding whiteness of the lime that covered the villages and seemed to suddenly appear like bits of chalk scratching against the red earth of the plains or against the steep cliffs of the leaden gray mountains. A sad and dramatic voyage until the sudden appearance of Rute which rose up in the distance under the dark blood of a dying sunset!

My sister put me up in the top floor of her house. Since I was exhausted from the trip, I went to sleep immediately. But before going to bed I performed my customary hygienic ritual of opening wide the windows of my new room, to which I had brought with me my exaggerated desire for absolute quiet and my feelings of panic at the possibility of becoming sick again. I was awakened by a cool, fresh dawn that cast a pink glow across my eyes. I was no longer gazing out at the Guadarrama Mountains or seeing the thin aerial grayness of Madrid's urban landscape. A steep, narrow street that led in one direction to the fields and in the other to the mountains was all I could now glimpse from my room. But the apartment fortunately had a small terrace, and from there I could look out over a part of the town, white, hilly and presided over at its highest point by the tragic Mount of the Cross. I could also see a wide panorama of red and yellow fields covered with orderly rows of olive trees and grapevines. All of Rute created the impression of something hard and almost sinister.

One of the walls of my room, the one against which I rested my head to sleep, formed part of an adjacent prison cell. Shouts and voices began to penetrate my sleep. I spread out the manuscript of *Mar y tierra* on my work table and got ready to patiently copy it on the typewriter. That was the first task I had assigned myself for the day after my arrival. Since it was winter and there was a heavy rain-fall, I decided not to explore the town or meet anyone until the weather improved. As I copied my poems and put them in final form, others began to emerge that were also about the sea, and they enlarged and enriched my book. During the whole time I devoted to this task, Claudio de la Torre's "You might win first prize" stayed with me and became woven into the final verses of my ballads.

On one of those nights at about ten o'clock, when the rain and wind were at their worst, there was a loud pounding on the front door of the house. I heard my brother-in-law step out on the balco-ny, evidently surprised by the racket. The strange dialogue reached me in bed through my always open window.

"Who is it down there at this hour?"

"The mule-driver."

"Who?"

"It's Andrés, Don Ignacio—Doña Colo's mule-driver."

But Andrés—what's going on?"

"Well, Doña Colo wonders if Don Rafaelito would like to drop by her house."

"But it's pouring rain and it's also very late!"

"... drop by to have tea ..."

"Tea? Tell Doña Colo that Don Rafaelito is probably asleep by now ..."

At that moment, and thinking that something pleasant and enjoyable was going to happen that night, I intervened in the conversation from my window:

"Tell your *señora* that I will be right there, Andrés."

"What do you mean!" shouted my brother-in-law, hearing my voice. "Weren't you sleeping?"

"No! Andrés, tell Doña Colo that I will be there. I'm coming right down."

I got dressed again in a minute. At the door the mule-driver was waiting for me with a huge red umbrella. The water was running down the street like a river. We began to walk silently. The wind from the mountains was coming right at us, and as we were walking slowly the water formed small whirlpools around Andrés' wooden shoes. Someone came stumbling out of the darkness.

"Good evening, Andrés and company."

"Good evening, Lino."

We continued in silence.

"Lino?"

"The fellow of the *'peo.'*"

"What did you say, Andrés?" I asked him.

"Of the *'peo,'*" he repeated somberly. "All of Rute knows him."

I was not able to ask any further questions since Doña Colo's door was soon there before us, half opened and expectant.

"Come in, come in, Don Rafaelito. What an honor! We were beginning to think you would not come."

Doña Colo, known more formally as Doña Clotilde, a rather large lady dressed in black with a matching wide ribbon around her neck that supported a huge double chin, was looming there in the middle of the front yard holding out her hand to me.

"This way, Don Rafaelito."

I walked into a charming dining-room filled with lace, green glasses set on a sideboard and pale lemons peering over the edges of the wineglasses. Spread out on the round tablecloth were darkly glazed earthenware cups, a bottle of local brew and a huge fruitbowl crammed with cascading grapes.

"Girls!" called Doña Colo.

Two rather faded-looking young ladies with red carnations in their hair suddenly appeared on the scene, one dressed in a blue sweater and the other wearing a yellow one.

"This is my María, Don Rafaelito, and my Carmen."

Two flaccid hands, deathly cold, fell into my own, to the accompaniment of a rigid nod of the head.

"A pleasure," I managed to mutter, somewhat taken aback.

"Sit down, Don Rafaelito. Come on, girls, what are you doing?"

They decided to sit down. No one dared to speak.

"Well, Don Rafaelito," began Doña Colo, "we know that in Madrid all the elegant people like to have tea. Isn't that true?"

"Yes, señora, that is true."

"We were very anxious to meet you."

"I wanted to meet you, too, señora."

"How should we do it, I asked my Carmen and my María. Let's invite Don Rafaelito to something he would like!"

"Please, please, Doña Clotilde!"

"Doña Colo, Don Rafaelito, is what everybody calls me."

"Señora!"

"Then it began to rain, but we said how could a little rain bother Don Rafaelito, since he lives in Madrid?"

"It doesn't bother me at all, Doña Colo; I was pleased to come."

There was a pause.

"How do you take your tea?"

"The same way you do."

"We like it with a dash of anisette."

"I beg your pardon, señora?"

"With a splash of anisette—it's very good for burping."

I had never heard of this before, but ... "I like it that way, too, Doña Colo."

"It's really delicious—the bottle is right there. Take as much as you like."

I poured a stream of alcohol into my cup. The three ladies did the same.

"Carmen, go and get the sweets—although we prefer to drink ours with grapes."

"Don't bother, Carmen, I will have mine with grapes, too."

"Please don't be formal, Don Rafaelito. You can use the 'tú' form with Carmen."

"Fine. That's what I'll do from now on."

"What I was saying—we take ours with grapes. These are the hanging variety, winter grapes; we keep them in the dark, hanging from the ceiling of the storeroom. Look how beautiful they are; take a bunch."

I helped myself. A long silence ensued. I lifted the bunch of grapes for a minute and then slowly dipped it into the cup. I then brought it to my mouth and bit off the first grape.

All three of them, each one with a bunch of grapes in hand, looked at me uncomfortably.

"Is that the way it's done in Madrid, Don Rafaelito?"

"Yes," I calmly replied. "That's the elegant thing to do."

"Then, girls, that's the way it is. If Don Rafaelito says so . . ."

And the three of them in unison dipped their grapes in the tea and then lifted them, dripping, to their mouths.

"What do you think of my two girls? (urp)"—Doña Colo had just released her first burp.

"Very good-looking, as all Andalusian girls are."

"They're Rutenians! My María is beautiful. She has a lot of flesh on those bones of hers. If you could only see it! Her whole body —urp! (Doña Colo's second burp)—is covered with dimples and folds . . ."

"Mama!" protested the two girls, both blushing.

"Just look, Don Rafaelito, the way things happen. My María deserves the very best. She's so silly! On the other hand, that one—it just goes to show you, Don Rafaelito—the skinny one! Well, she's found herself a rich sweetheart and she'll be married by the end of the year!"

Carmen, the poor skinny one, tried to say something but—urp, urp!—two consecutive burps made speech impossible.

"See what I mean, Don Rafaelito? Just like I told you! It's the anisette! There's nothing better for gas! I'm going to give you another glass."

"Whatever you say, Doña Colo." At that moment (urp!), I had finally launched my own burp. "Look, why don't we just forget it? Don't bother to give me another glass. I don't think I need it now."

"Bravo, bravo, Don Rafaelito! You finally did it too! How do you feel? The anisette here in Rute is something special! You'll see how well you're going to sleep tonight!"

Having finished our tea amidst all kinds of burps to the accompaniment of Doña Colo's chatter and the silence of her two daughters, we played cards, a game called "The Standing Donkey," a silly and innocent little card game but the only one I remembered from my childhood days. Since it was still raining cats and dogs and it was already past midnight, I asked Doña Colo's permission to leave.

"As you wish, Don Rafaelito; it has been a great honor . . ."

In the hallway I shook the firm hand of Doña Colo and the frozen ones belonging to her daughters.

"Don't get lost, Don Rafaelito."

"Certainly not, Doña Colo."

Since I didn't want the mule-boy to accompany me, his huge red umbrella protected me from the rain until I reached home.

This was my first night out in Rute. It had been wonderful and worthy of an Arabian tale from *A Thousand and One Nights.*

The following day at lunch I entertained my brother-in-law by telling him about my visit to Doña Colo and the burping choir.

"Well, you haven't seen anything yet," he said to me. "There are stranger people than that around here. This is a rather alcoholic village; people here exercise their elbows a little too much. You'll see what I mean."

"Have you ever heard of Lino?" I asked him.

"Who? The flatulent one?"

"Yes. The one they call the '*peo.*'" Last night we passed each other in the street when I was walking with Andrés."

"Didn't he tell you the story?"

"There was no time. Besides, I don't think it would even have occurred to poor Andrés to tell me about it. He seemed a bit stupid."

"It really is a funny story."

I prepared myself to hear another Arabian tale.

"You may know," began my brother-in-law, "that although there is a theater here, very few traveling companies come this way. Several years ago one did appear. It was a great event. They advertised some work by Echegaray. I think it was *Mancha que limpia (The Stain that Cleans).* The whole town turned out to see it. There was a full house. Downstairs in the orchestra seats together with the Mayor, the Judge, the Town Notary—that was my job at the time —were the wealthy families that abound in these parts. Upstairs sat the less affluent: the olive-pickers, workers, and peasants from the surrounding areas. On stage the play was presented in the usual fashion, to the great satisfaction of the audience, which applauded the more brilliant scenes or speeches. The end of the drama was

180

finally approaching. Everyone in the theater, overcome with emotion, was holding his breath. Suddenly, from the top balcony, a noise was heard. What was it? An enormous and resounding fart. The actors were practically paralyzed. The Mayor stood up. Everyone in the orchestra section turned around and looked upward. 'Who did that?' shouted the Mayor. Silence. 'Let the person who did that stand up immediately!' he repeated, practically raging with fury by this time. No one dared to speak. 'Everyone in the top balcony is to be taken to jail and will stay there until there is a confession! Send the police upstairs!' At that moment a voice was heard: 'It was Lino!' 'Lino, Lino!' began to echo throughout the house. They took him away. The play, now that the excitement and emotion were gone, could only barely make it to the end. When Lino left jail a few days later, the whole village called him by the alias that is now all his own: 'peo,' or 'the fart.'* 'A real disgrace. That's what it is,' is the way Lino laughingly replies to anyone who asks him to tell the real story about his nickname."

I later came to know Lino under the bright light of day. He was an amusing man, filled with vitality and always with a happy expression on his face. Just like so many poor Andalusians, he seemed to live on air. He only earned a few *pesetas*—very few—and these he picked up during the olive harvest. He immediately tossed them away on alcohol, and then for the rest of the year he again lived on air! I became a good friend of his. Whenever I saw him, I would give him a few coins which he repaid by telling me jokes, and then he would race off to drink up the money immediately at the nearest corner bar. Lino the fart! I wonder whatever became of him.

One night I suddenly realized that my book *Mar y tierra* was finished. There was nothing to add. The typescript, in three copies, was perfect. It already had the look of a book in print. I often took it with me into the fields in the morning. There, beneath the olive trees or seated on a bench along the Bridge of Swallows, I read it aloud without finding it necessary to make any corrections. I thought about it often ("You might win first prize!"). What should I do with it now? What publisher in Madrid would seriously consider publishing such a work? Poetry was not a profitable business. Even Juan Ramón

---

*The correct Spanish word here is *pedo*. However, the intervocalic consonant is consistently dropped in Andalusian colloquial speech.

Jiménez, in those days, used to publish his own books, barely five hundred copies of each one. Why shouldn't I follow the advice of Claudio de la Torre? I had to make up my mind. Time was passing and the deadline for submitting my manuscript was approaching. One afternoon, after the *siesta*, I made a package containing two copies, went to the post office and sent them special delivery to José María Chacón y Calvo. In a separate letter, I asked the Cuban author to see that the work was presented to the National Literary Competition. A few days later I had a reply from him: the copies had arrived late but a few magical *pesetas* offered to some employee at the Ministry had managed to fix everything.

More relaxed, although not without feeling certain moral and aesthetic misgivings for having succumbed to the temptation of presenting my work to an official competition, like any two-bit poet, I tried to forget about my audacity and even got ready to start a new book. The first thing I needed was a title. From the very beginning of my new career I had tried to give a certain focus to my work, treating it as a unit, almost like a closed circle, in which the poems, although in appearance separate and independent, really formed a definitely harmonic entity. What could I choose this time? I was affected and even overwhelmed by the atmosphere of Rute, that dramatic Andalusian village located at the base of the Mount of the Cross, a town like so many others that lay hidden away in those mountains, saturated by religious terror, riddled with old popular superstitions and incited by forcible repression of all the senses to occasional explosions of the darkest and most incredible crimes. It was a rich village with an unusually large number of suicides, drunks and mentally disturbed inhabitants who, after having invoked the spirits, wandered off to hunt for treasures through the nocturnal hills. These diabolical expeditions almost always ended up in beatings, shootings or stabbings.

After eliminating many other possibilities, I thought I had finally hit upon the most suitable title—*Cales negras (Black Lime)*—in my attempt to condense all the darkness, tragedy and mystery which lay hidden beneath the blinding whitewashed facades of Rute.

I began the first series of ballads. The blue tones of my beaches and salt-flats of Cádiz were not possible here. The music was different and the rhythms more syncopated; the shades of light were not the same and even another language was spoken in this region. In spite of the sun, the harsh and cutting voice of the shadows was to cast a cloak of mourning over almost everything I would write at that time. From among the things I saw, the things I was told or imagined, I would extract the petty, underlying motivations. This constituted the dramatic essence of my new poems, some of which were to have the quality of popular songs more suited to guitar accompaniment than the more refined lute of traditional ballads.

There, in the highest part of town, lived a beautiful girl known in the village and surrounding areas as *La Encerrada* (The Captive.) She was never seen except with a veil covering her face at early morning Mass and was always accompanied by someone. There were many nights when I would climb up the hill to the street where she lived, spending hours walking up and down in front of her house, hoping to catch a glimpse of her from behind the closed windows and balconies of the building. But my efforts were unsuccessful. The strangest and even most ridiculous stories circulated concerning this young lady, and the whole town would repeat these tales with added embellishments originating from their own wild imaginations. Her mother and her aunts, who watched over her, were hated by the men in town who would dream about the girl, desiring her openly and shamelessly. Even my own dreams were filled with thoughts of her and a sad feeling, a silent love, took hold and instilled in me an anguished desire to release her from those dark protective shadows that were ruining her beauty and sacrificing her youth behind four walls.

During the black, wintry hours of dawn when the hungry olive-pickers would set out for the groves, I quickly walked toward the church and hid myself among the columns lining the atrium, excited at the prospect of seeing her arrive, delicate and terrified, her proud head buried in the folds of her mantilla. She would not be simply accompanied, but rather held prisoner by two—and sometimes even four—of her aunts, formidable scarecrows with their wide-eyed, challenging expressions. The girl heard Mass in a kneeling position, her body completely immobile and resting her head between her hands. When it was over, she would disappear again, walking proudly and without the slightest sign of self-consciousness as she went out into the tenuous light of dawn, returning to her prison in the upper regions of the village.

Neither in the street nor in church was I ever able to see her eyes during the whole time I lived in Rute. I never found out either if from behind the bars and shutters of her house she had ever attempted to look in my direction in that desert-like stillness of the

183

night. I only learned later that "The Captive" of my early Rute ballads had committed suicide, an act of violence intimately related to a sad and very ancient tradition of her village. No one ever told me what had actually caused her to take her own life, but based on what I already knew about her and her terrifying watchdogs, almost twenty years later I was able to weave my own fable of love and old women in a work I called *El adefesio (Grotesquerie)* that attempted to recapture the sense of physical and moral horror of this incident.

After writing "La encerrada" I composed other ballads—"La maldecida" and "El prisonero"—which comprised a series of works inspired by the prison cell that I knew existed on the other side of my bedroom wall. Spring was approaching and the warm morning sun induced me to stroll to the outlying areas, walking along the road to Loja. I would sit on the large rocks bordering the ploughed fields and then always return home with some new ballad for my *Cales negras*, a book which although only recently begun was already demanding of me a precise design, a particular profile that later was always to be one of the clearest characteristics of all my poetic activity. From one of those walks through the fields I brought back "La húngara" ("The Hungarian"), a poem dedicated to a lovely Magyar girl who wandered through the countryside with her family in a green wagon decorated with flowers, birds and little mirrors; I also found inspiration for several "Pregones," light, happy verses which exalted the wild flowers, the olive-laden breezes and the inhabitants of that mountainous region.

One night my brother-in-law told me that he would soon have to make a trip to Iznájar and wondered if I would like to accompany him. This was a smaller but even more extraordinary village than Rute, located high up in the mountains. It had a Moorish castle that was like a huge decayed molar but still displayed above the mouth of a deep chasm the merlon-crested thrust of its towers.

During our ascent in a little automobile that was more like a mule, another notary who had joined us for the trip volunteered some background material:

"Iznájar is a town of spiritualists. Don Ignacio knows all about that."

"Spiritualists?"

"Spiritualists. But don't be frightened."

"Well, spiritualists," interrupted my brother-in-law, "that's what they call them, but ..."

"They themselves think they are."

"You know the stories they tell."

"Of course I know them, Don Ignacio, just as well as you do."

"They're a wild, crazy bunch of people."

"Wild and crazy in a way, but interesting and even amusing at the same time. Since Don Rafael is a poet, he's going to like this town."

"Who are these spiritualists? Do you know any?" I asked the notary.

"I know many of them. There are some among the rich and, naturally, many among the poor people of the fields who are obsessed by the idea of finding treasures."

"Treasures?"

"Yes, that's what it all boils down to," muttered my brother-in-law, a sarcastic smile on his lips.

"That's the principal reason for those sessions, to look for treasure, but first they have to find out where it might be hidden. But all this is combined with a mixture of strange superstitions, bits and pieces of history and past events that are still very much alive in the memory of these people. Don Rafael is going to be as interested in them as I am. You may not know that I am also a very modest writer of sorts. Don Ignacio can laugh, but what else would you expect? I was born and raised in these hills."

I realized that my brother-in-law saw all of this differently and did not find it particularly amusing that his friend the notary was telling me these stories.

"Ignacio," I said to him, "I have been very much impressed with Rute. There is something dark and overwhelming tucked away in these mountains and I would like to know about everything that happens up here."

"What does happen, Don Rafael, is extraordinary, although at times also unpleasant, as in the case of the Iznájar spiritualists. I could tell you many stories about them, but let me just briefly relate one of them so that your brother-in-law won't get too upset. The most suitable title for this tale would be 'The Surest Way to Find a Treasure.' On certain Fridays," the notary began, "the spiritualists very secretly announce one of their sessions. Although these could be held in any house in town, they generally meet in a particular place—a cave or someone's home—hidden away in these mountains. Once they have gathered together and are sitting there completely in the dark, the most prestigious of the spiritualists, who also has the

185

reputation of being a sorcerer, invokes the spirits, asking them who of those present that night is going to furnish the magic candle, a type of wand which is capable of indicating the site of the buried treasure. After the names of those who have to furnish the sperm for the candle have been revealed, as well as those who are to help in the digging, they gather around in the most total darkness imaginable and form what they call 'the great magic circle' around the leader of this ritual, who holds in his hands a type of clay mortar. This is a solemn moment . . ."

"If you consider masturbation to be solemn."

"This is a solemn moment. When the semen from the chosen few is in the mortar, the great spiritualist mixes it with a piece of wax to form the magic candle, whose wick, made from the intestines of a small goat, gives off a flame that no gust of wind can extinguish. When the candle is lit, everyone moves in circles around it, hopping and shouting until the chief spiritualist holds it over his head and leads the way out of the room. Holding onto each other by the waist with both hands and thus joined in single file to their leader, they silently wander along the dark cliffs as if in a daze. They can spend several hours in this activity. If anyone utters a single word, the ceremony would have to be stopped and begun again the following Friday. The whole thing is like a parade of sleepwalkers. Finally, wherever the candle is totally consumed and lets its last drop of life fall to the ground, there the treasure is to be found."

The notary remained silent for a few seconds while he lit a cigarette.

"And then what happens?" I asked him impatiently.

"Then the chief spiritualist invokes the spirits of Fátima and Zoraida, uttering a prayer to the Virgin Mary, while the rest of the group kneels and devoutly repeats this oration. With the knives everyone carries with them, they begin to dig in the earth."

"And then?"

"Then, they don't find a thing," said my brother-in-law.

"Oh yes they do," the notary calmly replied.

"Have you by any chance ever seen one of their treasures?"

"No, I haven't. But remember, Don Ignacio, the time that olive-picker was discovered hanging from an olive tree, and later some ancient gold coins were found sewn into his mattress?"

"That's what they said, but I never saw them."

"Well, I *did* see them. And they were coins dating back to the time of the Moors."

"Here in Andalusia almost everything dates back to the time of the Moors."

"I don't know if everything does," the notary said, somewhat annoyed, "but the coins definitely were from that period. I am sure of that."

Our brave little car made its last superhuman attempt to reach the hilly outskirts of Iznájar. We stopped in the main square, dominated by its castle, now in a state of ruin but nonetheless still quite grandiose. Looking up, the notary said jokingly:

"You can't deny, Don Ignacio, when you look at that tower . . ."

"I know what you're thinking: it dates back to the Moors—just as you do. One has only to look closely at you to see that."

And my brother-in-law, grabbing his friend by the arm, entered the Town Hall.

Iznájar seemed to be deserted. From time to time a local resident passed by and looked at me as if I were some strange creature. Where could the spiritualists be hidden, I wondered as I climbed up alone toward the castle? What anguished loneliness one feels in these mountain villages! Rute, which had struck me as being such a melancholy place, was like the happy sound of bells compared to Iznájar. I reached the abandoned castle; there wasn't a soul around. I climbed the crumbling steps to the top of the tower. All of its thin narrow windows, except for the four highest ones, had been sealed up. The countryside, spread out down below, seemed like a setting for one of García Lorca's ballads. Yes, it was death that looked back at me from the distant peaks and valleys. There in that very tower I wrote a poem that had some of the same mysteriously dramatic qualities found in much of Lorca's poetry. These were the identical funereal and harsh lands that had been described by him!

> *Prisionero en esta torre,*
> *prisionero quedaría.*
> *(Cuatro ventanas al viento.)*
> *——¿Quién grita hacia el norte, amiga?*
> *——El río, que va revuelto.*
> *(Ya tres ventanas al viento.)*
> *——¿Quién gime hacia el sur, amiga?*

_____*El aire, que va sin sueño.*
(Ya dos ventanas al viento.)
_____*¿Quién suspira al este, amiga?*
_____*Tú mismo, que vienes muerto.*
(Y ya una ventana al viento.)
_____*¿Quién llora al oeste, amiga?*
_____*Yo, que voy muerta a tu entierro.*
_____*Por nada yo en esta torre*
prisionero quedaría!

Prisoner in this tower,
Prisoner I would stay.
(Four windows to the sky.)
_____*Who shouts to the north, my love?*
_____*'Tis the river racing by.*
(Three windows to the sky.)
_____*Who moans to the south, my love?*
_____*The air that moves with open eye.*
(Now two windows to the sky.)
_____*Who sighs to the east, my love?*
_____*You, yourself, who soon will die.*
(Now one window to the sky.)
_____*Who cries to the west, my love?*
_____*Walking in death to your grave, 'tis I.*
_____*Then as prisoner in this tower,*
Nothing could make me stay.

Late in the afternoon we began our descent to Rute. In the car the notary tried to get my brother-in-law to speak.

"And you?"

"I?"

"Yes, you also have your own collection of spiritualist stories."

"But the ones I could tell, that is, the *one* I know, is less horrifying than yours."

"The final outcome could have been even worse, Don Ignacio."

"But it didn't turn out that way. It simply ended up by being amusing. It happened last year. One Sunday morning, a few minutes before going to Mass," began my brother-in-law, addressing himself to me, "a strong-looking, healthy young fellow accompanied by an old man approached me:

"'Don Ignacio,' he said, 'I have brought my grandfather here to make his will.'

"'Come back tomorrow,' I requested. 'Today is a holiday. It's Sunday and I'm on my way to church.'

"'That's impossible, señor. There is no time to lose.'

"'I'm very sorry, but . . .'"

"'For the love of God, notary,' begged the old man, his voice quavering, 'we are in a great hurry. Something has to be done right this minute.'

"'Right this minute? Why?' I was by then quite intrigued.

"Both the grandfather and the grandson stared at me with wide-open eyes, but they remained mute.

"'It's almost noon. Mass will begin any minute. What's the trouble?'

"'Well, my grandfather is going to die this afternoon.'

"'What! This afternoon?'

"'Yes, señor, this afternoon. I only have a few hours left.'

"'The spirit has contacted him.'

"'All right, all right! Come back in a little while. You can explain all that to me later.'

"'Have pity on us!'

"'We live so far from here.'

"'I don't want to die on the road,' whined the grandfather, grabbing my hand.

"'Don't worry, you're not going to die.'

"I began to walk away.

"'We will pay you double, señor,' offered the young man, as he blocked the doorway. I became indignant.

"'Get out of my way immediately.'

"'How unfeeling you are!'

"'What's to become of me now?'

"'Don Ignacio!'

"'Don Ignacio!'

"Their shouts followed me out into the street until I turned the corner and reached the entrance to the church, arriving just in time for the beginning of Mass."

"And the grandfather? He probably died that night without a will. The spirits never lie," I said jokingly to my brother-in-law.

"Hardly! I saw him a few days later in the square. He was alone, looking quite sturdy and in perfect health.

"'What's this I see? You didn't die after all?'

"'Well, Don Ignacio, it's this way. It seems the rain that afternoon scared away the spirits.'

"'You can thank your lucky stars that I didn't put you and your grandson in jail.'

"'In jail? My grandson?'

"'Your grandson and the whole lot of you.'

"'I don't understand, señor.'

"'Never mind. Just don't have anything more to do with spirits and you'll live a good long life.'

"I left him there, but after taking a few steps I turned my head and there he was standing in the same spot, probably wondering what I had meant. Do you realize what the grandson was trying to do, in cahoots with his famous spiritualists?" asked my brother-in-law looking both at his friend and at me. "You don't have to be a fox to figure that one out. They wanted the grandfather to make a will so they could kill him that very night and collect the inheritance. They're all half mad in these villages."

"That *is* a strange tale," commented the other notary.

"It dates back to the time of the Moors," replied my brother-in-law, smiling.

Rute welcomed us at night with closed doors and the stumbling gait of a few drunks roaming the streets.

I began to get bored. The spring season had fully arrived. Doña Colo's daughters could be seen in the square wearing more flowers than ever in their hair. I was no longer enjoying myself. I spoke to no one except my brother-in-law and my sister. I had grown tired of attending Mass to look at "The Captive," who seemed each day to be held more *incomunicada* by her aunts and was becoming progressively more afraid to look up in church or during the torturous walk back to her house. Without any real enthusiasm I continued taking my morning walks in the country when the weather was good, always ready to stalk some little ballad for my new book. I was really fed up with my provincial solitude, but I did not have either enough energy or money to return to Madrid.

One day a solution unexpectedly presented itself. It was eight o'clock in the evening, a few minutes before dinner, when it happened. I was in my room, daydreaming, and waiting to be called to the table. I heard someone climb the steps in great haste. And then, suddenly, there was my brother-in-law standing in the doorway, almost breathless, holding a telegram in his hand.

"Excuse me," he said, "but since your mother is not well"—she was then beginning to suffer from heart trouble—"I took the liberty of opening it. Thank God, it wasn't that. Here. Read the good news."

And he handed me the telegram, embracing me at the same time. I read the contents almost without believing what I saw and thinking it was all a joke: "Awarded National Prize for Literature stop Congratulations stop Love stop José María."

"To be perfectly truthful," I said to my brother-in-law, "I had forgotten all about this."

What wonderful news! Now people would forget that I had ever been a painter! This was the first thought that came into my head while I stood there with the telegram still clutched in my hand.

A few days later, I silently left Rute along the road to Lucena in order to catch the express train for Madrid.

CHAPTER V

How slowly I work! A simple page of prose is as difficult or even more difficult for me to write than an entire poem. Everything I do turns out to be too rhythmical. I struggle against this; I make corrections and even mutilate a sentence to make it sound less like a verse of poetry. I read it over carefully and find that I don't like it at all. What else can I do but continue with the Grove as I have up until now and apologize for my inability to keep from getting lost among its branches; for filling it with the same musical, metrical and jaunty gusts of air that have shaken these same branches ever since the opening chapter.

*W*HEN I REACHED Madrid I leafed through the old newspapers they had saved for me at home to discover who else that year had received National Literary Prizes: Gerardo Diego and José Ignacio Alberti. How surprised and happy I was! The national award for criticism had gone to my uncle for his essay on the life and work of the painter Eduardo Rosales, and the second prize for poetry had been given to Gerardo Diego for his *Versos Humanos (Human Verses)*.

My family was delighted. Their lost-sheep-of-a-son and that poor student who had not even been able to finish high school was beginning his poetic career with some signs of success. The money, of course, impressed them even more. Five thousand *pesetas* was really a magnificent sum in those days, especially for someone who used to walk everywhere to save streetcar fare. I began to make plans long before I even collected the prize. I would immediately buy the Barbieri *Anthology of Traditional Ballads* and the complete works of Gil Vicente; also an overcoat, for although I was not particularly susceptible to cold weather, I came close to freezing without one; and a new suit as well, because the ones I had were becoming threadbare; then . . . I would keep a little for my travel expenses, but the rest of it—ah, the rest of it I would fritter away by eating ice cream with my friends! Those were basically my projects, all of which I was later to carry out almost exactly as planned once the money was actually in my pocket.

But the first thing, the very first thing, was to thank the members of the Selection Committee and particularly my ecstatic friends, Claudio de la Torre and José María Chacón. Both of them invited me to dinner on separate occasions. My victory had been fairly, clearly and unanimously won. Thanks to their enthusiasm and their faith in me, I felt eternally saved. With that prize, I was suddenly born into the literary world of Spain. From many provinces where no one previously knew anything about me and had certainly not heard of me as a painter, I received warm congratulations. The young writers of Madrid, including those living in the Residencia, began to look at me differently. From this moment on I would no longer be that thin, half-tubercular little painter who amused himself by writing verses in his free time.

José Moreno Villa, a member of the Committee, was already known to me. I went to see him first. I found him drinking beer, of which he was very fond, in the gardens of the Residencia which had been his home for many years. Pepe Moreno, as he was affectionately known by all the other residents, congratulated me with that elegant smile that always seemed to be suspended from his little moustache. How old could Pepe Moreno have been in those days? He belonged to a somewhat strange generation that had appeared on the scene a few years after the disciples of Juan Ramón Jiménez. I was not too familiar with his poetry. He was not a "celebrated" poet like Machado and Juan Ramón, and he was never really to become one. By this I mean that his name was not mentioned frequently by the "new wave" of poets, those of us who could recite by heart poems written by those other two great Andalusian poets whom we considered our "maestros." In that period, only one book by Moreno Villa had fallen into my hands: *Garba*. It was his first collection, published in 1913, and to be frank, it had not impressed me very much. The poems did not display the kind of elegance and refinement I had hoped to find in a poet from Málaga. It is true that from time to time they were imbued with an Andalusian fragrance of jasmine which served to create a lightness of tone and a heightened sense of gracefulness. But something harsh, abrupt and grating was there in the structure of all those poems that made it difficult for me to enjoy them fully and retain any of them in my memory. It was hard to penetrate fully or enter freely into that poetry. And with his later work, the poems Pepe Moreno continued to write up until the years immediately preceding the civil war, I experienced the same feelings.

In spite of the wealth of culture and his fine sense of humanity, his poems seemed to be in a wild and unfinished state, making it at times impossible for one to move comfortably through them. I remember his love poem, "Jacinta la pelirroja" ("Jacinta the Redhead"), published in 1929 and perhaps his most original work of that decade. It is a dialogue between the poet and his beloved. I have only recently reread this poem and found certain passages to be reminiscent of the lyrical conversations between Juan Ramón and his Platero. His anti-rhetorical language, the confidential tone, its breadth and even obvious charm never fully succeeded, however, in creating that unobstructed, open path that every poem should offer to its readers. His prosaic expressions and his jarringly abrupt tonal deviations somehow destroyed the poetic unity.

But perhaps this constituted an outstanding and even positive characteristic of José Moreno Villa's personality during that period. I clashed with it, however, and that reaction on my part was painful to me, since all of us had warm feelings for this poet, this versatile and talented man—a fine prose writer, a great art critic, a curious painter. We all wished he might have the same stature as those who had come before and would come later to contribute to the greatness of Spanish poetry in this century. But starting particularly with his "Salón sin muros" ("Room without Walls"), I think that Pepe Moreno's poetry, once he had returned to his solitude and former celibacy within the enclosure of the Residencia, became sharper, less entangled and, one might even say, less splintery. And yet it is unquestionably due to that almost cloistered love affair with Jacinta that his poetic voice became more profound, more measured and in tune with the verses themselves, and he succeeded in harmonizing the dissonances and initiating the concert that would allow us to hear the most beautiful notes of his music, "the music that he carried within," when he eventually became a "pilgrim on foreign shores." He was also to compose some fine poems on the Spanish Civil War and I will come back to him—Pepe Moreno recently died in Mexico—in some future volume of this *Lost Grove*.

But now, in these pages, I stand alongside a smiling Moreno Villa, shy, gentle and surrounded by students and the flowering gardens on that peaceful spring afternoon which served as a pleasant background for a meeting I had arranged with him to express my gratitude.

I don't remember if Pepe told me then about the battle he had had with another member of the Selection Committee who opposed my receiving the prize. Such an amusing and revealing scene would have been difficult to forget. There was probably some reason why he didn't tell me about it at that time. It could have been due to the presence of someone unknown to both of us during my visit. I read about this argument in the pages of his autobiography *Vida en claro (Life Seen Clear)*, which appeared in Mexico in 1944 and is a delightful, interesting work. But I discovered this only recently, a few days ago, more than thirty years after the event! I quote it here since it constitutes a particularly vivid leaf among the branches of my memory. Pepe Moreno writes:

I would like to describe this scene with the Selection Committee without leaving out how I managed to put my own foot right in it. The Committee was comprised of Menéndez Pidal and the Count de la Mortera (Gabriel Maura) for History, Arniches for Theater, Antonio Machado and I for Poetry. Perhaps I am leaving someone out. Gabriel Miró served as secretary to the Committee. Everything went beautifully until we came to poetry. Maura first suggested the so-called "Shepherd Poet," Miguel Hernández. I objected immediately. Maura supported his suggestion by blurting out a particularly awkward sentence: "His poetry smells of lambswool and sausage." I replied to the effect that this would be cause enough for a poet to make his readers vomit. And then I really went too far: "That," I said, "is as repulsive as a painting by Luis Menéndez Pidal whose works are as black and smoky as blood pudding." In the heat of the discussion I had forgotten that his brother, Ramón, was sitting right there. Miró intervened with great tact and the others suggested that *I* recommend a candidate for the first prize. "I have rarely been as sure of the appropriateness of my vote as I am now," I began, "and I am convinced that among all the candidates, the one who promises to be of most lasting importance is Alberti, with his book *Marinero en tierra*." And then Antonio Machado, who had been silent up until then, agreed that this was definitely the best work. Maura and the others accepted this proposal, but the Count had also another candidate to suggest, in addition to the "Shepherd Poet"; that was Gerardo Diego. He proposed that Diego be awarded the second prize by switching the award for theater to poetry. That was exactly what we did.

This amusing anecdote as told by Moreno Villa was, I am certain of it now, totally unknown to me. How could I have forgotten such a thing? But I still can't help wondering today why of all the members of the Selection Committee, the only one I never did personally thank was Gabriel Maura, Count de la Mortera!

My second visit was to Gabriel Miró. I think I went alone, somehow overcoming my frequent attacks of timidity. He lived on Rodríguez San Pedro Street in the Argüelles section of Madrid and in the same apartment house where Dámaso Alonso also had his residence. He received me in his study, which was tidy and simple, with its table next to the window completely covered with books and piled high with stacks of paper. I think some of those sheets of manuscript contained the opening chapters of "Nuestro Padre San Daniel" ("Our Father Saint Daniel"), the first part of his great and final novel, *El obispo leproso* (*The Leper Bishop*). I remember most about Miró's physical appearance his heavy eyelids and the sharp but sad expression that peered out from beneath them. He was broad-shouldered, solidly built, extremely kind and charming. I spoke to him of that letter he had written to me years ago containing words of praise for some poems of mine which Juan Chabás had sent to him. He had written that letter in Polop de la Marina in the region of Alicante where he owned some land and a farmhouse, a peaceful place where, during the summer months, he devoted himself to his patient and harmonious literary activities.

"Referring to my early poems, you wrote in that letter that those verses 'contained words of penetrating beauty.' I, like you, in those days at least, was very much taken by the beauty of language. The beauty, clarity and plasticity of your prose style is particularly attractive to me."

"That's only natural! In the Levante, just as in Andalusia, everything is clear and transparent. The light there causes even the most distant objects to have the sharpest of outlines. Even what might ordinarily be blurred or fuzzy, there becomes precise and brilliant!"

"I have come to express my gratitude . . . ," I began uncomfortably, after a brief silence.

"Gratitude? Come, now!" he interrupted, standing up.

"I would like to introduce you to my wife and my daughter, Olimpia. My other daughter is not here."

Both ladies appeared on the scene immediately. They were unpretentious and as pleasant as he was himself. After we had talked a little about my book, which they had seen in manuscript form, they offered me almonds and those exquisite sweets, made from secret convent and monastery recipes, which Miró has described so perfectly and artistically in his own novels. It was a pleasant, intimate afternoon filled with familial affection. Gabriel Miró was a good man with some of the same saintly qualities as Antonio Machado. He earned a modest salary as an employee in the Ministry of Public Education. His beautifully wrought literary works which the Church consistently and silently opposed, but which were also admired by a devout and enthusiastic minority, did not bring in enough income for the family to live on. It was necessary for him to die, five years later, in order for the rest of the family to begin to receive the honors and fruits that this author only barely achieved during his lifetime. Always the same sad, cruel indifference with which Spain treats most of her great writers!

After that visit, I was to see Gabriel Miró again only on very rare occasions. Not long before his death, I ran into him and Pedro Salinas in the Atocha Circle. I walked with them both as far as the Cibeles Fountain. Miró had a defeated look about him, and I noticed the dark rings under his eyes as well as his jaundiced complexion. A month later he was dead, having died there in Madrid, far from the blue sea he had always carried with him in his eyes.

After having made my visit to Miró, I especially wanted to pay my respects to the one member of the Selection Committee whose vote meant the most to me and had filled me with pride: Antonio Machado. Without any prior appointment, I appeared at his house on General Arrando Street. I was greatly disappointed. He was not there, nor was he even living in Madrid at the time. His mother, a small, refined and charming-looking old lady, came to the door: "My son is in Segovia. He hardly ever comes to Madrid. Sometimes he spends his vacations here."

Without entering the apartment, I kissed her hand and left.

I still had not collected the prize money nor had I gone to the Ministry to pick up the original manuscript of my book. After finding out when this could be done, I raced off one morning to that hideous building. In front of the window where I was to receive in one lump sum the first five thousand *pesetas* I had ever earned in my life, I met someone who had come there for the same purpose: Gerardo Diego. I don't think I had ever seen him before. When we left the building, we had already become friends and on that clear spring morning in Madrid we walked together toward the Salón del Prado, carrying on an animated conversation. One poet from Cádiz and another from Santander, the two opposite poles, had just met.

From that day on I saw Gerardo as I was always to see him: timid, nervous, passionate, withdrawn, odd and cheerful in his own special way, and with something of the village monk about him. I was familiar with some of his poetry and with his book *Imagen (Image)*, which I had at home. He had already written quite a bit, but his most important works, the *Manual de espumas (The Manual of Foam)* for example, were still unpublished. His latest book, *Versos humanos*, with poems written from 1918 to 1925, was the work that had just received the award in literature together with my own *Marinero en tierra*. But, as he explained to me, those verses were not in the least like the daring, free-flowing, syncopated, kaleidoscopic and unpunctuated poems in *Imagen* or the *Manual*. His last book contained works that were closer to the more subdued classical and traditional forms of which he was a true master. The *pesetas* that a few minutes ago he had tucked into his wallet were not meant for Gerardo Diego, the "Creationist," the friend and colleague of Vicente Huidobro and Juan Larrea, but for the serene poet who followed in the tradition of Góngora, Jáuregui, Bocángel, Medina, and Medinilla. "Terraced roofs and cellars" were the terms Gerardo used to describe these opposite tendencies. With his cellars, from a monetary point of view as well as from several other points of view, the poet from Santander was not always to receive significant recognition while he lived.

That very night, as I sat in my room looking through the manuscript, a torn, yellowish piece of paper fell from the pages. The cramped and somewhat shaky writing said

Mar y tierra,
Rafael Alberti—
This is, in my judgment, the best book of poems in the competition.

Antonio Machado

I read and reread that note with great joy and emotion! I have kept it all these years in the first page of an old edition of *Marinero en tierra*, the only copy that by some chance I was able to salvage from the Spanish Civil War and still have in my possession.

I had yet to visit Menéndez Pidal and Arniches, the amusing and even almost brilliant author of theatrical farces, the future father-in-law of José Bergamín. It was Bergamín himself, a rather close friend of mine, who took me to the Arniches' house. They invited me to lunch, an invitation I accepted with some misgivings since in that period of my life, after so many years of isolation, I was not only timid but a bit uncultured in my reactions and in the art of social graces. Don Carlos Arniches, a man who had brought laughter to several generations in Spain and America, presided over the table, but he was somewhat serious and withdrawn in manner as he sat there, as if hiding behind his small glasses. He didn't open his mouth once during lunch. I was asked to sit between his two beautiful daughters whom I had admired during their strolls along the Paseo de la Castellana before even meeting them. Their light-hearted reaction to my timidity and awkwardness made it easier for me to survive this experience. Rosario was Bergamín's girlfriend, and Pilar was engaged to Eduardo Ugarte, a young author of comedies, whose plays were about to be presented in public. The other guests were Arniches's wife and the couple's two sons: Fernando, who was in the military, and Carlos, an excellent architect. What I remember most clearly about this meal was how inept I felt and how I had absolutely no idea what to do with all those little plates covered with napkins. I am grateful to Rosario and Pilar for having made those hours at least bearable. I began to breathe again normally only when I was back in the street with Pepe Bergamín.

199

Pepe was one of the many children of an illustrious, witty lawyer from Málaga who was also politically involved in the affairs of the Monarchy. From Don Francisco, Pepe had inherited, among other things, two characteristics that were to clearly mark him as an obvious branch of the paternal tree: his strange and highly personal ugliness as well as his amusing and even complex ingenuity which at times was as frightening as the flash of an Andalusian knife hurled below the heart, the worst kind of knife wound possible. He was faithful to his own beliefs and totally loyal to his friends, as every man ought to be. But he was equally extreme in his attitude toward his enemies, as every man also ought to be. A special type of Catholic, he was the kind of individual our Holy Inquisition would have condemned in an earlier period, and more than once, to the purifying flames of its bonfires. He was opposed to the existing dictatorship, which he referred to in sharp, biting aphorisms created for those strange theatrical pieces he had written but which were impossible to perform in public. The intricate mechanism of his language was as complicated as Quevedo's, or even more so. His passions were comparable to those of Unamuno, with whom he maintained a warm friendship which on Unamuno's part was quite generous, since the elder Bergamín, as a Minister of the Monarchy, had expelled Don Miguel de Unamuno from his Rectorship at the University of Salamanca.

No one had yet begun to write with more fervor and enthusiasm about Spanish poetry than Pepe, and he was soon to become the best commentator of our creative activity in this area. He himself was a poet but his work was conceptual, difficult, innovative, although at the same time undeniably and inextricably linked to the poetic jungle of Spain's Golden Age. He composed sonnets which were worthy of a preferential place in the most selective anthology, and this applies particularly to those published during his painful exile. His devotion to Juan Ramón Jiménez was only comparable to that which the then extraordinary and virulent poet from Moguer also professed towards him. A few years later—and it was Jiménez who was responsible for the break—this admiration changed to mutal hatred. A book of aphorisms, El cohete y la estrella (The Comet and the Star), was the only book that Bergamín had published up until that time. It had appeared in the collection of the Biblioteca Indice and Jiménez himself, who was the editor of this collection, had included on the first page a lyrical portrait of the author, undeniable proof of his friendship and admiration for Pepe's literary talents. That was the start of the literary career of one of the most singular and labyrinthine authors of our generation. I think it was through him that I learned that Juan Ramón had really liked several of the poems in my *Marinero* which had appeared in *La Verdad*, a poetic supplement edited in Murcia by Juan Guerrero Ruiz, an enthusiastic friend of Juan Ramón and of the new poetry.

I decided to go see Jiménez. (This was not the first time I had paid him a visit. Three years earlier, during the period of my exhibition at the Ateneo, I had visited him with Juan Chabás and given him a painting, *The Castle of You Will Go and Never Return*, a decorative and innocent geometric work done in brilliant colors. I don't think he liked it very much. I never knew what he finally did with that painting.) The companion of my second visit was José María Hinojosa, "the vivid, graphic, and harsh poet," son of rich landowners from Málaga, who was to fall under the bullets fired by his own peasants during the confused, early hours of the civil war. Juan Ramón himself opened the door for us. What a strange mixture of joy and fear I suddenly felt in the presence of that greatly admired man with his violently black beard and his Arabic-Andalusian profile turned in my direction on that late afternoon. Twenty years later, during my exile in Argentina, I included in my collection *Retornos (Returns)* some verses meant to commemorate this meeting:

> *Le llevaba yo estrofas*
> *de mar y marineros,*
> *médanos amarillos,*
> *añil claro de sombras*
> *y muros de cal fresca*
> *estampados de fuentes y jardines.*

> *I carried to him stanzas*
> *Of sea and sailors,*
> *Yellow sandbanks,*
> *Bright shadowless indigo*
> *And walls of fresh lime,*
> *Engraved with fountains and gardens.*

Yes, I had brought him the manuscript of *Marinero en tierra* containing verses in which I had concentrated all my feelings of nostalgia for Cádiz, far from that beautiful bay which he, since the days of his own childhood in that very same Jesuit school in the Puerto, had also stored away in his heart. He lived there in his apartment, only infrequently going down to the center of town, but listening to all the sounds of the city from that high balcony set in the quiet neighborhood of Salamanca, among the honeysuckle and morning-glories which his thin fingers, talented cultivators of distant gardens, had trained to grow along the walls to form delightful arabesques:

> *Estaba él derramado*
> *como cera encendida en el crepúsculo,*
> *sobre el pretil abierto*
> *a los montes con nieve perdonada*
> *por la morena mano*
> *de junio que venía.*

> *He was spread*
> *Like melted wax at twilight*
> *Across the open ledge*
> *Facing the mountains with snow pardoned*
> *By the dark hand*
> *Of the approaching month of June.*

Our friendship, bright and almost continuous then, openly flowered in that spring twilight against the background of the blue and distant peaks of the Guadarrama Mountains. The writer Antonio Espina was with him that afternoon.

I quote here, with some additions and deletions, from the chapter which I dedicated to this poet in my book *Imagen primera de . . . (First Image of . . .):*

In those years, 1924–25, Juan Ramón had begun to feel a sense of anxiety about the new wave of Spanish poetry that was beginning to appear with such passionate impetus and fervor. He had already commented on the fresh and youthful flame of García Lorca, the noble tones of Pedro Salinas, the lineal perfection of Jorge Guillén, the Madrid-flavored lyricism of Antonio Espina, the initial simplicity of Dámaso Alonso, and he was preparing himself to receive there on his balcony the most recent poetic breezes which would soon reach him under the names of Altolaguirre, Prados, Cernuda, Aleixandre. ... Never was a Spanish poet more beloved and respected by such a sparkling generation of poets, utterly convinced, as they were, of the freshness and purity of the spring where they went to quench their thirst, and eager to follow the guiding star that offered itself to them.

Juan Ramón was then editor of the journal *Indice* as well as of the publishing firm that went by the same name and whose list of publications had recently been enriched by two new titles: *Signario* by Antonio Espina and *Presagios* by Pedro Salinas.

That afternoon, with a copy of *Signario* in hand, the poet was protesting about the typographical errors that it contained. He had discovered errata, blurred letters and jagged lines, all of which kept him awake at night. "Besides," he told us, "in the edition of the *Fábula de Polifemo y Galatea* by Góngora, edited by Alfonso Reyes, the printers also made some hideous mistakes; Spain has lost its great printing tradition. Just have a look at an English book." He showed us a recently published volume of Keats. "How elegant, how delicate and charming it looks! This is the sort of thing I would like the Biblioteca Indice to do, but apparently here in Spain that is not possible."

As I have said, in those days Juan Ramón still had a violently black beard, the perfect profile of an Andalusian Arab and an opaquely soft voice that at times sounded almost like falsetto. On that afternoon, literature was the subject of conversation and various authors of his generation were mentioned: Pérez de Ayala, the Machado brothers, Ortega y Gasset ... During this visit, I came to realize Jiménez' extraordinary Andalusian wit and sharp tongue which he brought into play in order to make fun of people or caricature them. I was to see this particular talent of his often during our long friendship. That afternoon the principal targets of his derisive laughter were Azorín and Eugenio D'Ors.

"Have you seen the title of Azorín's latest book? *El chirrión de los políticos (The Creaking of Politicians)*. 'Chirrión!' What a word that is! I received a copy of the book with a personal dedication. Naturally, I went personally to his house to return it to him. Azorín," he continued, "lives in one of those houses that smells of Madrid stew and cats' piss. He sleeps all bundled up in a bed with mosquito netting over it that is decorated with strands of pink ribbon. On his night table, as an object that he undoubtedly considers to be in the most refined taste, there's a painted plaster figure of a little black boy, the kind used in advertisements for La Estrella brand of roasted coffee, which was a gift from his constituency when he was elected deputy from Alicante. No matter how humble or modest his way of life may be, a writer is known by the house he keeps."

After a visit to Pérez de Ayala's house one day, Jiménez broke off his relationship with him, because Ayala had shown him a room where the whole ceiling was hung with sausages and salamis, a small detail that nonetheless was repugnant to Juan Ramón and one that he could never forgive. "In order to portray reality with total authenticity in one of his novels," continued Jiménez, "Ayala told me that he had gone to live in a house of prostitution, taking with him a trunk full of clothes because the study of the atmosphere in that place was going to take some time." He detested Eugenio D'Ors, particularly since the day when that poor Catalonian philosopher had greeted him politely in the street by removing his grey *"chapeau melon"*—a derby or mushroom hat, as it is called in Spain—an article of clothing that Juan Ramón considered to be ridiculous. "This Xenius (a pseudonym often used by D'Ors) is creating total confusion with his linguistic mixture of Catalan and Spanish. I'd be happy if you, Alberti, could draw him dressed as a ballerina with his fat arms raised above his head, and with a caption that reads: 'Xenia the Esperanta.' He'll probably end up dancing the rhumba in Cuenca," concluded Jiménez, with a mixture of amusement and anger.

In José Ortega y Gasset's house—and let the reader not forget that it is Juan Ramón Jiménez and not I who is the visitor here—he discovered, on the piano, a small plaster reproduction of the Venus de Milo of the type they sell in downtown Madrid for twenty cents, and I think there was also a bronze paperweight representing the scene of Don Quixote charging the windmill with a desperate and screaming Sancho Panza standing by. These ornamental details were sufficient reason for Juan Ramón to make biting comments against the person of Ortega, and then to proceed with a criticism of the philosopher's style and work.

I will probably never put in writing the things he told us about Antonio Machado, whether they were real or invented, because of the respect I have always felt for that saintly poet.

204

Juan Ramón's house was completely the opposite of those he criticized. With the help of Zenobia Camprubí, his admirable and patient wife, he had been able to decorate it in a naturally simple and elegant way. There, in the one room which has always remained very mysterious in my mind since even in subsequent visits I was never permitted to enter it, the poet worked indefatigably all day long and a good part of the night. When he was thus engaged, it was impossible to see him and he thought nothing of refusing to receive guests.

This poet, like so many others, became frantic when someone unexpectedly tried to disturb his privacy or break into that silence so necessary for doing totally satisfactory work, a kind of invasion that happens too frequently when one lives in a large city. During those hours of deep creative activity, Juan Ramón was even annoyed by visits from his wife. She told me that on more than one occasion, the astonished eyes of her friends would see—through the living-room doorway—a screen that seemed to be self-propelled, moving by some diabolical trick like a strange, modern temptation scene in the style of Hieronymus Bosch. Behind it crept the poet, carrying the screen as he walked by, his head sunk in his beard, wishing to remain unseen as he went from one room of the apartment to another.

In that desired solitude, in the middle of Madrid, Juan Ramón produced, polished, retouched, entangled and disentangled his *Work,* as he himself called it. He was no longer the poet of *Arias Tristes* and *Pastorales,* books that revealed to Rubén Darío the delicate and deep sadness of our Andalusia. Nor was he any longer the poet of those ballads and refrains dedicated to spring, the elegiac creator of *La soledad sonora (Resounding Solitude)* or even of the more complex and finely wrought *Sonetos espirituales (Spiritual Sonnets), Estío (Summer),* or *El diario de un poeta recién casado (The Diary of a Recently Married Poet).* It had also been a long time since Platero, that immortal little donkey, walked throughout the world, nevertheless not ceasing to trot softly along the streets and paths of his native Moguer. Juan Ramón had by this time abandoned the musical groves, the delicate and transparent landscapes that he himself had brought to Spanish poetry. He was now, in the burning darkness of his creative work, the revitalized poet of *Piedra y cielo (Stone and Heaven), Poesía (Poetry), Belleza (Beauty)* and *Unidad (Unity).* His poetry had begun to be like an unadorned diamond. No rhyme or assonance, nor even the delightful and at times rhythmic play of free verse; only the very essence of the poem, stripped of excess trappings.

Arranco de raíz la mata
fresca aún del rocío de la aurora . . .

I tear out the bush by its roots,
Still fresh from the dew of dawn . . .

From a stanza in one of the brightest and most sparkling ballads which appeared in an early book of his, I had extracted two lines which served as an inspiration for one of my ballads which had pleased him so much:

La blusa azul y la cinta
milagrera sobre el pecho . . .

The blue blouse and miraculous ribbon
crossing his chest . . .

That small sea of poems, my allusions to the salt-flats, to the beaches and castles along the shores of the Bay of Cádiz, brought back memories of his own adolescence in the Puerto, and we discovered that many of his *Marinas de ensueño (Daydreaming Seascapes)* were visions of a faded nostalgia for the Bay of Cádiz as seen from the windows of the infirmary or through the trees—the eucalyptus and the pine—at San Luis Gonzaga, the Jesuit school where we had both studied in our youth.

I was quite overwhelmed by the way Juan Ramón Jiménez welcomed me that afternoon on my second visit. His preference for me over such a long period of time was unusual, and I mention it now with pride. He instilled in me feelings of inspiration, enthusiasm and a sense of self-confidence I never had before. I left him the manuscript of *Marinero en tierra* I had brought with me. A short time after that a selection of poems from this collection appeared in the journal *Sí,* a series of notebooks containing poetry and prose that he was editing under the title *El andaluz universal (The Universal Andalusian).* And even more flattering was the beautiful letter signed by him which appeared in another issue of these same notebooks, a letter which I have always included as a prologue to the various editions of *Marinero* and in my poetic anthologies.

Once again in the street, I said goodbye to Hinojosa. I did not return home until the early hours of the morning, although I don't know where I spent that May night. I moved blindly, without any particular direction, as a man drunk with happiness, feeling the way any aspiring young poet might have felt after paying a visit to Góngora or Baudelaire. Some of the *pesetas* from the prize sang in my pocket. I stopped to buy ice cream in all the ice-cream parlors that crossed my path, inviting any stranger who accepted my invitation to join me in this strange activity. I had on a new suit—that is, a pair of slightly pink pants and a sport jacket to match that was made of a material that looked like blotting paper and which my family thought resembled a bullfighter's outfit. A brownish tie with a wide knot hung from an excessively ample shirt collar, and my nose was almost hidden by the rounded peak of a light gray English hat. People were staring at me, but I paid no attention to them as I ate and offered ice cream to everyone in sight. A good bit of my prize money was to evaporate in thin air that spring as I helped to quench the thirst of friends as well as strangers.

I also found a publisher for my *Marinero;* Don José Ruiz Castillo, owner and director of the collection Biblioteca Nueva. He called me because I had painted a portrait of one of his children some years earlier. I was astounded by his insinuation that I pay at least part of the printing costs. How could that be possible? I told him it would be better if the work remained unpublished. Besides, I had reserved the money which was still left to buy books and to take an automobile trip with my brother Agustín through Castile. Don José, generous and pleasant as he was, soon realized his mistake. He would edit my book, paying all the expenses, and he even intended to send my manuscript to the well-known printing firm of Adelantado in Segovia, which he had contracted to work for him.

The following day I rushed off to see Daniel Vázquez Díaz. He had promised to do a portrait of me for *Marinero*—it turned out to be a Rafael Alberti almost in full profile and with a book in his hand. The lines of the sketch were quite good, but the artist, who always had managed to capture an exact likeness of his models, didn't come even close this time (I told myself that it would eventually look like me when, in my old age, I finally received the Nobel Prize). In the meantime, three young composers—Gustavo Durán, Rodolfo and Ernesto Halffter—who were enthusiastic about the rhythmic and melodic qualities of my ballads, had written music for three of them.

Of this trio, the marvelous song which Ernesto composed, *La corza blanca (The White Deer)*, became known throughout the Hispanic world shortly after it was published. The other two, *Cinema* and *Salinero*, were also beautiful and have been widely sung. The fact is that Ernesto Halffter, then a true musical prodigy, had succeeded in creating something masterful, simple and melancholic, which was very much in keeping with the mixture of old and new styles present in my lyrics as well as with the theme that I had taken from Barbieri's *Cancionero*. Ernesto's *La niña que se va al mar (The Girl Who Goes Down to the Sea)* also became famous, but it was not included in that original edition for reasons of space.

With the coming of spring and the prestige that the prize had brought with it, my visits to the Residencia de Estudiantes became more frequent. It was a happy time, at least for us. In the Residencia gardens I met Pedro Salinas and Jorge Guillén, who were about the same age, some ten years older than I, and, like Gerardo Diego, professors of literature in Spain and abroad. Both were soon to become great poets. Salinas was the more outgoing of the two: talkative, quick to smile and very *"madrileño."* Everyone called him Don Pedro, even though they spoke to him in the familiar *"tú"* form. Guillén, from Valladolid, was perceptive, refined, withdrawn, pale and extremely tall with glasses behind which one could see the small, penetrating eyes that were capable of precisely delineating the most diffused and nebulous phenomenon. José Moreno Villa had written in his autobiographical *Vida en claro*, a book composed in exile, that all the recent poets had appeared in pairs: Machado and Juan Ramón, Salinas and Guillén, Lorca and Alberti, Prados and Altolaguirre, but that he, like León Felipe, had come on the poetic scene unaccompanied. A curious observation which I now realized was true and certainly apt in the case of these two Castilian poets. That was how I saw them from the first, as a perfectly matched pair, much more harmonious in spite of their different poetic tones than the other groupings mentioned by Moreno Villa.

I knew *Presagios*, Salinas' first book, with its seminal lyrical portrait of Juan Ramón Jiménez during those years of great creativity in Spanish poetry. I was almost totally ignorant of Guillén's work and had read only a few poems that had perhaps appeared in the *Revista de Occidente*. I was impressed by the crude realism of certain poems in Don Pedro's book which jarred somewhat with the rather intimate, restrained or controlled tone of the rest of the works in the collection.

> *Un viejo chulo le dijo*
> *(La chiquila era inclusera):*
> *"Bendita sea tu madre!"*

> *An old pimp said to her*
> *(The little girl was an orphan):*
> *"May your mother be blessed!"*

How could such a popular note, this kind of neighborhood slang, appear with such abruptness in a poet whose works were so basically refined? When I came to know Don Pedro better I discovered the answer. In spite of Paris, Cambridge or New York, Salinas was still very much a resident of Madrid, and every so often in his conversations these bursting geraniums would sprout: "barrio" slang, colorful expressions laced with sugarpaste and rotgut whiskey. Our friendship was sealed from that day forward and it grew stronger with the publication of my *Marinero en tierra*, developing generously by degrees and reaching its high point when my book *Sobre los ángeles (Concerning the Angels)* was finished and he gave an interpretive lecture on this work. His talk was illustrated with angelical examples that ran the gamut from the medieval representations of the Beatitudes to the metaphysical geometrics of Chirico. I always loved Salinas, and respected him for what he really was: an older brother to our generation. (So, of course, was Guillén.) His severe poetic truth, although so distinct from my own or from that of other southern poets, always attracted me with the serene and human qualities that revealed, even in its most extravagant moments, a gentle heart incapable of expressing sudden violent tremors or deep bitterness. The poetry of a kind, cordial man, with a sincerity of tone which although almost always contained within a more complex technical framework nevertheless reminded one of the tranquil voice of Antonio Machado. This was, after all, Castilian poetry in which Salinas from the very beginning displayed a simple, tense and unadorned poetic line with an internal skeletal structure that firmly supported the authentic flesh surrounding it. I believe it was García Lorca who introduced me to both these poets.

Federico continued there in the Residencia, throwing gardens and cells into noisy confusion. Along those springtime paths, with their murmuring poplar trees, he continued reciting his *Gypsy Ballads* which were increasing in number each year, the songs becoming more varied and richer in texture. But Lorca, loving the presence of a live audience and pleased with his role of wandering minstrel, insisted on not publishing them. The whole group was still there: Pepín Bello, Luis Buñuel, Dalí, Moreno Villa,—and the appreciative "claque" which surrounded Federico. It was the time of the "Anaglyphs," the "Fartometer," of Buñuel's ferocious jokes, of the "Order of the Brothers of Toledo." Moreno Villa speaks about the Anaglyphs in his autobiography. They consisted of a type of miniature poem, spontaneous and amusing associations which, to quote Moreno, "consisted of three nouns one of which, the middle one, had to be the word *gallina* (hen). The secret was to find a third noun that would be impressive because of its peculiar and unexpected phonetic quality." Here Moreno is mistaken. The difficult and at the same time amusing aspect of a good anaglyph resided in the fact that the third noun could not have the slightest relation to the first one.

Pepe Moreno gives, among others, two fairly acceptable examples:

El buho	*El té,*
el buho,	*el té,*
la gallina	*la gallina*
y el Pancreator.	*y el Theotocópuli.*
The owl,	*Tea,*
The owl,	*Tea,*
The hen	*The hen*
and the Almighty.	*and Theotocópuli.**

There was soon a real epidemic of anaglyphs; even very serious types like Américo Castro were not free from temptation. Different kinds were invented, but they were generally rejected. It was actually

*Theotocópuli (Domenico) is the name of the painter who is better known as *El Greco* (c. 1544–1614).

Federico who gave the final blow by creating the baroque style of anaglyph. I remember this one:

Guillermo de Torre,
Guillermo de Torre,
la gallina
y por ahí debe andar algún enjambre.

Guillermo de Torre,
Guillermo de Torre,
The hen
And there must be a swarm there somewhere.

As a result of this innovation, a period of decadence set in and the anaglyph was forgotten.

Another invention which, naturally, was kept secret turned out to be "The Fartometer." First a small candle was placed inside a square wooden box. At a certain distance from the flame, but at the same height, dangled a piece of string. In one of the sides of the box was a small opening that was also on the same level as the tip of the flame and the piece of string. The idea was to gauge the intensity of the wind which each contestant could propel through this opening. An extremely potent fart would be necessary for the flame to curve and set fire to the string. It was a typical schoolboy's game. I can't remember if some of those very sedate professors who lived in the Residencia ever decided to participate.

As for the "Order of the Brothers of Toledo"—that was something else again. In spite of the rigorous entrance requirements, I was accepted that year. Founded some time ago by a group of friends and fellow residents, the principal task of the membership was to wander, particularly at night, through that marvelous and magical city located on the banks of the Tagus. The members of this brotherhood would generally take up lodgings in the Posada de la Sangre where Cervantes had written his exemplary novels and which also served as the setting for some of those stories.

The inn, although somewhat modernized in certain details, still preserved at the time the totally Spanish atmosphere of those road-side lodges or taverns where mule drivers and travelers would stop, so authentically but poetically described from experience by the author of *Don Quixote*. In accordance with the rigid clauses of the rules governing the Order, the members of the brotherhood would leave the inn when the cathedral clock had struck 1:00 a.m., an hour in which the whole city of Toledo seemed to shrink and become even more withdrawn into its silent and phantasmagoric labyrinth. On the night of my initiation into the secrets of the Order, we went out into the street with all the brothers except me carrying bedsheets which they had carefully removed from their rooms and hidden under their jackets. Luis Buñuel was to serve as the Brother Superior. The mysterious and poetic spectacle which had been prepared for dawn was meant to bring back to life the prevalent theory of the existence of ghosts in the atrium and square adjacent to the Convent of Santo Domingo el Real. After weaving and unweaving our way among the deep cracks of the sleepy town, we reached the convent at the moment when its barred windows suddenly lit up, becoming filled with veiled hymns and prayers recited by the nuns. While the prayers continued to be heard in monotonous succession, the members of the Brotherhood, who had left me standing alone at one end of the square, began to cover themselves with their sheets, crouching behind the columns of the atrium. They could be seen moving slowly and separately behind the pillars, white and realistic-looking ghosts from another time gliding through the somehow unreal silence of that Toledan penumbra. I was beginning to feel more frightened as my imagination got the better of me, when suddenly the sheeted visions began to move violently and shout in my direction: "This way! This way!" while they disappeared down the narrow alleys, leaving me abandoned, alone, and lost in that frightening maze of Toledo. I did not have the slightest idea where I was and there was not the remotest consoling possibility that someone might be around to show me the way to the inn. Besides the fact that there was no one in the streets of the city at that hour, if a stranger in town doesn't ask for directions in Toledo every hundred feet or so, even during the day, he might as well consider himself definitely lost. This, then, was one of the worst tests to which the novitiates of the Brotherhood were subjected.

And so I began to walk down the first narrow street, feeling a certain satisfaction in not having a compass to guide me, since I had made up my mind to be lost until dawn. Walking through a darkened Toledo on a moonless night such as that one is like becoming suddenly wafer-thin, to be whittled down to a mere profile, a flattened human mold, willing to be wounded even more, to be scraped against the rough edges of such a strange crevice; it is to become air, the whisper of water along those shrunken passageways, those deceitful open ditches that are suddenly blocked by sheets of metal, where no exit is possible. It is like walking along paths that have been trodden before, to become silent footsteps, only the resonance and final echo of a lost shadow.

I had become just such a lost and confused shadow when suddenly, in one of those unexpected clearings—an unforeseen opening that suggests the presence of a square, the corner of an alley which creates a small space to make room for the wall of a convent, a church, an elegant residence—there rose up before me an uncombed and romantic ivy-covered barrier through which something could be glimpsed that made me strain my eyes to discover what it might be. It was a white slab, covered in places by the dark hair-like strands of ivy which partially obliterated the writing that had been carved into it. The flickering of a lamp hanging from a nearby niche in the wall helped to decipher the written message: "Garcilaso de la Vega was born here." The inscription continued in small letters which were difficult to read, but the figures indicating the birth and death of the poet were clearly visible: 1503–1536. And it seemed to me then as if Garcilaso, a Garcilaso formed by tender dark leaves, had broken loose from that climbing ivy and had begun to walk with me through the nocturnal silence of Toledo, waiting with me for the coming of dawn.

> *Cerca del Tajo en soledad amena*
> *de verdes sauces hay una espesura,*
> *toda de yedra revestida y llena,*
> *que por el tronco sube hasta el altura . . .*

> *Near the Tagus River in pleasant seclusion,*
> *Is a thick grove of green willow trees,*
> *Adorned by creeping ivy in profusion*
> *Climbing to the heights among the leaves . . .*

It was the hour of dawn when, with these verses of Garcilaso on my lips, I found the Posada de la Sangre and threw myself into bed, happy about my first adventure as an initiate into the mysteries of the Order. A few hours later, at lunchtime, what a good time the brothers had at my expense as we all sat facing a huge pot of partridges, the famous culinary specialty of the Venta del Aire! Under the arbor that covered the open patio where our banquet took place, pencilled portraits of the principal brothers of the Order had been sketched on the whitewashed walls. Their creator, Salvador Dalí, was also included among them. Someone had told the innkeepers not to paint over them, since they were valuable works of art by a famous painter and that they were worth a fortune. In spite of this warning, they were obliterated years later by the new owners of the restaurant.

Summer was approaching. The Residencia was, as usual, getting ready to begin its program for foreign students. A few days earlier, when I had gone to thank Don Ramón Menéndez Pidal for his vote as a member of the National Literary Prize Committee, he had invited me to read some of my poems on the opening day of this summer session. It was the first time that I was to recite before an audience of people I did not know. I was calm enough when the moment of my recital finally arrived, but I lost part of my aplomb when some gentleman with a Don Juanesque beard took me by the arm and, as I stood there between his beard and the wall, offered me the following bit of advice:

"You must realize, young man, that you are Andalusian and you're going to recite before foreign students who are coming to Madrid to learn Spanish. Read slowly, pronouncing all your words carefully, including the final syllables, and please be particularly careful with the way you pronounce your *ll*'s and your z's."

When I was walking toward the auditorium, somewhat frightened by that admonition, I asked a friend the name of that handsome bearded gentleman who was so worried about my Andalusian accent.

"That's Américo Castro, the famous philologist. I'm surprised you don't know him!"

Before a young audience of English and North American students, among whom were some very beautiful girls, I recited poems from my *Marinero en tierra*, with a forced Castilian pronunciation. Everything seemed to be going quite well, but when I came to the verses of that sonnet "A un capitán de navío":

> *Por ti los litorales de frentes serpentinas*
> *desenrollan al paso de tu arado cantar . . .*

I pronounced the *ll* of *desenrollan* so perfectly that, as I stood on tip-toes to emphasize such perfection, my foot slipped off the podium and I almost broke a leg.

Once outside in the gardens, I was greeted and congratulated. Don Américo was pleased. My reading had not been so bad after all. Someone approached and threw his arms around me in a hearty embrace. It was Amado Alonso, a young philologist from the province of Navarra; a charming, frank and good-natured individual who looked a bit like some *pelota* player. He introduced me to his companion, a willowy English girl who happened to be the most beautiful student in the program that summer. We became friends, but he was to leave Spain shortly thereafter. I think he went to England where he married his beautiful pupil. (I came across him later in Buenos Aires, surrounded by his lovely children, and we renewed our friendship. He was working for the publishing firm of Losada. Because of political problems in Argentina, he had to leave for North America, where he later died of cancer. His *Spanish Grammar* and his books on linguistics are still used in many educational institutions.)

The heat was becoming intense. People were beginning to abandon the Residencia. Federico was already wandering through the fields of Fuente Vaqueros in his native Granada. Without his presence, the Residencia seemed lonely and sad. Dalí had also left. That summer I received a postcard from him, with a photograph of the castle in Figueras, in which he wrote: "Greetings, Alberti. How are things? Affectionately, Salvador." Above the highest window of the fortress, Dalí had written: "This is where the members of the clergy used to pee." The mailman couldn't control his laughter. "Excuse me, " he said, "I couldn't help but read that."

My *Marinero en tierra* was still at the printers in Segovia. I would not have the galley proofs until the end of summer. I was getting ready for my trip. In my brother's small car I planned to explore the regions of Old Castile. Agustín was a good driver, and I would be the only passenger. In the meantime, having nothing else to do, I used to roam the streets without any fixed destination, with a book of poetry under my arm, finding it enjoyable to read beneath the shelter of the trees.

One morning, as I strolled up Cisne Street, I noticed that coming down the opposite side of the street, slowly and somewhat withdrawn, was the shadow of a man who although terribly aged I immediately associated with the portrait of a younger Machado that had appeared on the flyleaf of his Collected Poems—published by the Residencia—and which I counted among my most prized possessions. It was he, or his shadow, there was no doubt in my mind; a sad shadow in a state of decline and moving with the steps of a sleepwalker, of a soul immersed in itself, absent, totally removed from the world around it. What should I do? Could I awaken this shadow, tearing it from its dreamlike state? If I don't dare now, I said to myself, I'll never have another chance—and I ran towards him, fearing that he might suddenly disappear into thin air.

"Don Antonio Machado?"

After a tremulous moment of silence, as if he needed time to search his memory in order to remember his own name, two staccato-like sounds were all I heard: "Yes . . . yes."

"I am Rafael Alberti. I wanted to meet you and thank you."

"Ah . . . ah!" he murmured, still not totally awake, as he took my hand in his. "There is no reason to thank me."

And he absented himself again, a shadow lost among the gallery of itself, wandering off down the street, "sad and poorly dressed" [*mal vestido y triste*—quoted from Machado] on this bright summer morning.

> *Misterioso y silencioso*
> *iba una y otra vez . . .*

> *Mysterious and silent*
> *He wandered back and forth . . .*

This was the way Rubén Darío had described him, and these lines, in effect, offer a perfect image of Antonio Machado up until the moment of his death.

Finally, early one morning, I left the heart of the Castilian *meseta* with my brother. I was to begin my second book, which was also to consist of songs and ballads. In my little notebook I had already written a title: *La amante (The Beloved)*. Who was the person with that name with whom I was to wander through the countryside of Castile as far as the coast of Cantabria where there was another sea, a northern sea which I had not yet seen? Someone, a distant beautiful friend from those days of recuperation spent in the Guadarrama

216

Mountains. I was still the landlocked sailor who set out to travel over unknown plains, mountains, rivers and villages, but this time not accompanied by the blue peasant girl who stood looking out at the Sea of Cádiz. Pedro Salinas, whom I unexpectedly met in the main square of Burgos, years later offered an exact image of what I looked like on that trip: "An official courier, a messenger from the king, who carried from sea to sea a state secret, from the silvery salt-flats of San Fernando to the sullen cliffs of Santillana de Asturias." I was just as Salinas so delightfully described me, although at the time I would never have thought so. But I did give myself away after my visit to Aranda de Duero:

¡Castellanos de Castilla,
nunca habéis visto la mar!

¡Alerta, que en estos ojos
del sur y en este cantar
yo os traigo toda la mar!

¡Miradme, que pasa el mar!

Castilians of Castile,
Who have never known the sea!

Watch and listen closely!
In southern eyes and southern song,
I offer it to you. Gaze at me!

I bring to you the sea!

Rhythmically, melodiously and lightheartedly I traveled with my absent beloved through more than a hundred villages. My songs poured out, covering almost all of them as well as the endless number of paths and roads that joined them together. A joyous itinerary, always open to the possibility of laughter. But the most incongruously amusing episode, and I have always been a great admirer of incongruity, happened in Medina de Pomar.

I was visiting this town's beautiful collegiate chapel with my brother Agustín. In the church, an old and crafty priest who was showing us around stopped solemnly before the sanctuary of the main altar, a bright and dazzling jewel surrounded by religious relics.

"This receptacle," slowly whispered the old man, "contains the splinter of a bone from the body of St. Francis. There is also a tooth here that belonged to St. Blas, the patron saint of toothaches. Here is one of the Virgin's needles. Over there, one of St. John's tears, and now for the most amazing thing of all . . ."

He suddenly stopped speaking as we held our breath. He had reached the central and highest part of the sanctuary. Next to his flat, dirty finger brilliantly sparkled a small box containing still another relic.

"And here . . . you would never guess what's in here."

My brother, a firm believer, waited somewhat unctuously for the priest to continue. I, on the ōther hand, could scarcely keep a straight face.

"Well, here we have nothing less than the foreskin of Jesus Christ."

Even Agustín burst into laughter.

"Don't laugh. It is the true foreskin of Christ!" stated the priest as he signaled to us to be silent. "The real *thing*," he repeated, "and the one worshipped in the Cathedral of Jaén is apocryphal."

Previous to this devout scene in Medina de Pomar, I had lived for a few days in Santo Domingo de Silos, the marvelous Romanesque monastery hidden behind the Demanda Hills of Burgos. It was well after nightfall when we reached that Benedictine shelter whose founder and ancient patron saint had been glorified in song by Gonzalo de Berceo, a member of that same religious order. After subjecting us to the creaking sounds of bolts and locks, a mysterious little monk opened the heavy main door and beckoned us to enter. In response to our "Good evening," he only replied with a silent nod of his head. It was the hour of silence for the community of Saint Benito. An oil lamp dangled from one of his hands and from the other hung a rosary of thick beads. A blast of cold air filled with the perfume of an invisible garden indicated to us that we had come to the end of the frightening hallways along which we had been following the illuminated hand of the monk. It was pitch black. Only the cold, which was becoming more intense, and the pulsating sound of a fountain made it possible for our eyes, blind to the night around them, to imagine the presence of those arches of the lower cloister, a true marvel of the ninth century. We had to wander along stairways, passageways, and under other arches, still following those flannel-covered footsteps of our guide and feeling somewhat uncomfortable, until with a final nod the monk closed the door of the cell which the hospitality of that brotherhood of Silos traditionally and generously offers to the traveler.

The strains of a pure Gregorian chant awakened us before dawn. The entire community of the Order filled the upper cloister on the way to the church. We followed the procession and then listened to the singing of the Mass. The peasants of the village, who were congregated there, all seemed to know the canticles by heart and they sang them in unison with the monks. A perfect harmony spread out in waves through the nave of the temple. This same concert could be heard at dawn every day of the year, and not even the raw winter cold or snow caused a break in this routine. When the Mass was over, those humble peasants gathered up their farming tools, which they had temporarily left in the square, and placing them on their shoulders moved out into the fields.

After a breakfast served on white tablecloths and in clay crockery that seemed to have been placed there by the artist Zurbarán himself, the monks gathered around us. We kissed the hand of the abbot, Father Luciano Serrano, a famous historian who, as I was to be told by several members of his flock in the intimacy of the night, was hated by all the inhabitants of the monastery. There was a poet amongst them, a kind and educated individual, whose poetry was not, however, very good. His name was Justo Pérez de Urbel, and he was extremely knowledgeable about the symbolism of the paintings and Romanesque arches in the cloisters. I heard him tell marvelous things about that structure, lectures which I have never forgotten. He showed me the codex of Gonzalo de Berceo, a treasure which had been preserved by the Order from the time of its composition, and from those manuscript pages I inhaled the holy and primitive aroma of Spanish poetry. (How sad it is that Justo Pérez de Urbel eventually turned out to be one of the most avid partisans of the Franco regime!)

The brother in charge of the apothecary, a man of small stature and playful mien, became quite friendly, and he eagerly showed me around the pharmacy located in the dark depths of the convent. I tried to get him to give me the secret formula for the famous Benedictine alcholic brew which was then called "Liqueur of Santo Domingo de Silos," due to the somewhat fierce litigation that the French brethren of the Order of Saint Benito had brought against their Spanish counterpart. Business is business, even though the Holy Ghost may be involved in the transactions. I jokingly proposed to the pharmacist that he poison the abbot whom nobody liked, but who would have to be tolerated until his death since this was a lifetime position granted by a secret vote cast by all members of the community. Only the Holy Father of Rome had the power to remove him. Why was this abbot so hated? He was condescending and tyrannical, besides being terribly arrogant. Those humble monks, the majority of whom were of peasant stock, felt humiliated by him, and they were fed up with his haughtiness and lack of generosity. They endured it with resignation, however; what else could they do? They had voted for him, but who could have imagined that such a pleasurable privilege was to have the effect of placing the mitre of Saint Domingo on the head of the Devil? Because they had, in effect, reached the point of believing he was the Devil incarnate and under orders from the demons of Hell. That was how he had been described to me by Bernardino, the brother in charge of the garden, an old, delirious figure then practically on his deathbed. The abbot, for some reason or other, had gone off to Rome, and Bernardino, an old Carlist guerilla with a price on his head for having committed several murders, but protected by the right of asylum granted to the monastery, believed it to be his duty to inform his brothers of one of his most terrifying nocturnal visions.

"Gather around me, my children. I am going to confess to you all I have just seen. Our abbot is in mortal sin. He cannot visit the Holy Father. Every time he tries to climb the steps of the Vatican, a legion of demons swoops down from the tower. They carry him up there with them, but only to subsequently dash him to the ground from on high. He will not be received by the Pope until he confesses and is absolved."

A few hours later, Bernardino called all of his brothers together again.

"Let us rejoice, brothers," he said to them, although he was already in the throes of death. "Our abbot is now in God's graces. He has confessed to his sins. At this very moment he is speaking with the Holy Father. I can now die in peace."

This and other similar visions of Friar Bernardino at the end of his life had the whole monastery in a state of panic. Even after his death, the brothers would talk about them in terror. For them, he had died a saint. As for the abbot—they never did manage to get up enough courage to ask him about his experiences in Rome.

Unforgettable nights during my brief stay in Silos! Breaking the rule of silence, some of the more daring members of the brotherhood came to visit me in my cell. I would offer them sherry and they would bring me samples of their famous liqueur. Until the last stroke of midnight, they would stay with me, tilting their glasses, and more than once they remained in my cell way past that hour. Since I was under no obligation to take Communion, I would continue drinking alone. How delightful and strange were those semi-clandestine meetings! The brothers enjoyed the Andalusian brew I offered to them, and it had the effect of stirring them up, making them both talkative and curious. Although the Order of Saint Benito does not impose confinement on its members, the world for them, with the exception of the abbot and other authorities, did not extend further than the neighboring villages and fields which they visited either on horseback or on foot, preaching the doctrine of Christ. For that reason, the world beyond their experiences was truly intriguing to them. What was Madrid like? What about Sevilla and Barcelona? And the theater, dances, bullfights? My descriptions, which were almost always somewhat frivolous and picaresque in tone, caused their eyes to open wide and their faces to become flushed with excitement.

"But the theater is nothing compared to the vaudeville shows," I said to them maliciously one evening.

Very few of them had ever heard the word, and they didn't have the slightest idea what kind of a spectacle this might be. I then gave them a brief demonstration. I grabbed the monk's cowl from one of them and, wrapping it around my body like a typical embroidered silk shawl known as a *mantón de Manila*, I would sing to them the most popular songs in Madrid at the time:

> *Soy la maja moderna española*
> *que en la Castellana se pasea . . .*

> *I am the modern Spanish maja*
> *Who strolls along the Castellana . . .*

My exaggerated gestures, my hip movements, the way I manipu-

221

lated the cowl, all fascinated them to such an extent that they broke out in spontaneous applause, lifting their glasses and offering a toast which might have been dedicated to me or to Raquel Meller, the singer I had been imitating. After a few other demonstrations, they agreed that if it was all just as I had presented it, these music hall shows had nothing at all to do with Hell and damnation. The Devil could rest easy.

Monks such as those I found in Silos—liberal, educated and frank at the same time—were quite unusual, and I was not to see the likes of them very often in later years. Their library was also a marvel. I noticed that there were books of poetry by the French Symbolists, and I even held a copy of Verlaine in my hands. The monastery almost constantly received visits from famous men. More than once Miguel de Unamuno walked through its cloisters and created some anxiety for the community with his doubts and paradoxes. In the visitors' book I saw his signature as well as those of Zuloaga, Eugenio D'Ors, Gerardo Diego and other well-known artists and writers. I left them a poem in honor of the Virgin of March and Child who, with her bovine eyes, looked out over the lower cloister not far from the cypress tree and the hollyhock that grew in the garden. Those were memorable days we spent at the Monastery of Santo Domingo in the gentle shadow of Berceo and so many innocent souls steeped in the aroma of the Middle Ages and the black bread of the fields! (It seems that now those wonderfully pure and liberal souls have succumbed, and those who possessed them have prostrated themselves at the feet of the Caudillo. The Benedictine Order has accepted a task which other religious brotherhoods rejected: to be the caretakers of the Valley of the Fallen, the necrophilic monster of the present regime which has cost the poor Spanish people so many tears and literally millions of *pesetas*.)

Traveling with my "beloved," I finally reached the sea:

> ¡Perdonadme, marineros,
> Sí, perdonadme que lloren
> mis mares chicas del sur
> ante las mares del norte!
>
> ¡Dejadme, vientos, llorar,
> como una niña, ante el mar!

222

Sailors, forgive me!
My little seas of the South
Can only weep
Before the grandeur of the North.

Winds, let the child within me
Shed tears before the open sea!

I was tremendously impressed by the Cantabrian Sea, that dark and angry body of water so different from the blue meekness of my Bay of Cádiz. Starting from Laredo, I traveled along the coast of Santander and the Basque provinces until I reached San Sebastián, leaving a song behind in each seaside village. Once back in Madrid, I composed the last one—number seventy—which was a kind of farewell to that friend of mine, more imagined than real, that ideal traveling companion who had accompanied me over the lands of Spain I had not known before.

A pleasant surprise awaited me on my arrival: the galley proofs of *Marinero en tierra* were on my desk. This was the first time I had ever seen such things. I had no idea how to make corrections, but I invented my own symbols and returned them, special delivery, to the printer. The book appeared in the autumn in a suitably correct edition that included the portrait by Vásquez Díaz, the musical scores by the Halffter brothers and Gustavo Durán, as well as the letter from Juan Ramón Jiménez. A yellow band encircling the book announced in large black letters: "National Prize for Literature 1924–1925."

The first copies I dedicated were for the members of the Selection Committee. I delivered the one inscribed to Juan Ramón to him personally, and I waited with some anxiety for the critics to have their say. This was not long in coming. The first shot was fired from the pages of *El Sol* by Enrique Díez-Canedo in a flattering article in which he stressed my relationship with Lorca and the increasing importance of the poets from the south of Spain. Other critics followed suit: Gómez de Vaquero, Fernández Almagro, Bergamín, Marichalar . . . Almost all of them spoke about Federico, some establishing differences and others concentrating on our affinities. The Lorca-Alberti battle had begun, a dispute that was to go on for some time

223

and in which the participants almost always came to blows, while the two protagonists continued to be friends, viewing the conflagration from a distance.

Brickbats rained down on me from the provinces, but the reasons were absurd and the critics who wielded them clearly displayed their bad faith and noncomprehension. The anonymous commentator of a Catholic newspaper, after affirming that "Alberti proceeds from some Nordic hamlet to the rhythmic accompaniment of an iridescent sea," went on to call me "a monster from Avernus," "corrupter of poetry," and other equally delightful epithets. Another critic was disturbed by my poetic rhythms, "the intentional limping of the verses which makes reading them impossible." This was a stupid and unfounded remark about a book as simple and traditional as *Marinero en tierra*. (Many "very important people" had reacted in the same way to Federico's poetry and his recent works for the theater. At first, actresses such as Lola Membrives, as well as López Heredia and Company, would laugh openly at his *Gypsy Ballads* and his early dramas, but this was done behind Lorca's back and only after they had bestowed upon him the great honor of allowing him to read to them. Things changed when Margarita Xirgu and Josefina Díaz presented *Mariana Pineda*, *La zapatera prodigiosa* and *Bodas de sangre*, with resounding success. The box office is after all, for certain actresses, the mother of intelligence.)

After the triumph of *Marinero*, the editors of the *Revista de Occidente*, which Ortega y Gasset had been publishing since 1923, asked me to write for them. I submitted a series of poems from *Marinero*, along with others from *El alba del alhelí*, the book that I had begun in the mountains of Córdoba under the title of *Cales negras*. In France and in England, translations of my works had begun to appear. (Those in English brought royalties; the French ones did not.) And so I was in a happy frame of mind. I wanted to write more. But it was difficult for me to do this in Madrid, since there were too many interruptions by people who, for one reason or another, were interested in seeking me out. One morning I took the train and headed once again for Rute.

CHAPTER VI

*I continue writing in the woods of Castelar, with the impending
arrival of another autumn season. I always get up at the same
hour: six-thirty in the morning. Sunrise now is not until after
seven. The dew sparkles everywhere like pulverized glass. The bitter
juice of a lemon and a short bicycle ride clear my head and sharpen
my memory. I have breakfast and, weather permitting, I sit
outdoors to work.*

IN RUTE, news of the "awardment" had
already made the rounds. Doña Colo and her two daughters appeared almost immediately at my brother-in-law's house.

"We have come to greet the famous poet. Well, well, Don
Rafaelito! You certainly are the sneaky one! We knew you liked to
write verses, but, but—we never expected anything like that! I mean,
we're overjoyed!"

I was also congratulated by the notary friend of the spiritualists,
somewhat of a literary man himself, who embraced me affectionately
and addressed me as "colleague," "renowned bard," "beloved of the
Muses." In the streets the sullen inhabitants, who had barely greeted
me before, did so now, even with smiles on their lips. Shortly after
my arrival I locked myself in my headquarters—it was winter and
very cold—there on the top floor of the house, against the wall ad-

joining the prison. I was practically finished with my second book of poems, *La amante*. The only project I planned to carry out during my residence in Rute was to finish what I had started on my first visit here, that is, the *Cales negras*, whose definitive title would be *El alba del alhelí*. Christmas was approaching. For the benefit of my young nieces and nephews I wrote a series of songs inspired by the little figures of the *belén* that I myself had put together for them . One of those songs:

> *Aceitunero, que estás*
> *vareando los olivos,*
> *¿me das tres aceitunitas*
> *para que juegue mi niño?*

> *Olive-picker, shaking the branches*
> *Of the olive trees all day,*
> *Could you give me three tiny olives,*
> *So my little boy can play?*

was to be made famous, with only slight modifications, years later by the dance company of La Argentinita, and it was sung throughout all of Spain as a song written by an anonymous composer. Another series, *El pescador sin dinero (The Penniless Fisherman)*, was inspired by the way in which I somewhat foolishly spent the money I had won on people I hardly knew.

New popular cries, images and refrains were beginning to give shape to the book, creating a well-defined profile, an over-all design that I have always insisted upon, almost without my realizing it, in everything I have ever written. When the work had taken shape and had grown in volume, I divided that part of *El alba del alhelí* which had been composed in Rute into two sections: "El blanco alhelí," in which I grouped the less substantial, but more playful and gentle poems; and "El negro alhelí," which contained the more dramatic and darker works such as "La maldecida," "La encerrada," "Alguien," "El prisonero." The third section, "El verde alhelí," was to be dedicated to the sea which I would soon visit. My departure from Rute coincided with a letter from García Lorca, a delayed reply to several letters of mine which I had written to him during this brief vacation. Since it was a very short note, I can still remember what it said:

Dear cousin: Yesterday afternoon there was a terrible storm here. Tell me, please, if you had one there too. I am working, totally immersed in poetry which both wounds and overwhelms me.

Adiós!
¡Al molino del amor
por el toronjil en flor!
¡Adiooós!

Goodbye!
To the mill of love,
Through the flowering grapefruit grove!
Good-byyye!

When are you coming to Granada?

Love, Federico

I never did go to Granada, neither then nor later. But that same night I left by car for Málaga with the friend of the spiritualists, the good notary who still called me "illustrious bard, colleague, and beloved of the Muses."

About that nocturnal trip I only remember, as if seen through a thick mist, our stop in Antequera where, while we filled the car with gasoline, I silently recited some octaves from the *Fábula del genil* by Pedro Espinosa, the great classical poet who had been born there. We arrived in Málaga right before dawn. From the palm trees in the park I saw the eyes of Málaga open to the sea while the coastline of the city took on the color of pink carnations. At nine o'clock in the morning I raced off to the Imprenta Sur.

Neither Prados nor Altolaguirre were expecting me. They had never met me, but they guessed who I was. It was a marvelous meeting. At that very moment they were setting the type for the second or third issue of *Litoral*, the best Spanish journal of poetry published during the happiest years of our generation. Manolo —Manolito— hurried over to greet me, knocking over a bottle of ink in the process, descending on me like an angel that had dropped from a tower. Meanwhile Emilio Prados, his eyes glancing over his glasses, stood looking at me silently with an enigmatic smile. They

Canción

Con el junco de una acacia
corazón,
yo dibujaba en el agua
del lago cosas fantásticas,
con un junco, corazón.

Se abrieron en flor las ondas
corazón.
Y se llevaron mi alma
sabe Dios si a otras riberas,
corazón;
también de cosas fantásticas,
con un junco, corazón.

were the lonely heroes of this press. From that tiny workshop came the most immaculate pages of poetry being written in Spain at the time, each page patiently set by hand, letter by letter. In those days, these two typographer-poets were preparing their first books: *Tiempo* and *Canciones del farero* by Prados and Altolaguirre's *Las islas invitadas*. Emilio Prados was already what he would later become and continues to be to this day: a darkly tormented poet, an underground lightning-bolt, always struggling to cross swords in the open with some highly concentrated sentiment compressed into being by insufferable tortures. At times, by the feeble light of the lantern he holds in his hand, he is able to come out of that deep mine of his, but this never lasts very long since his world, a special mixture of Hell and Paradise, is to be found there in those subterranean galleries which only *he* knows and where he forges his hidden but luminous sparks.

With Prados one could walk through the streets, but with Manolito such a thing was impossible. He would bump into everything, walking in a zigzag pattern, and end up with the sleeves of his jacket coated with the chalky white dust he had rubbed off the walls. Without warning he would be off the sidewalk, ending up in the middle of the street, or he sometimes remained behind, disappearing into the doorways or lobbies of the buildings from which we would have to rescue him, only to be searching for him again a few minutes later. He was totally absent-minded. He had the face of a Scandinavian poet—his mother's last name was Bolin—his hair stood out wildly in little snail-like curls and he always had a smile on his lips, lips that were always ready to utter some witty or amusing remark. Everything about him made you think of a little calf that had escaped from Limbo, a strange angelical invention left to wander astray on earth. Manolito had lost his mother recently. And the date of her death, according to his own confession, was to be the most important day in his life as a poet and as a man. Many of the poems contained in *Las islas invitadas* which he read to me then were already marked by that anguish, by the deep sorrow one finds in the purest and most inspired Andalusian songs:

> *Era mi dolor tan alto,*
> *que la puerta de la casa,*
> *por donde salí llorando,*
> *me llegaba a la cintura ...*

> *So high was my pain,*
> *That the door of the house,*
> *Through which I left in tears,*
> *Only came up to my waist . . .*

With Manolo and with Emilio I spent many unforgettable hours in Málaga. We walked along the beaches together, seeing the nets stretched out under the sun, shimmering with anchovies. We strolled through the Limonar and climbed up to the castle of Gibralfaro, that old Moorish fortress. When one evening they both accompanied me to the pier to say goodbye, I realized that there, at the edge of the Mediterranean, I was leaving behind the friendship of two poets who were also two new branches of that Andalusian tree which formed part of our beautiful generation. Before my departure I had given them the manuscript of *La amante*, which they were to publish that same year (1926).

An ugly, broken-down barge with an even uglier name, *Enriqueta R*, transported me to Almería. My sister Pepita, whom I dearly loved, was waiting for me on the dock with her young lawyer husband (who was to suffer a horrible death during the first days of our Civil War). I stayed with these newlyweds for several months. I liked Almería; it was like an African outpost. After a night during which the warm desert breeze known as the *Terral* had swept through the city without ever letting up, the roofs of all the houses were buried under layers of sand. Although it was spring, the sun's rays gave off a summer heat, but a warm blue sea made it possible for me to swim almost every day. On the beach or seated among the palm trees in the park, I began to write the poems which were to comprise the last section of *El alba del alhelí*. I became friends with a beautiful Philippine girl whose parents had left her with my sister for a brief stay when they moved to Madrid. We walked together on the roofs and terraces and listened, as I had done back in the Puerto, to the kitchen conversations that rose up through the wide mouths of the chimneys. How beautiful it was at nightfall to stand together on those terraces watching the lights of the ships at sea go on one by one, and to see the emerging outlines of the constellations above us in the sky! And what had to happen, happened: we fell in love. It was then that my sister very wisely suggested that it might be better for me to return home. I did leave, but I took with me a large stack of poems and some of the happiest memories of my youth.

230

I reached Madrid with my third book totally finished. What was I to do now to begin again? The short, rhythmical and musical poetry I had written up until then no longer appealed to me. It was like a lemon that had been squeezed dry, and the problem was to see if it could still yield drops of a different kind. What was the sense of trying to squeeze it even more? Had I not tried other forms in my *Marinero?* I would start out by writing tercets, still making use of my favorite themes of the sea but adding others that were pounding inside my head.

Our enthusiasm for Góngora was beginning to grow at that time, encouraged by the proximity of the tricentennial celebration of this poet's death. I urgently needed a title. How could I proceed without one, since it would serve to contain the new lyrical avalanche which I felt was overtaking me? Shortly after composing the first poems, I found a title: *Pasión y forma (Passion and Form)*. It was to be the poetry of a painter: plastic, lineal and sharply delineated. That delicate, soulful tremor of my earlier songs was going to be enclosed in a rock-crystal coffer, in a hard, protective urn that would nonetheless be white and transparent. I would submit the metric versification to the most strict and precise pressures. I would obsessively pursue linguistic beauty, the most vibrant, harmonious sounds, and create images that at times within the same poem would succeed each other with a kind of cinematographic speed. Among all the other inventions of modern life, the movies had an overwhelming effect on me, since I felt that this medium brought with it a new vision, a new feeling that in the long run would obliterate once and for all the old world that now lay crumbling among the ruins of the most recent European war. And putting aside the tercets and sonnets and even the deliberate influence of Góngora, I stated with jubilant conviction that:

> *Yo nací—¡respetadme!—con el cine,*
> *bajo una red de cables y aviones,*
> *cuando abolidas fueron las carrozas*
> *de los reyes y al auto subió el Papa.*

> *I was born—have some respect—with the movies,*
> *Beneath a network of cables and airplanes,*
> *When the coaches of kings were abolished*
> *And the Pope drove off in a car.*

I did not know then if the respect I demanded was valid or if I was mistaken in asking for any such thing. I later came to see that it was not only film, in which I had schematically centered the starting point of my new style, but everything else I mentioned above that would lead mankind in this century to be the champion, the sunbearer, the luminous hero of a previously unknown humanity.

Pasión y forma was a good title, but on the advice of José Bergamín it was changed eventually to *Cal y canto (Whitewash and Stonesong)*, with its vague and incomplete connotations.* I began to publish the first poems of this collection—"Oso de mar y tierra," "Sueño de las tres sirenas" and "El jinete de jaspe" appeared in the *Revista de Occidente*. In *Litoral* I published "Narciso," a work comprised of tercets that was meant to be a modern version of the Greek fable. Many people thought these poems were successful; others, sharpening their nails, began to speak of neoclassicism, of submission to traditional forms, of the return to strophic verse. I was well aware of what I was doing. Even more important, I knew what was needed. Imitations were cropping up everywhere of the popular or traditional songs which Federico, in his way, and I later, in my own, had dispersed in all directions. A frivolous, effortless and even vulgar *Andalucismo* was threatening to invade everything, creating a dangerous epidemic that could have the effect of destroying us all. There was an urgency to stop this flow and to erect dikes to hold back the rising tides.

I remember that in an interview I had with a reporter from *La Gaceta Literaria*, which was published early in 1927, I had stated, jokingly but nonetheless with some annoyance: "I am not Andalusian but Norwegian, by intuition and because of my personal fondness for Gustavo Adolfo Bécquer." I proposed to make of each poem a difficult obstacle course. Góngora appeared on the scene at a very opportune moment. The glorification of this poet and the infiltration of his labyrinthine underbrush into our own poetic jungle would help us exorcise the evil. Even Federico, whose *Gypsy Ballads* were still unpublished, temporarily laid his Andalusianism to rest and wrote his "Oda a Salvador Dalí" which, if it doesn't bear much relationship to Góngora, has even less in common with folklore traditions. That return to strophic poetry was to be defended with sincere ardor and cogent arguments by one of its fiercest enemies:

*The Spanish word *canto* has the double meaning of "stone" and "song."

232

Gerardo Diego. It would be interesting to quote here some of his observations:

> Poets of a previous generation did not know how to create perfect poetic strophes, just as composers then were equally unable to resolve a perfect sonata. Even painters could not then successfully incorporate architectural aspects into their paintings. A few years later we were assaulted by the magnificent hurricane formed by all those vanguardistic *isms*. Artists became concerned with the material itself or the novelty of content. It was impossible to achieve at the same time what could be called total harmony. Then there was a rebirth of tranquility and we ageeed that the essential thing was to create. Or, to put it another way, it was important to be in total possession of one's talents, to master them and to be fully aware of what we, as individual artists, were doing. . . . There were three possible ways to achieve this. For each work there existed a particular form that would be uniquely and fully suited to it; free verse . . . or, to call it by another name, the open stanza, the old strophic verse, or totally new verse forms. Is this rhetoric? Evidently, it *is* rhetoric. But everything is rhetoric, and fleeing from it is a kind of negative rhetoric which is much more dangerous. No. We must not flee from anything. . . . We will write *décimas*, sonnets, and even *liras* because that's what we want to do; . . . our feelings are sacred. And it is all logical and explains why painters today insist on drawing well and why musicians learn counterpoint and the art of the fugue. But there is a difference between what we were doing and what our reasonable ancestors of the eighteenth century did. For them the strophe, the sonata, or the quadrille paper were obligatory. For us this was not the case. We had already learned to be free. We knew that what we were doing was a form of equilibrium and nothing more. And it is equally certain that we would often feel the beautifully free desire to fly outside the cage, having carefully calculated the weight, the capacity of the engine and fuel consumption, so as to not become lost like a floating cloud. The stanza, always the stanza, above or below, whether it be a slave or even nameless.

Gerardo's ideas, although they were to appear only later, perfectly synthesized the feelings we all had and coincided with the first bugle blasts of our battle in defense of Góngora, whose centennial, the third one since his death, we were preparing to noisily celebrate. It was, however, still a year away. But it was necessary to begin taking our positions, to close ranks and to study the strategy we would follow in such a "colossal combat." It was already rumored that the Royal Academy would stand aside with their arms crossed; that is to say, the members of that body would declare a war of silence on the occasion of this important date. Góngora, in spite of having some timid followers in that learned corporation, was still officially and traditionally considered to be a devil with horns, "an angel of darkness," an executioner of the Spanish language, particularly in his two magnificent poems "Soledades" and "Fábula de Polifemo y Galatea," the works which formed the nucleus of our enthusiastic admiration.

We are now in the month of April of the year 1926 and seated in one of those charming Madrid cafés which we all loved. Those of us who had almost spontaneously gathered there were Pedro Salinas, Melchor Fernández Almagro, Gerardo Diego and I. As a consequence of our first conversation, the idea was born to convoke the first assembly devoted to Góngora, at which time we would present the general outline of our project. The plan was to definitively vindicate Don Luis de Góngora on the occasion of his tricentennial celebration. In attendance at this assembly, in addition to the four of us and some others, were Antonio Marichalar, Federico García Lorca, José Bergamín, Moreno Villa, José María Hinojosa, Gustavo Durán and Dámaso Alonso. The plan was to distribute in twelve notebooks or publications all the papers which would be presented: six containing the poetry of Don Luis and six for the testimonials. The editing for the first six volumes would be under the direction of Dámaso Alonso (Soledades), José María de Cossío (Romances), Pedro Salinas (Sonetos), Jorge Guillén (Octavas), Alfonso Reyes (Letrillas) and Miguel Artigas, the author of a prize-winning biography of the poet (Canciones, décimas, tercetos). The remaining volumes were to be the responsibility of Gerardo Diego (Anthology in Honor of Góngora from Lope de Vega to Rubén Darío), Antonio Marichalar (Contemporary Prose Works Concerning Góngora), Moreno Villa (Album of Sketches) and Ernesto Halffter (Musical Album). The Report of the Centennial would be written by anyone who offered his services. I would be in charge of the poems dedicated to Góngora written by those poets who were invited to the homage. I was also granted the great honor of being named secretary to the group. Marichalar was charged with the most delicate and difficult mission, which was to have the *Revista de Occidente* publish all the projected volumes, something which the journal's editor-in-chief, José Ortega y Gasset, agreed to immediately. (I have been able to refresh my memory and fill in the blanks by consulting the *Crónica del Centenario* [*The Centennial Chronicle*], which was published by Gerardo Diego in *Lola*, a supplement to the magazine *Carmen*, issues 1 and 2, 1927-28, a poetry review edited by Gerardo himself.)

In the following meetings we planned the celebrations that would be held in honor of Don Luis—an act of faith to make up for three centuries of misunderstanding: the presentation of one of Góngora's theatrical works, concerts, an Andalusian street fair, exhibitions of engravings and drawings, conferences, meetings, etc. At the proper moment, a letter of invitation would be sent to all those collaborating in this testimonial. As secretary, I would be in charge of this activity. However, since there was still plenty of time to begin the battle and as summer was already upon us, the Góngora group disbanded with a firm promise to meet again in October.

I returned to my own work, *Pasión y forma*, adding sonnets and a few ballads which seemed to impress Salinas when I read them to him. I published some of them in *Mediodía*, a somewhat offbeat poetry magazine started by a group of young poets from Sevilla. I also began a series of comic works, almost burlesque in tone, which were obviously precursors of my book about film comics as well as gentle precedents of *El burro explosivo (The Explosive Donkey).* * That summer I met the painter Benjamín Palencia who did a very good

---

El burro explosivo was a short book of poems of a popular nature published by Alberti early in the Spanish Civil War in a series called the Editions of the Fifth Regiment. These poems were meant to be read by or to the soldiers of this regiment, and they are often crude as well as obviously political. The title is taken from an incident among the miners of Asturias during the insurrection there in 1934. The miners loaded a *burro* with charges of dynamite, with the intention of exploding this living bomb against the military forces of the Government. The donkey, however, always turned back when it had gone halfway to its destination, with the wicks sputtering and getting shorter and shorter. The striking miners tossed stones to keep the animal moving in the right direction, but during one of these starts and stops the donkey exploded and disappeared. Alberti, in his brief introduction to this collection, says that these poems are themselves "loaded with dynamite."

portrait of me, and we were later to become very good friends. Palencia belonged to a new group of excellent painters, almost all of whom had lived in Paris: Bores, de la Serna, Peinado, Ucelay, Pruna, Angeles Ortiz, Cossío and even Dalí, who in those days had become a member of the group but who was subsequently to go his own way, embarking on a foolish and scandalously productive career which, in spite of his great talent, would eventually lead him to that Vatican-Franquista opportunism in which he is so deeply immersed today; Dalí eventually became one of those putrefactions of his own invention. Juan Gris was considered by the entire group to be somewhat of an older brother. Miró was to come later. In Spain there was a group of painters younger than Palencia which included Gaya, Luna, Flores and others.

Benjamín, with his innocent peasant-like face, was an indefatigable worker. When he showed his drawings to us (and he turned them out by the thousands), he actually papered the floor of his workshop with them, leaving the visitor only a tiny spot for his feet. The series of drawings was interminable. He had just made a trip through Extremadura, sketching whatever shepherd or child had happened to come into the range of his pencil. I am convinced that this province owes Palencia a monument. Some day they will erect one in his honor and all the enthusiastic inhabitants of those fields will come to pay homage. The landscapes he painted, depicting those strange fields, constitute, for me at least, the very best of his artistic production. (I do not know what he is doing at the moment. The little I saw of his recent work exhibited here in Buenos Aires did not appeal to me as much, but once again I greatly admired those landscapes of uninhabited, clean and cultivated fields that dated from his early Extremadura period.)

Jose María de Cossío, a new and friendly addition to our Gongoristic meetings, was responsible for my being introduced one afternoon in the lobby of the Palace Hotel to a very exceptional individual who was to become, after his hideous death, the subject of one of the best poetic elegies ever to be written by a Spanish pen. This was Ignacio Sánchez Mejías, who was then only a bullfighter. (I say "only," because shortly thereafter he became a playwright and, with the help and advice of García Lorca, the guiding light and impresario of the Spanish ballet company whose main star was his friend, Encarnación López—"La Argentinita.") Ignacio was then in excellent physical condition, but approaching that age when in the difficult art of bullfighting one begins to lose a certain grace, quickness of movement, speed and profile. These qualities, however, were possessed in the extreme by another new friend, a young *matador* who was at the peak of his career: Cayetano Ordóñez, the "Niño de la Palma." I remember that Cossío, a passionate admirer of my poetry, asked me to recite some poems of mine immediately, almost at the very moment when Ignacio had thrown his arms around me while telling one of the hotel bellboys to bring us a good bottle of *manzanilla*. I was then deeply committed to composing tercets. The last ones I had written were entitled "Corrida de toros" ("Bullfight") and "El jinete de jaspe" ("The Jasper Horseman"). I began my recital. Sánchez Mejías listened to my poems attentively with a broad smile on his masculine face.

> *Caracolea el sol y entran los ríos,*
> *empapados de toros y pinares,*
> *embistiendo a las barcas y navíos.*

> *The sun spirals and the rivers rush in,*
> *Soaked in bulls and pine forests,*
> *Charging the sailboats and the ships at sea.*

"Terrific!" he commented, interrupting me but signaling with his hand for me to continue. When I had finished reciting, I told him that such an expression coming from a person who had fought and killed more than seven hundred bulls not only seemed to me to be suitable, but that it also filled me with pride. Then Cossío asked me to recite "Las chuflillas," a light playful poem that had been dedicated to the "Niño de la Palma," who was greatly admired by me, by Bergamín, and by Cossío himself. In this case, things didn't turn out quite so well.

"That's a sad excuse for a poem!" muttered Ignacio, after a rather harsh silence.

(Bullfighters, like our great poets of the seventeenth century, have never been particularly appreciative of or friendly toward professional colleagues. That commentary by this great *torero* of Sevilla confirmed what I already knew.)

I can proudly state that of all the members of my generation I was the first one to know Sánchez Mejías and become his close friend. Ignacio was not from a lower-class background, as the majority of bullfighters are. He was the son of a well-known doctor in Sevilla, and he had even attended high school for several years. But the typically Andalusian love he felt for the bulls had led him to practice his bull-fighting skills with other young enthusiasts in the open fields and pastures, and it was there that he came to know Joselito, his future brother-in-law, who eventually became one of the greatest bullfighters of all time. This is not the place to tell about his passionate and violent career in the bullring, a story that has already been excitingly told by José María de Cossío in his monumental treatise *Los toros*. I will only write about my personal relationship with Ignacio from that afternoon when we first met until the advent of the Republic.

What an extraordinary man and how intelligent he was! He was extremely sensitive to poetry, particularly our poetry which he loved and enthusiastically encouraged us to continue writing. He was a friend to us all.

> *Aire de Roma andaluza*
> *le doraba la cabeza . . .*

> *An aura of Andalusian Rome*
> *Gilded his head . . .*

was what García Lorca wrote in his "Lament" on Ignacio's death. In his physical appearance and in every other way, Ignacio was not an Andalusian gypsy, but belonged rather to the serious and sharply profiled Andalusian type often identified with the Sevilla existing in the days of the Roman Emperor Trajan. But in spite of his pensive air, he was usually very lively, witty, sarcastic and even a bit annoying with his frequent and sometimes infantile games. I have seen him take a home-made reed pea-shooter from his pocket and aim it at the legs of girls who were passing by in the streets, and then immediately hide the weapon as they turned to look in his direction.

Just like those men and boys who leap from the audience into the bullring to test their skill, Ignacio enthusiastically threw himself into our Gongoristic battles, becoming extremely fond of the "Soledades" and memorizing the most difficult and complicated arabesque verses of Don Luis. Shortly before the date of the tricentennial celebration, he called me to come to Sevilla. There was to be a gathering to commemorate the seventh anniversary of the tragic death of Joselito. From the train station he took me to a room at the Magdalena Hotel and, locking the door with a key, he warned me:

"You can't eat or drink until you write a poem dedicated to José. The celebration in his honor will take place tonight in the Cervantes Theater."

A few hours later I recovered my freedom by reading to Ignacio a work entitled "Joselito en su gloria" ("Joselito in His Glory"), composed of very simple quatrains that I later repeated at the celebration amidst the *olés* and applause of a frenetic audience composed of gypsies and bullfighting fans who had been devout followers of that young *torero*. A somewhat vulgar gentleman with a monocle, who was seated next to me, took part in this homage by presenting a flowery discourse. He was Felipe Sassone, a mediocre imitator of the most ridiculous plays by Benavente.

During my brief stay in Sevilla, I met the young poets who were affiliated with the poetry journal *Mediodía*. They were enthusiastic and even heroic in the face of the frivolous and fun-loving indifference that existed in the Andalusian capital. I can remember Collantes de Terán, Rafael Porlan y Merlo, Justo Sierra, Rafael Laffon, Romero Murube, all of them with their look of young Sevillian bullfighters, a poetic entourage, already experienced and talented fighters within that Spanish literary circle which was becoming wider and more beautiful by the day. Included in that group was also Adriano del Valle, a shipwrecked victim of *ultraísmo* who had now become a true devotee of brilliant *churrigueresco* gardens.

And there was Luis Cernuda.

Dark, thin, extremely refined and meticulous, he spoke very few words that day. (And even later, throughout the many years of our friendship, he remained a man of very few words.) I discovered that he was living on a street called the Calle del Aire (The Street of Air). What an extraordinary coincidence, considering the poet he already was and what he was to become in time! The Imprenta Sur in Málaga was preparing to publish his first book. The title? *Perfil del Aire (The Profile of a Breeze)*. No one could have painted a better portrait of him. We were already familiar with some of his poems, his *décimas* or his heptasyllabic strophes of an unusual linear perfection; unadorned purity, transparency. In the beginning, the critics tried to relate his poetry to that of Jorge Guillén. But soon those who searched for similarities found themselves frustrated and disappointed. Cernuda had opened his eyes for the first time on the Calle

239

del Aire, and his own personal air, even though it was caged behind the delicate wires of his *décimas,* awakened, in its flight, vibrations and music of the South which were very different from the sounds created by the Castilian poet. Floating on the breezes that issued from that crevice which constituted the Calle del Aire, this poet from Sevilla was one day going to reach the very heart of a dreamlike world where he would find the gentle and melancholy strains of another poet, also from Sevilla, Gustavo Adolfo Bécquer. And for a time Cernuda was to live in the shadow of Bécquer as a sleepless resident of oblivion. There had never been in the city of Sevilla a poet more "universal and Andalusian," to quote the words used by Juan Ramón Jiménez to describe himself.

Another poet—"the very greatest!"—was introduced to me by Ignacio that very afternoon of my arrival. I was in my hotel room.

"Come in, Don Fernando."

A somewhat stocky, strongly built individual, bull-like in stance, filled the door frame and then walked toward me, his arm outstretched to shake my hand.

"Here he is: Don Fernando Villalón Daóiz, the best new poet of all Andalusia."

Fernando Villalón, who was cracking the bones of my fingers as he squeezed them between his own, laughed at the way his friend had introduced him. Actually, he was a very well-known rancher of Sevilla, a breeder of brave bulls, a kind of sorcerer, spiritualist, hypnotizer and also the Count of Miraflores de los Angeles—but an incipient poet as well.

Fernando and I became friends immediately, both of us tremendously excited by our mutual familiarity with the same vivid landscapes bordering the Bay of Cádiz, the salt-flats of San Fernando, the wineries of Jerez and the Puerto. Being so physically close to all those places, why shouldn't we take a trip? And after two days of authentically wild drinking filled with expressions of enthusiasm for our Lower Andalusia, we took off, without even packing suitcases, in an absurd little automobile driven by Villalón himself. We headed for the Puerto de Santa María to visit the San Luis Gonzaga School where we had both been students some twenty years earlier, as had Juan Ramón Jiménez. What a frighteningly amusing excursion that was, since Fernando not only took his hands off the wheel while he explained his literary projects to me, but he would often stop the car suddenly and grab a wooden pole he had on the back seat. Leaving me there alone in the middle of the highway, he'd run off through the fields in pursuit of a wild hare! I swore to him that I would go back to Sevilla by train.

Fernando was an extraordinarily cultured and pleasant human being. A son of that romantic and feudal Andalusia, he would often sit beneath the olive trees and break bread with the workers in the fields. Very much a man of the people, his inseparable friends were the foremen who watched over his bulls, gypsies, stable boys, the variegated staff of employees who worked his ranches, and any young, budding bullfighter who might invade his pastureland. When I met him he was already on the verge of bankruptcy. His absolutely poetic way of doing business had ruined him financially, plunging him into a situation bordering on poverty. If Villalón was, as I myself discovered, exactly the way people described him—a unique and extraordinary individual—this reputation was not based on the few works he had written, but on his fantastic way of life and his strange personality. His real poetic vocation had not surfaced to any serious degree until he was well into his forties. It was for this reason that Sánchez Mejías had introduced him to me without any trace of irony as a new poet. His most recent poetic outburst had just unexpectedly appeared in a first book of poems published under the title *Andalucía la Baja (Lower Andalusia)*.

"That Fernando is really something! Imagine writing little poems at his age!"

Those envious street-corner gossips, those who admired him without really understanding him—all Sevilla, that is—were scandalized at the time of my arrival there by the "rancher's latest act of madness," which had the effect of reviving other either real or imagined incidents in his life that were told, retold, embellished and completely deformed as they went from mouth to mouth, flowing down the Guadalquivir.

It was said that his ideal goal as a breeder of brave bulls was to succeed in coming up with a fighting bull with green eyes, and that in order to hunt for sweet-water Nereids he had exchanged his magnificent olive groves for a deserted, flat and sandy inlet located in the delta of the Guadalquivir River, a kind of barren little island that disappeared totally when the tide came in. It was also said that in order to experience Nirvana, he had lived for more than six months in a dark cellar accompanied by a goat and a frog, eating only small quantities of vegetables. When we passed through the town of Cuervo, a small village on the way to the Puerto, Fernando himself told me that a curse had caused all the fountains of the town to run dry and that on the afternoon this happened, black dogs with white heads appeared on the horizon and howled all night long until the coming of dawn. People also said —but what *didn't* they say about Villalón in all those cities and villages? He also told me about his magical tricks which helped him to discover lost paintings by Murillo. He would buy any old canvas he saw, because with only a simple glance he could tell that under the first layer of paint was hidden another work created by that famous and popular painter of Sevilla. But the results of these discoveries which he showed to me in his house were nothing more than mediocre paintings dealing with religious themes and partially destroyed by the various acids he had used to clean them. Some of them were actually punched full of holes.

He was planning to write at that time a kind of history of bullfighting which he would call *From Geryon to Belmonte*, since he affirmed that the first known bullfighter was Hercules, who stole brave bulls from the mythical king of Tartessos, the name the ancients had given to Andalusia. Fernando insisted in propounding the most extraordinary theories which were always refuted by Ignacio during long hours of discussion. I witnessed these verbal battles on several occasions, and I assure you they were extremely serious and often ended badly. Like the time when the rancher-poet insisted on demonstrating to Sánchez Mejías that the Three Wise Kings of the Orient in their trip to Bethlehem to pay homage to the newborn Christ Child had first passed through Cádiz, something which Ignacio would not accept. As a result of this dispute, their close friendship almost came to a sad end.

When, a short time after the publication of *Andalucía la Baja*, this Count of Miraflores de los Angeles published his *Romances del 800 (Ballads of the 800)*, he became totally integrated, due to his marvelous power of assimilation and his poetic talents, into the new and ever-expanding poetic generation.

When I returned to Madrid around the middle of May, Góngora was on fire. We already had the names of those who had enlisted in the cause, the poets who had been invited to collaborate in the special issue of *Litoral* to be published in Málaga. They were Aleixandre, Altolaguirre, Adriano del Valle, Cernuda, Rogelio Buendía,

Pedro Garfias, Romero Murube, Moreno Villa, Juan Larrea, Hinojosa, Prados, Quiroga, Pla, and others, as well as the original group of organizers. Antonio Machado was included in the list, although he never actually did keep his promise. Three great poets who refused in writing to participate in this homage were Don Miguel de Unamuno, Don Ramón del Valle-Inclán, and Juan Ramón Jiménez. Manuel Machado and Ramón de Basterra did not even bother to answer our invitation. Of the prose authors who had agreed to collaborate—Miró, Marichalar Espina, Jarnés, Ramón G. de la Serna, Fernández Almagro, Giménez Caballero, Alfonso Reyes and others—original manuscripts were received only from José María de Cossío and César Arconada. It was obvious that this part of our project was a complete flop. Like the bad example set by the three important poets mentioned above, there were others who did not bother to reply: Pérez de Ayala, Ortega y Gasset, Fernando Vela and Eugenio D'Ors. However, art work was contributed by Picasso, Juan Gris, Togores, Dalí, Palencia, Bores, Moreno Villa, Cossío, Peinado, Ucelay, Fenosa, Angeles Ortiz and Gregorio Prieto. Two well-known composers, Manuel de Falla and Oscar Esplá, had completed their testimonial contributions, using texts from the work of Don Luis. Falla composed the *Sonnet to Córdoba* for chorus and harp, and Esplá's work for voice and piano was entitled the *Epitalamio de las Soledades.* Neither the Halffter brothers nor Adolfo Salazar lived up to their commitments. The non-Spanish composers, Ravel and Prokofieff, who had planned to join us, were never even heard from. This was a great disappointment.

This is probably the moment to reproduce one of those negative replies, actually the only one that I, as secretary of the group, did *not* receive, since its author had published it in the first installment of his *Diario poético (Poetic Diary)*, a work then in progress. Unfortunately, the letter from Unamuno and the oversized postcard from Valle-Inclán were lost during the Civil War. I can more or less remember the general tone of Don Miguel's reply, which he sent to me from Hendaye during his exile in the south of France. He expressed his feelings of incompatibility with the aesthetics of the poet from Córdoba, whom he violently criticized for his lack of humanity, his coldness and his Latinate pedantry. In his letter, Unamuno then suddenly diverted his anti-Gongoristic sentiments and launched into a terrible diatribe against Primo de Rivera (the dictator who was responsible for Don Miguel's expulsion from Spain), calling him "a camel in heat" and a series of other only slightly less vicious names. The message from Valle-Inclán was more insolent and less rational, a rather absurd reaction from a Gongorist such as he, although his Gongorism had been somewhat subdued as a result of his submersion in the calming waters of Rubén Darío. I do not know if Gerardo Diego still has copies of these letters. Luckily, Juan Ramón's reply is available, since it was published by Diego in his *Centennial Chronicle*. It is an example of one of the sharpest and most revealing shots fired during that famous battle.

Note in Opposition
Madrid, February 17, 1927

My dear Alberti:

Bergamín spoke to me yesterday about the Góngora affair. The general tone and coverage which Gerardo Diego wishes to give to this matter sponsored by the *"Revista de Desoriente"** has had the effect of dampening any enthusiasm I might have had for participation. Góngora needs a more disciplined and firmer director who knows what he is doing, and certainly there is no need for gratuitous provincial ideas which consider themselves, poor things, to be universal truths. You and Bergamín undoubtedly understand what I mean.

Yours truly,
K.Q.X.

Amusing, but annoying, since this K.Q.X.—and here I copy the exact words from Gerardo's *Chronicle*—"is Juan Ramón Jiménez himself, according to his own confession, although the seriousness of those accusations contained in the note do not seem to me to be congruent with the playfulness of signing in code. However, what else

*"*Revista de desoriente*" is a pun on the *Revista de Occidente (Occidental Review)*, edited by Ortega y Gasset, which had incurred Juan Ramón's disfavor by allowing Alberti, Gerardo Diego and their friends to use it for their tribute to Góngora. *Oriente* in Spanish means "east," while *occidente* means "west." Jiménez is implying that the editors of the journal were misguided or disoriented in this instance.

can we do but go along with him and, searching for a reasonable and conciliatory interpretation, we will call him for the time being Kuan Qamón Ximénez, a particularly delightful name."

Juan Ramón was bored during that period of this life by having to live alone in his attic apartment, frantically tangling and untangling his Complete Works, and hardly in contact at all with the world outside. He would hear occasional rumors about what was happening out there through the comings and goings of a few acquaintances, but he was beginning to be tired of everything, including us—his most faithful friends—and this fatigue had spread to the initials of his own name, J.R.J., which he exchanged during those days of Gongoristic exaltation, and not without a certain amount of Andalusian wit, for K.Q.X. I once heard him say that these were "the three ugliest letters in the alphabet."

Naturally, Gerardo's response to Kuan Qamón Ximénez arrived "addressed to Alberti and in all seriousness," but only after the excitement of the Góngora homage had already died down, due to the fact that K.Q.X. did not publish his reply to our invitation until late in 1927 although he had dated it in February.

I quote below, and in its entirety, the letter from Gerardo in which certain things are clarified.

Note in Favor
Madrid, December 3, 1927

My dear friend Rafael:

I have read today the note in opposition which K.Q.X. offered to me through you. I would like to rectify two historical errors which I have noticed in the text and I would like these corrections to appear in the *Centennial Chronicle*. The general tone and organization of the homage to Don Luis was, as everyone but K.Q.X. already knows, agreed upon by several colleagues, that is, by the six people who signed the invitation and by many others. All this is already mentioned in my scrupulously truthful *Chronicle*. The *Revista de Occidente* simply served as our publisher, and therefore the Góngora affair has no other relationship with this journal than one of gratitude to them for having kindly offered to print whatever we sent to them with no conditions attached. Therefore, the condemnation directed at me in that brief note should be shared equally by you, Salinas, Lorca, Bergamín, Dámaso, etc. I have done nothing more, as you all know, than encourage you to work and to submit for your approval a general editorial plan. If this deserves condemnation by K.Q.X., I accept it with pleasure, knowing that all you other sinners are in this thing with me. As for the rest—you and Bergamín undoubtedly know by this time what I mean—we have already sufficiently discussed K.Q.X.'s lamentable attitude.

Your good friend,
Gerardo

This is perhaps the most unpleasant memory I have of the Centennial celebration, since it relates to Juan Ramón. There were other incidents, but they were of a journalistic nature and concerned *La Gaceta Literaria* and its editor, the aspiring fascist Ernesto Giménez Caballero, and also the newspaper *El Liberal* because of an article written by an old ex-*ultraísta*, López Parra, which described an intentionally disruptive scandal that had been organized by that same Giménez Caballero. The issue in this case was a Requiem Mass that had been celebrated in the church of the Salesas Reales for the soul of Don Luis, a soul that was undoubtedly roaming the infernal regions.

As for pleasant and enjoyable memories, there are many of them. Among others, I will mention the "auto-da-fe" in which we condemned to flames the works of some of Góngora's most conspicuous enemies both among the ancients and our own contemporaries: Lope de Vega, Quevedo, Luzán, Hermosilla, Moratín, Campoamor, Cejador, Hurtado y Palencia, Valle-Inclán, etc. On that night of the 23rd of May there was a "water" show against the walls of the Royal Academy. Indelible wreaths of uric acid colored most of them yellow. I had stored up my own supply all day long and I was able to write the name of Alemany—the author of *Góngora's Vocabulary* —on one of the sidewalks. Astrana Marín, a critic who attacked Don Luis almost daily while at the same time directing his anger against us, received his just deserts when we sent to his house, on the morning of that special day, a beautiful wreath of alfalfa into which had been woven four horseshoes and, as if that weren't enough, we had affixed to it a *décima* by Dámaso Alonso whose first four lines are all I can remember at the moment:

Mi señor Don Luis Astrana,
miserable criticastro,
tú que comienzas en astro
para terminar en rana . . .

[These four verses constitute an untranslatable play on words based on the name of this critic, Astrana. *Astro* means *star* and *rana* is the word for *frog*. After calling Don Luis a miserable critic (using the rather insulting suffix *astro* to denigrate him even more), an attack is made on his name. "You who begin as a star *(astro)*/ only to end up as a frog *(rana)*.]

As can be seen, our generation was not all that solemn. Not even the most proper members of the group, such as Salinas, Guillén, Cernuda or Aleixandre were stuffy types. (Naturally, these poets were not precisely the ones who had participated in the fluvial act perpetrated against the walls of the Academy.) Times had changed. We were no longer looking for ascetic leaders. And although Juan Ramón Jiménez, with his imposing beard, was in some way such a type, our respect for him never reached the point of idolatry. This sense of happy independence could be clearly seen in *Lola,* the charming and noisy supplement to the journal *Carmen.* And so, in that banner which we unfurled in the wind to honor and defend Góngora, each one of us displayed our own sovereign heraldic symbols alongside our mutual oath of allegiance to the great poet. We would not submit to anyone, not even to Góngora himself, once the battle had been won.

The fact that the poetry of that hook-nosed and dangerous beast from Córdoba happened, many centuries later, to coincide with some aspects of our own work, and that the date of his tricentennial had come at the right moment in our lives, should not suggest that we were even vaguely under his vassalage. The Gongoristic contagion was not only deliberate, but temporary. It did not extend beyond the year in which the homage took place. The most visible traces remained in the poetry of Gerardo and in my own work, and this was nothing to be ashamed of. But when I was finishing the last stanzas of my "Tercera Soledad (paráfrasis incompleta)" ("Third Solitude [Incomplete Paraphrase]") in honor of Don Luis, the wings of the first poems of my *Sobre los Angeles (Concerning the Angels),* were beginning to flash in the darkened heavens of my bedroom. For

247

that reason, when my dear friend Pablo Neruda, in writing about Lorca, affirmed that he "was perhaps the only poet over whom the shadow of Góngora did not spread the sheet of ice that in 1927 had the effect of sterilizing the great youthful poetry of Spain," I sincerely believe that he is mistaken. The example of Góngora did not sterilize anyone. On the contrary, our entire generation emerged from that necessary vindicating struggle even stronger and with more clearly defined goals.

Some aspects of that victorious battle can be seen through the following list of accomplishments: Dámaso Alonso's edition of the *Soledades*, an extraordinary work which continues to be studied; the *Romances* under the editorship of Cossío; and the *Poetic Anthology in Honor of Góngora*, with a prologue by Gerardo Diego. The other volumes, which were to be edited by Salinas, Guillén, Artigas and Alfonso Reyes, unfortunately were never published. But the most important results of this extravagant celebration of Góngora can be summed up by the words of Dámaso himself:

> The recent generations have been formed by reading and admiring the author of the *Soledades*. And much of this youthful enthusiasm has found its way into the body of the so-called 'official criticism.' It turns out to be almost amusing to compare what was said about Góngora in the literary manuals written before 1927 and what is being said now. The clarity and beauty of his poetry are now obvious and there is no need to see his work as a struggle against dilapidated fortresses and excessively outmoded armaments.

And nevertheless, nevertheless, it may be that the genial poet of Córdoba will soon revert back to being the Angel of Darkness and be forced to struggle again—this is his intermittent and hidden punishment—to reach the light. But in the meantime, may the lesson—I should say the example—of Góngora continue to awaken each morning within every one of us. In opposition to the repetitious and facile techniques of the present moment with its almost anonymous type of free verse, against false and prefabricated hermetic poetry, against sloppiness and lack of enthusiasm, against the senseless noise created by so many loquacious quacks, let the hand of Don Luis be seen again with its vigorous and demanding sense of discipline. Let us never have to be forced to plead with anguish as did the magnifi-

248

cent and unfulfilled poet Guillaume Apollinaire when he addressed his future critics:

> *Be indulgent with me when you compare me*
> *with those who were perfection and order.*

What a great year—1927! Variegated, fertile, happy, amusing, contradictory, especially for me, since I was almost on the verge of becoming a bullfighter when for the second time my health began to give me trouble, and I felt within me the first signs that a terrible storm was brewing. My friendship with Sánchez Mejías was reaching a dangerous stage. He stubbornly insisted that I become a member of his retinue in the ring. Was that a joke? Perhaps. But Ignacio's obstinacy began to worry me. So that I might become accustomed to seeing bulls at close range, he sent me a telegram from Sevilla asking me to go to Badajoz in whose bullring I would make my debut by participating in the preliminary entrance parade and then, wearing my *traje de luces,** I could then watch the fight from behind the *barrera,* or protective fence. Naturally, I never did go. He was very angry with me, and my failure to appear made him double his efforts to have his way and satisfy this capricious idea of his. Ignacio was ferocious when he decided to do something, and it was almost impossible to keep out of his way.

And so with his *idée fixe* that I was to become a bullfighter, he managed to get me into the ring one afternoon in Pontevedra where Ignacio appeared on the program together with the bullfighters Cagancho and Márquez and where the Portuguese Simao da Veiga performed as *rejoneador.** From his seat close to the front row, José María de Cossío witnessed this strange event. To top it all, in the midst of those *toreros,* dressed in their gold and silver outfits, I was the only one wearing a black and orange suit, a suit of mourning which Ignacio had kept since the tragic death of his brother-in-law Joselito. Trying to hold in my belly-button, I paraded around the ring accompanied by the sounds of *pasodobles** and the echoing

---

*The *traje de luces* ("suit of lights:") is the spangled and glittering costume worn by bullfighters. *Rejoneador* is a bullfighter who fights the bull while mounted on horseback. *Pasadoble* is a type of marching music which is traditionally heard at bullfights, particularly during the opening parade or grand entrance of the *matadores* and their assistants. It is also a popular dance step.

trumpets. Afterwards—oh! When the first horned creature, huge and baffled, made his charge and passed alongside the boards and my chest, I understood the astronomical distance that separates a man seated before a sonnet and another standing exposed beneath the sun and facing that sea, that blind limitless lightning-bolt that a bull becomes when he is released from the bullpen. Luckily, the public in Galicia was not at all like the fans in Andalusia or Madrid who demand their pint of blood, and I was able to remain unnoticed behind the barrier throughout the entire spectacle. After leaving the bullring, I cut off my *coleta*—that is, I considered my bullfighting career to be over. It had only lasted three hours.

Ignacio, that very afternoon, also unexpectedly retired from bullfighting, having announced his decision to Cossío when he dedicated the last bull to him. "I dedicate this bull to you," he said, "which will be the last one I will ever kill." Ignacio abandoned his courageous career to become involved in another one where the gorings are occasionally even more severe. He was to exchange the arena for the stage—from a killer of brave bulls to playwright. A drama with the title *Sinrazón* (Unreason) that had been bubbling inside his head, would be performed for the first time the following year, but I will speak later about that particular evening.

The rumors about my taurine activities reached as far as Juan Ramón's apartment terrace. Ever since the Góngora affair, Jiménez had begun to sharpen his Andalusian knife and had already begun cutting with it here and there. "I have heard," he said, "that Alberti is involved with gypsies, *banderilleros* and other low-living types. There is no question that he has now become a lost soul." The commentary contained a certain amount of truth, but as for my perdition —here I sit, with fifteen or twenty books more to my credit, as I think back with a smile on what he said thirty years ago.

If it was bad that Juan Ramón considered me to have lost my way as a result of my association with Sánchez Mejías, it was much worse for him to have said the same thing about Federico García Lorca merely because he had begun writing for the stage, even though this was well in keeping with Lorca's obvious theatrical vocation which had been clearly apparent from the very beginning. Federico had made his debut as a young playwright some time ago when, with the helping hand of Martínez Sierra, he had presented at the Teatro Eslava his play *El maleficio de la mariposa (The Evil Spell of the Butterfly)*. This ingenuous, infantile little work was booed by the

audience who made jokes every time the characters in the play
—cockroaches and other insects—opened their mouths to speak. But
now the play to be performed was different, although it had also
been written years earlier. This was *Mariana Pineda*, a popular ballad in three scenes about the heroine of Granada who had sacrificed
herself for love and freedom.

In his excellent and extremely useful book, *Federico García Lorca y
su mundo (Federico García Lorca and His World)*, José Mora Guar-
nido, who was a very close friend of the poet, says that Martínez
Sierra himself was supposed to present this work, but under the
pretext of possible political complications that might ensue as a result
of the liberal tone of the play, he decided not to do so. "As a result,"
Pepe Mora was to tell me years later in Montevideo, "*Mariana
Pineda* seems to be a protest against the dictatorship of Primo de
Rivera, but it is not that at all." It was to be Margarita Xirgu, a
courageous, great and generous lady, who dared to put this play on
at a time when the frighteningly bearded Don Ramón del Valle-
Inclán had begun his duel to the death against the drunken sword of
the dictator. I was present at opening night. The old-timers and
members of the new generation were gathered, if my memory serves
me, in the Fontalba Theater. The place was buzzing with excitement.
Everyone feared the possibility that the performance would be prohibited by the authorities. The stage settings, executed by Salvador
Dalí and inspired by Federico's own sketches, were full of wit and
poetry. There was a long and significant ovation when Marianita,
already condemned to the gallows and abandoned by her lover, sang
out in favor of freedom as a real civil heroine. The following day
almost all the newspapers had favorable comments to make about
Federico's play, considering him to be a "young author who shows
great promise." We were delighted with his success. But Juan Ramón, alone on his terrace, was unhappy: "Lorca! Poor Lorca! He
is lost."

Years later and shortly after the opening of *Bodas de Sangre [Blood
Wedding]*, a work that he probably never even saw, Juan Ramón was
to say "that the play was simply a kind of operetta." He did not like
the idea that some of the young poets, who had come into being under his protective shadow, would devote themselves to the theater,
something that we understood very well and which would be easy
but boring to explain. When he found out that I was working on *La
pájara pinta (The Spotted Bird)* for the Podrecca Marionette Com-

251

pany, with music by Oscar Esplá (a work which, by the way, I never finished), he was also unhappy about that, since he felt I was just wasting my time. In that year of 1927, The Universal Andalusian, K.Q.X., or "He Who Is Tired of His Name," began to show clear signs that he was becoming a bit weary of us all. And the real battles began. At times they were caused by mere trifles, by boredom or by rather tyrannical demands of a literary nature that seemed capricious and unjust, but which nonetheless often created a situation that bordered on hysteria. The truth is that the real motives for those battles are still completely vague in my own mind; it is a secret that Juan Ramón carried with him to his grave. How could one explain that he would even be at odds with José Bergamín, the most enthusiastic and hyperbolic eulogist of his poetry, whom we considered to be his permanent private secretary? The break between these two men became definitive when Juan Ramón told Bergamín that he did not know how to use punctuation correctly and that he should only limit himself to writing aphorisms and forget about composing long prose works for which, according to Jiménez, he was not at all suited. And how can one explain his attitude toward such fine human beings as Salinas and Guillén, poets whom he enthusiastically praised at the beginning and then considered to be "blank rhetoricians," engineers, or something equally uncomplimentary—a great insult to their excellent poetry with its precise outlines and solid foundations, particularly in the case of Guillén? But he directed his strongest feelings of hatred at Gerardo Diego, whom he called a *loquitonto,** insulting at the same time Huidobro and Larrea, two very close friends of Gerardo. (The repeated criticisms of Neruda were to come much later.) What did Juan Ramón Jiménez really want? What was he afraid of? Was he perhaps worried that he would lose his baton and suddenly find himself alone, without his orchestra, making gestures in the air inside an empty hall? But in spite of everything he was still loved and admired from a distance. I myself saw him only infrequently after 1927, and even forgave him, although not always willingly, for his obviously unjust remarks.

Meanwhile, Ignacio Sánchez Mejías had come to know us all and almost always through the good offices of Cossío. His literary interests, which were becoming more well-defined each day through

Loquitonto is a Spanish expression that combines the words *loco* (crazy) and *tonto* (fool).

his relationship with us, had the effect of turning him into an ardent enthusiast of the new poetry, so that he encouraged his cattle-breeding friend, Fernando Villalón, to begin his poetic career even though he was over forty. With José Bergamín, who in those days was writing his *Arte de Birilibirloque (The Art of Magic)*, he had a special aphoristic-taurine relationship. In that strange and perceptive little treatise, Bergamín had formulated a theory of Spanish art and literature that was based on the most significant and contrary aspects of bullfighting—Joselito on one side and Belmonte on the other—an extraordinary theory elaborated with wit and ingenuity.

The luminous, classical and universal direction was embodied by Joselito; the more authentic, local and regional aspects were to be discovered in Belmonte. Examples to support this theory could be easily found; a painter and a poet who represented the first tendency were Picasso and Juan Ramón Jiménez. The second tendency could be seen in Zuloaga and Valle-Inclán. In that stirring up of an "anti-Belmontista" fire, Sánchez Mejías served as a somewhat energetic poker. What an unusual talent Ignacio had to immediately immerse himself in the most difficult part of a problem, to jump from something very serious to something else that was equally absurd and foolish! He was able to easily comprehend the modern schools of painting, the last Parisian "ism" that had just reached Madrid. He seemed to remember very little about his former life among the bulls, his glorious, courageous and golden afternoons in the bullrings throughout Spain and America. His friends were no longer people he had known before. Not even those aristocratic ladies who had always pursued him seemed to interest him any longer. He was not willing to split himself in two. He was now dedicated to one thing alone and would be faithful to it until his death.

Ignacio felt very much at ease with us, so much so that one day he shoved us all into a train and took us to Sevilla, to the Ateneo. He had arranged with the director, Eusebio Blasco Garzón—who died here in Buenos Aires after having served as the Argentinian Consul during the Civil War—for a series of readings and lectures to be given by the "seven avant-garde literary celebrities from Madrid," as we were called in the newspaper *El Sol*, or "the brilliant Pléiade," to quote from an article in a local paper that celebrated our arrival. This luminous constellation was composed of Bergamín, Chabás, Diego, Dámaso Alonso, Guillén, García Lorca, and me. The most amusing thing that happened during this trip was the composition of a sonnet decicated to Dámaso Alonso in which we all collaborated. The sonnet contained such unusual verses as the following:

Nunca junto se vió tanto pandero
menendezpidalino y acueducto.

Never before had there been joined together
So many menendezpidalian chatterers and an aqueduct.

[The adjective "menendezpidalian" refers to the Spanish scholar Ramón Menéndez Pidal (1869–1969) whose exhaustive investigations on Spain's medieval period and on the *Poem of the Cid* are remarkable achievements of erudition.]

Those evening sessions at the Ateneo were extremely successful. The inhabitants of Sevilla are a noisy bunch, given to exaggeration, and the audience cheered Guillén's difficult *décimas* as if they were beautifully executed passes performed by a *torero* in the bullring. Federico and I alternately read the most complicated fragments from Góngora's *Soledades*, to the accompaniment of enthusiastic interruptions from the audience. But the moment of uncontrollable delirium occurred when Lorca recited part of his *Gypsy Ballads*, which had not yet been published. People waved their handkerchiefs in the air as if they had just witnessed a superb performance in the ring, and the Andalusian poet Adriano del Valle put the finishing touches to his reading by standing up in his seat and tossing his jacket, his collar and his tie to Federico, in an act of uncontrollable frenzy.

During this trip García Lorca met Fernando Villalón, "the best new poet of Andalusia" according to Ignacio's usual introduction. The two poets became close friends almost immediately; it was a clear case of mutual admiration. One afternoon Villalón invited Federico and me to take a ride through the city. The three of us rode together through its intricate streets, a dangerous and delicate labyrinth of twistings and turnings which we maneuvered in that incredible car with which I had become achingly familiar on our trip to the Puerto. I will never forget the look of fright on poor Lorca's face, since his fear of automobiles was even greater than mine. Villalón raced through the streets, his hand on the horn, as if he were performing in the bullring with a display of *verónicas* and other bullfighting passes directed against the terrified pedestrians, while at the

same time he explained to us his future poem—"El Kaos"*—reciting the first stanzas of this work with his hands not even touching the
steering wheel.

That same night there was a party in Pino Montano, the beautiful
home of Sánchez Mejías on the outskirts of the city. The first thing
Ignacio did when we arrived was to disguise us all as Moors, wrapping us in thick Moroccan *chilabas*, an outfit that had the effect of
keeping us bathed in sweat until dawn. We didn't look like members
of the retinue of a royal caliph, but rather part of the chorus in some
popular operetta, and the most frightening-looking Moor of all was
Bergamín. Juan Chabás, on the contrary, looked almost authentic
and in character. We drank quite a bit that night, and from the
depths of those infernal garments we recited our poetry. Dámaso
Alonso amazed everyone by reciting from memory all one thousand
ninety-one verses from Gongora's *Primera Soledad*. Federico performed some of his spontaneous theatrical inventions that always
made us laugh, and Fernando Villalón, with my help, conducted several hypnotic experiments.

When that Arabic festival was on the verge of becoming uncon-
trollably wild and absurd, with drunken poets scattered everywhere,
Ignacio announced the arrival of the guitarist Manuel Huelva who
was accompanied by Manuel Torres, the "Niño de Jerez," one of the
true geniuses of the *cante jondo*. After a few rounds of manzanilla
sherry, the gypsy began to sing, gripping us all through his voice, his
gestures and the poetic lyrics of his song. His voice sounded like the
harsh cry of a wounded animal, a terrible well of anguish. But apart
from the sound, what was truly amazing were the words themselves,
the strange poetic verses of those *"soleares"* and *"siguiriyas"* with
their complicated arabesque structure and concepts.

"Where do those words come from?" he was asked.

"I invent some of them and I hunt for others."

"By the way," said Ignacio, "why don't you sing the one you call
'Las placas de Egito' ('The Plates of Egypt')?"*

Without giving us any time to react to such a weird title, Manuel

*The correct spelling in Spanish for the English word "chaos" is *caos*.

*The popular speech of Andalusia tends to simplify pronunciation by dropping cer-
tain consonants between vowels or when followed by other consonants. In this case
the Spanish "Egipto" becomes simply "Egito."

Torres burst out in a strange song that had been totally created by him. When he finished, and after a brief but emotional silence, we asked him to explain to us how this work had come into being.

With serious simplicity, the gypsy told us the following story:

"One night some friends of mine sent for me. I went, but in spite of their encouragement and no matter how much I drank, I couldn't get into the mood to sing that night. The little I did sing came out very badly; I just wasn't in the mood, and my voice showed it. Feeling very sad and disturbed, I walked alone through the streets without knowing what I was doing. As I was strolling along the Alameda de Hércules, I stopped in front of one of those outside stands that had been put up for the fair and began to listen to the sounds coming from a record-player someone had set up there. The plates turned round and round, and there was a song that told the story of some Egyptian Pharaoh. I continued on my way home with all that music swimming around in my head. When I was crossing the Triana Bridge, my voice suddenly cleared up and I began to sing what you have all just heard: "Las placas de Egito." ' "

We were almost speechless as it dawned on us that what this superb *cantaor* had heard coming from the phonograph (and Ignacio was to corroborate all this later) were records, which many people in those days called *placas* or plates, of the operetta *La Corte de Faraón (The Pharaoh's Court)*, very popular in Spain at that time. And what all of us had logically thought were probably the plagues of Egypt were for Manuel Torres "the plates." The gypsy had, in effect, followed in the tradition of popular art often composed out of ignorance or memory lapses which later become magnificent artistic creations. In this case, a new work of *cante jondo* had been born that did not bear even the slightest resemblance to its absurd model.

Manuel Torres did not know how to read or write, he only knew how to sing. But his consciousness of being a *cantaor* was admirable. That very night, with the confidence and wisdom one might expect in a Góngora or a Mallarmé if they had been asked about their aesthetic principles, Manuel told us in his own way that he never allowed himself to be carried away by the ordinary, the overly familiar or what others had done before, and he finally summed up his own thoughts with these masterful words: "In *cante jondo*," he whispered in his raspy voice, his strong, sturdy hands resting on his knees, "what one has always to look for and find is the black trunk of the Pharaoh." In some strange way he had come to the same conclusion as Baudelaire when he tells Death, the captain of his voyage, how he wishes to plunge: *Au fond de l'inconnu pour trouver du nouveau!*

The black trunk of the Pharaoh!

As was to be expected, of all those present it was Federico who was most overwhelmed by the emotional tone of the *cantaor* from Jerez, and he was almost frantic in the way he encouraged the singer to go on. No one on that magical and delirious night in Sevilla had found more applicable words to describe what García Lorca sought and discovered in the gypsy world of Andalusia and which he ignited through his ballads and songs. When in 1931 this poet from Granada published his *Poema del cante jondo*, written several years before, the following dedication appeared in the section entitled "Viñetas flamencas": "To Manuel Torres, 'Niño de Jerez,' who possesses the Pharaoh's trunk." The words of that great gypsy had remained fixed in his memory.

Our trip to Sevilla ended with the coronation of Dámaso Alonso in the Venta de Antequera. During the course of the banquet, Antúnez, a witty figure of the kind one only finds among Andalusians, appeared on the scene to entertain the guests. At the end of his absolutely surrealistic speech, he placed on Dámaso's shining head a green laurel wreath which, according to Gerardo Diego's chronicle describing this event (*Lola*, no. 5) "was cut from a nearby tree by the expert and particularly suitable hands of Ignacio Sánchez Mejías." This was a festival of friendship, of frivolity, of wit and poetry, in which could still be heard what were perhaps the last echoes of our battle in defense of Góngora.

Upon my return to Madrid, internal storm clouds would cause me to lose myself for a time in darkness and then become intricately caught up in those harsh, desperate and disconcerting final years before the inauguration of the Republic.

CHAPTER *VII*

*I am writing this new chapter in my new house at Pueyrredón
2471, Apartment 9A. It has been some time since I abandoned my
former residence in Las Heras and my poor little garden with
its poinsettia bushes, which was becoming progressively more
somber as tall and horrendous buildings began to close in around it.
I now live surrounded by light, above the beautiful trees of the
Plaza de Francia and where in the distance I can see the immense
river, the movement of trains, the loading cranes, the ships and the
flashing brilliance of planes shooting across the sky. I can breathe
again. The sun shines on my forehead and I can work happily.*

WHAT SHADOWY SWORD had almost
insensibly cut me off from the light, from the marmoreal form of my
earlier poetry, from the not yet distant song springing as it did from
popular sources, from my ships, inlets and salt flats? Why was I now
in that well of darkness, that obscure pit where I would thrash about
violently, almost in a state of agony, as I searched for a way that
would lead me to inhabitable surfaces, to the fresh air of life?

*Contra mí, mundos enteros,
contra mí, dormido,
maniatado, indefenso.*

258

Against me, worlds immense.
Against me, asleep,
Handcuffed, with no defense.

I could not sleep, the roots of my hair and my nails ached as I drowned in a sea of yellow bile, biting my pillow in an attempt to overcome the pulsating pain. How many real things in the semi-darkness had been pushing me in that direction, making me fall into that deep precipice like a crackling bolt of lightning! An impossible love that had been bruised and betrayed during moments of confident surrender; the most rabid feelings of jealousy which would not let me sleep and caused me to coldly contemplate a calculated crime during the long sleepless nights; the sad shadow of a friend who had committed suicide pounded against my brain like the mute ringing of bells. Unconfessed envy and hate struggled for expression, only to explode like a bomb buried deep beneath the ground. With empty pockets that could not even warm my hands, I took interminable and directionless strolls in the wind, the rain, and the heat. My family remained silent or indifferent in the presence of this terrible struggle that was reflected on my face and in my very being, wandering like a somnambulant through the rooms of our house and coming to rest occasionally on street benches. Waves of infantile fears that created even greater pangs of conscience, doubt, fears of hell, somber echoes from that Jesuit school on the shores of the Bay of Cádiz where I had loved and suffered; my displeasure with my earlier work; my sense of panic which urged me on, leaving me no time to concentrate on anything nor allowing me a moment of respite—all this and more, contradictory, inexplicable, labyrinthine. What was I to do? How was I to speak or shout or give form to that web of emotions in which I was caught? How could I stand up straight once again and extricate myself from those catastrophic depths into which I had sunk, submerging and burying myself more and more in my own ruins, covering myself in my own rubble, feeling my insides to be torn and splintered? And then there was a kind of angelic revelation—but not from the corporeal, Christian angels found in all those beautiful paintings and religious icons, but angels representing irresistible forces of the spirit who could be molded to conform to my darkest and most secret mental states. I released them in waves on the world, a blind reincarnation of all the cruelty, desolation, terror and even at times the goodness that existed inside of me but was also encircling me from without.

I had lost a paradise, the Eden of those early years: my happy, bright and carefree youth. I suddenly found myself cut off from my past without the consolation of those soothing shades of blue. My state of health had again taken a turn for the worse, and I felt a deep sense of emptiness. I began to withdraw from my friends, from the café *tertulias*, the Residencia, and even from the city itself. An inhabitant of darkness, I began to write blindly at any hour of the night without turning on the light in my room and with a kind of undesirable automatism, spurred on by a trembling, feverish and spontaneous urging that had the effect of making the separate verses of poetry literally smother each other so that it was often impossible for me to decipher them the following day. My language became harsh and cutting, as sharply honed as the blade of a sword. The rhythmic cadences crumbled into bits and pieces. Each angel appeared first as a spark and was then swept up in columns of smoke, into funnels of ashes and clouds of dust. But what I wrote was not all that obscure, and the most confused and nebulous thoughts took on the shape and reptilian movement of a flame-colored snake. External reality became woven into my own state of mind and shook the walls of my hideaway with tremendous force, causing me to hurl into the streets a stream of maddened lava: I was like a comet forecasting future catastrophes. No one accompanied me in my illness. I was totally alone.

This change in me did not go unnoticed, and there were rumors that I had become an unpleasant poet: inconsiderate, fork-tongued and completely intolerable. I envied and despised those who had been more successful. Almost all of them seemed happy: some were living off their family's money, others had careers that allowed them to live in peace—teachers, visiting professors at universities throughout the world, government employees or travel agents . . . As for me, what had I done with my life? I hadn't even graduated from high school. I was the proverbial black sheep, shunned by my own family, forced to go everywhere on foot, tossed like a leaf swept along by the wind and with the rain seeping through the torn soles of my shoes. I wanted to find work, to do something other than write. I even asked several architect friends of mine for a job as a bricklayer, but no one would take such a suggestion seriously. They saw this as some kind of a bad joke or my way of attracting attention. And nevertheless I insisted: a well-digger, janitor, the most menial or demeaning kind of work they could find. . . . I had to escape from that cave filled with demons, with long hours of insomnia and nightmares. It was then that José María de Cossío invited me to spend a few days with him at his old country estate in Tudanca. We arrived there one rainy night on horseback, guided by the light of a lantern we were carrying as we rode along the swollen creeks battered by the gusty winds.

In Tudanca, a town of about forty houses, we lived alone surrounded by the poor local peasants and receiving afternoon visits from the priest and the teacher, a thin, witty and intelligent old man. The house was a beautiful building constructed of wood and stone. It had a good library, monastery chairs and open hearth chimneys to protect us from the long winter with its penetratingly cold winds. The sun-porch opened out onto a small flower garden and fruit orchard. Although it was spring, we were grateful for the morning sun that rose up from behind the mountains after winning its hand-to-hand battle with the mist. That porch was where I decided to work. There I sat, reading or writing while Carlotta, a pretty peasant girl who helped around the house, would move in circles around me, sneaking glances at me from behind the trees. She was shy and easily frightened, though there were many mornings when she would awaken me by tossing garbanzo beans like soft bullets on my bed from a crack in the ceiling of my bedroom. But during the day Carlotta was like a skittish deer who shied away from any attempt to hunt her down.

Feeling somewhat relaxed, I was able to compose additional poems for my book. The dark clouds over the mountains, the battle of the winds, known by the inhabitants of that solitary region as the *Abrego* and *Gallego*, furnished me with new angels for my poetry. It was there in Tudanca that the short, controlled and concentrated verse line I had been writing gradually became longer and more in keeping with the movement of my imagination in those days. I wrote my "Tres recuerdos del cielo" ("Three Remembrances of Heaven"), the first spontaneous homage by any member of my generation to the memory of Gustavo Adolfo Bécquer. (There were to be others, but they were to come much later.)

But unexpectedly I laid aside those wings and that darkness and composed an ode to a football player by the name of Platko, a heroic goal-keeper in an important game between the Real Club of San Sebastián and the team from Barcelona that took place in Santander on May 20, 1928. I had gone to watch the game with Cossío. It was a brutal affair, with the Cantabrian Sea in the background and another sea of Basques and Catalans watching from the stands. It was football, but it was also a game of pure regionalism. The violence displayed by the Basques was unbelievable. Platko, a gigantic Hungarian goalie, defended the Catalan goalposts like a bull. There were injuries, clubbings by the Civil Guard and people dashing everywhere. At one desperate moment Platko was attacked so furiously by the players of the Real that he was covered with blood and lost consciousness a few feet from his position, but with his arms still wrapped around the ball. In the midst of applause and shouts of protest, he was lifted onto the shoulders of his fans and carried off the field. Since he had to be replaced by a substitute, the rest of his teammates immediately suffered a lowering of morale. But when the game was drawing to a close, Platko appeared once again, strong and handsome with his head all bandaged up but apparently willing to let himself be killed. The reaction of the Barcelona team was immediate. Within a few seconds the winning goal was scored against the Basques, who then abandoned the field, accompanied by the anger of many and the disillusioned applause of their fans. That night, at the hotel, we celebrated with the Catalans. Everyone sang "El Segador"* and waved separatist banners. And one individual who had accompanied Cossío and me during the game sang Argentinian tangos in a most professional and charming way: he was Carlos Gardel.

Very early that same morning we left with him for Palencia. It was a short, pleasant, and enjoyable excursion. Gardel was an innocent, affectionate and healthy human being. He took delight in whatever he saw or heard. Our ride through the streets of the city was deafening. The names of the shop-owners were particularly fascinating to us; they were primitive names that recalled the Christian martyrs of Roman and Visigothic times. Without being able to hold back our laughter we read such things as "Lace Shop of Hubilibrordo González," "The Café of Genciamo Gómez," "The Eutimio Bustamante Department Store," and this one in particu-

---

El Segador is a Catalan song which celebrates the War of Reapers (1640) in which men disguised as reapers, and pretending to participate in a harvest festival, began a revolt against the Spanish Monarchy.

lar—"Cojoncio Pérez Spare Parts"*—a happy, brief and unforget-table trip. Months later in Madrid I received a card from Gardel postmarked in Buenos Aires. He sent me a warm embrace and his best regards to Cojoncio Pérez. Both of us had found that name to be the most impressive thing we had seen in Palencia.

During the days I spent with Cossío in Tudanca, we visited other cities of the north: Santillana del Mar, Torrelavega, Gijón, Oviedo. . . . Near Santillana we made a great and exciting discovery: the bisons, deer and wild boar that lined the caves of Altamira. It was drizzling when we reached the spot. We stopped at the side of a road in front of the shack belonging to the caretaker who, in fact, was a priest. Protected by his red umbrella, we crossed some cultivated, flat fields that did not suggest the presence of anything else. However, at the base of a slight incline we came to a small door. Who could have imagined that through this door one entered the most beautiful sanc-tuary of all Spanish art! In the darkness we began to descend toward the center of the earth. A light went on, but we continued walking along a narrow passageway that became steeper and more humid as we moved forward. I didn't even dare to breathe as I looked at the rocks that bordered the path on both sides, eager to discover some sign of what we were about to see. There was nothing at all. All of a sudden, some hidden reflectors were turned on and—wonder of wonders!—we were in the heart of the cave, in the most astounding, painted underground area in the entire world. Since the vault of the cave was quite low, we could get a more complete view of that im-mense fresco painting, executed by these cave-dwelling maestros of our pictorial quaternary, by lying on our backs on top of the large slabs of stone set in the ground. It seemed as if the rock itself were bellowing. There, shimmering in small groups under a thin film of water that had filtered through the earth, were these red and black bisons. Some were charging and others were at rest. A millenary tremor seemed to shake the very walls. It was like the first Spanish bullpen packed with brave bulls straining to be set free. But there were no cowboys or ranch foremen to be seen on those walls. The animals roared in their solitude, bearded and frightening under the weight of centuries of darkness. I left the cave filled with the presence

*The popular Spanish word for testicles is *cojones.*

of angels which I released as soon as we came into the light, and I then saw them rise up through the rain with their eyes flashing in anger.

On leaving Tudanca I gave Cossío the manuscript of *El alba del alhelí*, since he had kindly offered to publish it at his own expense in his collection *Libros para amigos (Books for Friends)*.

From the north I raced immediately southward—that is, to the Puerto, passing quickly through Madrid. I don't remember who paid for the trip, but I do know that I reached my Uncle Jesús' house, where I spent several weeks surrounded by cousins of all ages and sizes. Uncle Jesús, so different from that distant and feared relation of my youth, was a kind and amusing man who was not unaware of a young poet's needs. One night he half jokingly and half seriously made me the following proposition: "Do you want to earn yourself a few *pesetas?*"

"Of course," I replied. "Tell me how."

"By writing some poetry for the Domecqs."

"Agreed. I'll write a great poem recounting the history of the House of Domecq: the epic story of its wines and brandy."

Uncle Jesús was a good friend of the famous wine merchants, and for all I know he might then have been their representative throughout Andalusia. He took me to Jerez to show me around. After visiting the best wine cellars and tasting the most diverse brews, we had lunch with Don Manuel Domecq, Viscount of Almocadén, a very refined Andalusian gentleman whose French ancestry, however, could not be denied. He even looked a little bit like Paul Valéry. He furnished me with all the necessary data for my poem. In less than a week I had composed a panegyric comprised of *sestinas reales** which sang the praises of his firm. I must admit that, given my mood at that time, I actually enjoyed writing the poem, since it had the effect of calming my feelings of anxiety. It was agreed that I would read my composition at a banquet to which, together with other special guests, Fernando Villalón had been invited. On the morning of the celebration I appeared in Jerez with my poem, written in calligraphy with India ink on large sheets of drawing paper and bound between two pieces of cardboard on which I had painted some colorful designs. After dessert was served, but before

---

**Sestinas reales* is a poetic composition consisting of six stanzas of six decasyllabic lines each.

264

we made our last toast, I recited this panegyric which everyone listened to in silence, applauding after I had finished, and presented the folio to Domecq.

In the afternoon we went to see his stables, where he bred his pedigree Hispano-Arabic horses, elegant and beautiful creatures who were grazing in the fields that bordered the Guadalupe River. There the Viscount took me aside and said: "You can choose the one you like the best. I was very pleased with your poem."

I was left speechless and stood there like a stone. Of course I was tempted by such a gift, but what was I supposed to do? I thought about it for some time before replying.

"Don Manuel," I finally said to him, "what would I do with a horse in a third-floor Madrid apartment? If I were still living here in the Puerto ..."

He laughed.

After dinner that evening, Uncle Jesús gathered his older children around him and he spread out on the tablecloth, in a fan-shaped pattern, ten crisp five-hundred *peseta* bills. It seemed at first like a fortune, but after I had made my mental calculations I realized it only came to a total of five thousand. I should have accepted the horse.

I didn't feel very guilty about having enjoyed that brief parenthesis filled with wine and football. But in the meantime, angels and demons had continued their activity in the innermost part of my being and I was slowly bringing them to the surface, covered as they were with my own blood, and then inserting them in that group of poems that was nearing completion. Tucked away in the drawers of my room, *Cal y canto* was waiting its turn, filled with the glowing sparks that had been struck during the Góngora battle. But it was not to have to wait very long. That same year the editorial section of the *Revista de Occidente* launched a series of publications devoted to the new wave of poetry. The first volumes in this series were *Cántico* by Jorge Guillén and Lorca's *Gypsy Ballads*. A new book by Salinas, *Seguro azar (Certain Fate)*, and my own work would appear shortly thereafter—that is, at the beginning of the year 1929, when another recently established publishing house (C.I.A.P.) also published my *Sobre los ángeles (Concerning the Angels)*.

García Lorca's *Romancero* was the most successful work of poetry to appear during that decade. Before coming out in print, it had already traveled part of the road leading to its tumultuous reception. The secret of his work lay in the clarity of those poems which nonetheless were clothed at times in a language filled with a mysterious sense of drama. Max Aub, a somewhat unknown member of that generation whose most fruitful work in the theater, fiction and criticism would appear later and is still appearing now from exile in Mexico, has expressed it very well: "With Federico's ballads, history repeats itself; we have a return of the dramatic tale, a return to Spanish poetry of a current that had been buried by modernism, by an attitude of art for art's sake on the part of those who did not know how or preferred not to join together the anecdotal and the poetic, since their concept of poetry would not permit such a mixture." But Juan Ramón himself had given the ballad new life, and this was his great contribution: an airy, flexible and musical poetry in opposition to the harsh and capricious metrical form of modernism. A short time later the poet from Huelva, Antonio Machado, wrote his "La tierra de Alvargonzález" ("The Land of Alvargonzález"), a terrifying Castilian story composed in a simple ballad style. But Federico's poems were different and the anecdotal aspects of the work were almost always shrouded in secrecy, so that at times, as in the "Romance sonámbulo" ("The Sleepwalking Ballad") or "La pena negra" ("Black Pain"), it was impossible to logically follow the narrative line. García Lorca, together with Juan Ramón and Machado, had constructed upon the foundation stones of the old Spanish "Romancero" another form of balladry that was strange and powerful, and this had the ultimate effect of strengthening and exalting this ancient Castilian tradition. That constituted his novel contribution, and it was responsible for his tremendous success.

Jorge Guillén's success with his *Cántico* was not of the same kind, but successful he was. In spite of what some people said, and even still say today, regarding influences and preferences, it became sharply clear in this book that the poetry of Jorge Guillén was undoubtedly the most personal and highly individualized poetic statement that had ever been made by any Spanish poet. Regardless of the opinion of many critics, this was poetry which was sparklingly clear, optimistic and jubilant like the circumference of a circle drawn without lifting the hand—exultant, vivid and admirable. Some apparently found it difficult to understand its formal content. Not everyone understands the beauty of a circle when it is not formed by a compass but by a trembling hand which is able to trace it with complete perfection and with one stroke of the pen. This was not prefabricated poetry, as Juan Ramón sarcastically suggested in his attack. It was poetry that grew directly from the objects it described in a dynamic ecstasy before the world; a transparent world in which even the shadows were clearly outlined and bathed in light.

A poet who is eternally young, elastic and forever confident, Guillén has been nourished by his canticle which has continued to surge upward until today. From its zenith, it can capture better than any other Spanish poetry the realities of the earth and also the very special and terrible reality of Spain. Look carefully at Guillén's last book, *Maremágnum*—prohibited (what a great honor!) by Franco's censorship—and see how it reads like a new great stanza of his *Cántico*. No one should be the least bit surprised by these lines in a poet who has from the very beginning been open and receptive to all things and to the air around him:

> ¡Salir por fin, salir
> a glorias, a rocíos,
> (certera ya la espera,
> ya fatales los ímpetus . . .)

> To finally emerge, go out
> Into glory, into the dew,
> (Hope now a certainty,
> The impetus now fatality . . .)

But I will speak more about the Guillén of today in a future volume of these memoirs.

For the moment I would like to return to Machado and recall my second meeting with him in the Café Español, an old nineteenth-century café located next to the Royal Theater of Madrid in the vicinity of the Plaza de Oriente. Mirrors coated with a mist left there by layers of dirty water reflected the shadowy image of dark ladies dressed in mourning, solitary gentlemen with their stiff old-fashioned collars, poor middle-class families with marriageable daughters well beyond their prime, sad and tightly closed flowers seen against the background of the worn velvet upholstery of the chairs.

A blind man, who was an excellent musician according to those who frequented the café, was playing the piano while a rather plump young girl moved from table to table in search of an invitation—a cup of coffee and a piece of toast that would be accompanied by a furtive pinch or two—from one of her father's admirers who sat

267

there deep in thought. From the street outside, with its autumn rain and cold, I looked through the bright and transparent curtains on the windows and caught a glimpse of the profile of Antonio Machado. I went into the café to greet him. I had just come from a small, intimate bookstore whose owner, a great friend to us all, had just obtained for me a rare edition of Rimbaud's poetry. I was as happy as a child that afternoon, knowing that I had this book tucked under my raincoat to protect it from the elements. Machado greeted me very affectionately, offering me a seat next to him while he introduced me to his friends. As I took off my coat I proudly showed him my beautiful book which he leafed through with an approving grunt, placing it then on a chair to his left on which was piled a collection of scarves and overcoats. I only remember one of the people he introduced me to, the old actor Ricardo Calvo, a very good friend of the poet. It was strange that afternoon not to see Machado's brother Manuel, who was usually his inseparable companion. The other gentlemen who surrounded him were odd, old-fashioned types who looked as if they had just come out of the back room of a village drugstore. I think my impression was correct, since during the whole time I was there the conversations revolved around provincial affairs, problems and questions that were far removed and unrelated to the cups of coffee that had been set down in front of them: some schoolteacher's transfer, somebody's illness, last year's harvest, etc.

"Oh, how stupid of me, how stupid of me!," I kept saying to myself later as I walked under the green lanterns and the tall statues of the Visigothic kings that lined the Plaza de Oriente. But ever since that afternoon I have always been able to look at my copy of Rimbaud with a certain melancholy smile, since that rare edition had suddenly become even rarer and more valuable as a result of the circular burns left there on its rust-colored front cover by one of Machado's cigarettes.

The year 1928 was sliding to an end. *El alba del alhelí*, José María Cossío's gift to me, was published that year in an edition of only 150 numbered copies, none of which were for sale. The critics hardly paid any attention to this book; it was almost as if it didn't exist. That didn't bother me very much, however, since I was really interested in the appearance of my two other works: *Cal y canto* and *Sobre los ángeles*. Now that I was totally free of this second collection of poems, I was beginning to concentrate on other things: a book of poetry with the title *Sermones y moradas (Sermons and Dwelling*

Places) and a drama *El hombre deshabitado (The Uninhabited Man)*, both of them well within the same electrically charged atmosphere of my angels. I had also begun another series of poems that was to mark a complete break with my earlier poetry, although it was still a product of the same state of confusion and anarchy in which I had composed my most recent works. The title? *Yo era un tonto y lo que he visto me ha hecho dos tontos (I Was a Fool and What I Have Seen Has Made Me Two Fools)*. We were living then in the golden age of North American comedy films that revolved around the genial figure of Charlie Chaplin. I dedicated the poems of this book to all those cinematic fools, who to my mind were real flesh and blood angels.

Suddenly a sensational event brought me again into close contact with my old friends. The theatrical company of Don Fernando Díaz de Mendoza, still in mourning for the death of Doña María Guerrero, had announced the opening of *Sinrazón*, the first dramatic work by Ignacio Sánchez Mejías. There was great expectation in the literary world, but even more in bullfighting circles, since the *aficionados* of Madrid were angry at Ignacio because of an ugly gesture he had made to those in the stands one Sunday afternoon in the bullring. When I reached the Calderón Theater, the whole place was buzzing. Up in the top balcony were strange types with handkerchiefs tied around their necks and holding huge clubs in their hands. Backstage, the members of the company were extremely nervous. Don Fernando, somewhat of an aristocrat and accustomed to gala openings, could not disguise his displeasure and anxiety. "Doña María must be turning over in her grave," he commented to Bergamín and me when we greeted him. Long before the curtain went up, the theater looked like a veritable bullring. There in the bleachers—that is, the top balcony—people were stamping their feet and whistling as they beat their sticks against the floor. Their behavior was repugnant to those sitting in the boxes and orchestra seats downstairs, who tried to quiet things down by protesting against this noise. Naturally, that only made things worse.

Finally, a bugle was heard—I mean the curtain went up—and there was instant silence. The stage was completely dark, but as a novelty the edges of the furniture were phosphorescent. The words of some invisible person were heard first—then the lights went on. The waiting room of a clinic appeared in all its modern whiteness. In the middle of the stage, standing before a table, a man dressed in white was questioning another individual who seemed to be somewhat distracted. The play had begun. Now, more than thirty years after that memorable night, I don't remember the work at all. It was not at all about bullfighting, as the audience had expected. The action took place in an insane asylum and dealt with the problem of madness or sanity, a theme which Ignacio resolved as gracefully as on one of his better afternoons in the bullring. A strange success, and also the first attempt to present Freudian theater in the Spanish language. At the end of the last act, the audience in the bleachers who had been prepared to demolish the great *torero* burst into applause and ovations which only increased in volume when Sánchez Mejías came out in front of the curtain to express his gratitude. The following day, the most demanding and punctilious critics awarded him an ear, the tail and the horns, accepting him as a new dramatic author. Evil tongues immediately spread the rumor that *Sinrazón* was not Ignacio's own work, but had been written by some of the young writers who were always around him. Nothing could have been more stupid or further from the truth. Ignacio was a man of genius and quite capable of creating a dramatic work that everyone admired.

For me, the year 1928 proceeded on its course with a lecture that Salinas dedicated to my *Sobre los ángeles* almost on the eve of its publication, a tribute which affected me deeply. Severe storms appeared on the political horizon of Spain at about the same time. But even before this, in an edition issued by the *Revista de Occidente*, my *Cal y canto* had its day. At the time of its publication, I had almost entirely dismissed this book from my mind, feeling that it was so distant and removed from the feverish atmosphere in which I was then living. It was published at the end of winter, when the trees were beginning to explode in their spring green. Bergamín was the first person to welcome its appearance, with an extensive essay written for *La Gaceta Literaria*. Other critics such as Quiroga Pla and Salazar Chapela also took notice of it, helping it along with its first steps. *Cal y canto* began its career by reviving the Gongoristic embers of an earlier time; I began to become interested in its fate. But suddenly the wings of the angels who had taken flight about the same time had the effect of darkening that earlier work completely, burying it in the rubble after it had barely started out on its happy voyage. Those burning, broken and violent creatures rose up against it in the midst of a convulsed spring season. The first student uprising in opposition to the dictatorship under which we were suffering had begun to shatter the tranquility of the streets. How confusing were those days when *Sobre los ángeles* appeared and was considered by Azorín to signal my having reached "the highest peak of lyric poetry"! But the angels had already abandoned me, tearing themselves from me and only leaving behind the painful emptiness of a wound. It was not, however, a time to weep. The moment I had darkly predicted in one of my poems was not merely approaching; it was there, right before me, inciting me to action:

> *Pero por fin llegó el día,*
> *la hora de las palas y los cubos . . .*

> *But the day finally arrived,*
> *the hour of buckets and shovels . . .*

I knew little or nothing about politics, absorbed as I was in my poetry within a Spain which until that moment seemed peaceful enough. But suddenly my ears heard words that had never reached them before, or at least had not meant anything to me before: Republic, Fascism, liberty—and I learned that Don Miguel de Unamuno, from his exile in Hendaye, was sending letters and poems to his friends which were really pamphlets directed against another Miguel—Miguel Primo de Rivera, the witty and fun-loving braggart from Jerez, supporter of the crumbling monarchy. These letters and poems spread like wildfire through the literary gatherings, the editorial offices of newspapers opposed to the regime, and reached the hands of angry university students. I saw how Don Ramón del Valle-Inclán, in his "headquarters" at the Café La Granja, in the streets, in the theaters and wherever he felt like it, fought his duel to the death against the "amusing" general. The general himself, in a memorable note that appeared in the newspapers, ended up by calling Don Ramón "that very great but very extravagant citizen." Without anyone realizing it was happening, as if by magic, a climate of violence had been created, and I was fascinated by it all. The shouts and protests, which in some dim way had existed within me, eating away at my own defenses, finally found an escape hatch and raced frantically into streets filled with fervent students.

We walked along the barricades that had been set up on the boulevards, stood firm against the mounted Guardia Civil and the gunfire from their Mausers. No one had called to me. It was my own blind impulse which guided me. The majority of those young men knew very little about me, but suddenly we were all friends. What could I do? How could I help them and not appear to be an instigator, one of those "foreign elements" which the newspapers blamed for any attack against the regime? Not even the poems of my *Sermones y moradas*, even more desperate and harsh than those in *Sobre los ángeles*, could be of any use to them. On the other hand, nobody then even considered that poetry might have any other purpose than to be intimately enjoyed by each individual. No one thought it could have any other effect on people. But the winds that were blowing were already heavily laden with ominous forecasts.

In the middle of this activity and on this battlefield which was not literary but real, Luis Buñuel appeared like some kind of meteor. He had come from Paris with his shaven head, his face even stronger-looking than ever, and his eyes unusually round and protruding. He had come to show his first film, made in collaboration with Salvador Dalí. It was one of the unforgettable sessions of the Cine Club which was still under the direction of the original founder of this group, the eccentric Giménez Caballero. The film caused a sensation, although many were disturbed by it; everyone in the theater was horrified by the image of a moon being sliced in two by a cloud, followed immediately by that other terrifying scene of an eye slit by a razor. When the audience, in a state of near shock, then asked Buñuel to offer some words of explanation, I remember how he stood up for a moment and said from his box seat: "It's merely a desperate and impassioned invitation to crime." Luis Buñuel was also living through a period of uneasiness, of violent protest, "expressing," according to Georges Sadoul, "that surrealistic sickness of the century in his *Andalusian Dog (Un Chien Andalou, 1928)*, the image of a youthful generation in a state of convulsed confusion." It was significant that this film would appear at a moment when Madrid was in such a feverish state and on the eve of great political events. Those winds of almost hurricane force were heading directly toward the breach through which so many of us would pass, with clear consciences, after having swept away the shadows of that deep, dark well into which we had fallen in recent years. Luis Buñuel was also to follow this path after having presented his *Andalusian Dog* and *The Golden Age (L'Age d'Or, 1930)*—those two masterpieces of surrealistic film-making—with the creation of *Earth Without Bread, (Las*

Hurdes, 1932), his magnificent documentary about poverty in the region of Extremadura. Again in the opinion of Sadoul, "This film explains and forecasts the Civil War during which the Falangists shot Buñuel's friend, the poet García Lorca, while Dalí, in New York, was painting a portrait of the Ambassador of Franco's Spain." Dalí, at the time of the filming of *The Golden Age*, and given the political direction his friend was taking, had broken off all relations with Buñuel and later accused him of being "brutalized by bureaucratic Stalinism."

It was a period of avant-garde movements, all of which reached Madrid somewhat late, and it also witnessed the grand finale of silent movies before the onslaught of sound. *The Cabinet of Doctor Caligari* had offered the first magical surprise in the midst of a silence that was filled with madness, cruelties and crime. I think it was through Buñuel's efforts that we were able to see, in the lecture hall of the Residencia, such films as *Intermission, The Shell and the Clergyman, Only the Hours* and *The Fall of the House of Usher*. Names that up until that moment were unfamiliar to us, such as René Clair, Germain Dullac, Cavalcanti and Epstein, flashed before our eyes in a procession of surprising images, a montage of unpredictable and absurd metaphors which were very much in keeping with the poetic and pictorial activity in Europe at the moment (Tzara, Aragon, Eluard, Desnos, Peret, Max Ernst, Tanguay, Masson, etc.). Among the masterpieces of film which were far removed from this extreme vanguard, from that golden age of silent movies, I still remember such works as *The Passion of Joan of Arc* by Dreyer, *Metropolis* by Fritz Lang, *The Gold Rush* by Chaplin, *The Mother* by Pudovkin, and particularly *The Battleship Potemkin* by Eisenstein. To this day I still have warm and tender feelings for those great and lovable fools Buster Keaton and Harry Langdon, as well as for the lesser figures of Stan Laurel, Oliver Hardy, Louise Fazenda, Larry Semon, Bebe Daniels, Charles Bower, etc., all of them heroes of a book I was in the process of writing, a book more or less created in the surrealistic mode, and whose title I had taken from a play by Calderón de la Barca: *I Was a Fool and What I Have Seen Has Made Me Two Fools.* I rarely went to the theater. What really impressed me was what I saw on the movie screen. Our stage, which was still invaded in those days by Benevente, the Quintero Brothers, Arniches, and Muñoz Seca, offered nothing to me. The only works of theater which still remain in my mind are the opening performances of *Sinrazón* by

Sánchez Mejías, *Tic-Tac* by Claudio de la Torre, *Brandy, mucho brandy (Brandy, Lots of Brandy)* by Azorín and *Los medios seres (Partial Beings)* by Gómez de la Serna, which was the most daring of all these plays, filled as it was with surprising touches of genius, but which then seemed to me too long and not very theatrically effective.

I barely saw Ramón socially, as was the case with almost all the writers of the generation which preceded mine. We greeted each other in the streets of our neighborhood where I would see him always with a pipe in his mouth, his face framed by those long sideburns that Goya had painted on all the young Madrid dandies in his popular scenes of the city. I was not a *pombiano*, and I think that Ramón never really approved of anyone who had not sat at the table of his famous *tertulias* at the Café Pombo. Once I allowed myself to play a somewhat stupid practical joke on him by sending him a tasteless pamphlet directed against Ortega and his acolytes from the *Revista de Occidente*, all members of Ramón's clan, which constituted a complete exposé of the group. This was delivered to him during one of those many noisy banquets that took place in the Café Pombo, and it may have been one held to honor Giménez Caballero. Although I did occasionally attend these gatherings, I was not too fond of café meetings nor of literary cliques. Ever since my first days in Madrid, I had been one of the "hatless" types, unaffiliated, and used to the fresh air of the streets. This was particularly the case in those days when I had become even more of a solitary, caustic poet, not a very frequent guest at social gatherings. But just as with everything else, I was not averse to peeking in on them from time to time. I was then a friend of Carmen Ybes, that delightful countess so admired by Ortega, and also of Isabel Dato, the daughter of the Monarchist minister Eduardo Dato Iradier who was the victim of an anarchist bullet. I was on friendly terms with the Duke of Alba and even more so with the Duke de las Torres, a one-eyed, pleasant and fun-loving individual. I would often visit the Bauers, the owners of the marvelous Alameda de Osuna that had been praised so highly by Antonio Marichalar in one of his fine books.

I was considered to be a friend to other members of the aristocracy, many of whom were shaken by the winds of freedom that were then threatening the Dictatorship. The street fighting first and then the coming of the Republic had almost entirely separated me from this group of people, and I only retained the friendship of an Argentinian countess who distinguished herself from the very beginning as a person of conscience, faithful to her liberal sentiments. She was Tota Atucha, the Countess of Cuevas de Vera. Both immediately after the Spanish Civil War, during my exile in Paris, as well as here in Buenos Aires, she has always been the same—a friend of truth and unafraid of political commitment—unassuming, quiet and sincere. She was an unusual human being and warmly admired by our group of Spanish exiles.

During the respite of that summer, I went back to the Guadarrama Mountains for reasons of health. I was suffering from a liver ailment and I had lost weight again so that I looked even more two-dimensional than I did during the early stages of my first illness. I could only eat vegetables cooked in olive oil, a dish I despised, and certain kinds of fruit. Nevertheless, against doctor's orders, I would stroll day and night until I collapsed in a state of exhaustion. Everywhere I wandered, up the side of a mountain, along a path, or in the most abandoned fields, I continued with my poems of *Sermones y moradas*, alternating them with those to be included in my book on *"the fools"* or my play *El hombre deshabitado* that was already pretty far along. In spite of all this activity, I was still confused and not convinced that my horizons had become any brighter. I was still under the yoke of my family. My books had not made that much difference. I had published five, but so what? The results were zero; not even the shadow of anything tangible. My pockets were as empty as they had ever been.

Upon my return to Madrid, the publishing house of Plutarco, whose editor was my Uncle Luis Alberti, suggested that I publish a new edition of *La amante*. I added a few poems I had found later as well as three pen-and-ink drawings. I sent these additions to them immediately, and the new edition soon appeared. The results came to a grand total of two hundred *pesetas*. I then banked all my illusions on the theater. I reread what I had already written of the play I was working on, and it seemed terribly difficult and obscure to me. Who would risk taking on anything like that? All actors were a pack of animals except for a few rare exceptions, and they were sniffing around Marquina, Benavente, Muñoz Seca and other playwrights like them. I tried to write musical librettos similar to the one I had begun for *La pájara pinta (The Spotted Bird)* and had never finished for reasons already mentioned, and the fragments I had were still unpublished. With a new libretto—*El colorín colorete*—I went to see Adolfo Salazar, suggesting to him that he send it to a French composer such as Darius Milhaud, for example. That idea was a complete flop, in spite of the fact that my script had been written in an invented language that needed no translation.

I think it was around that time that Manuel de Falla came through Madrid. He was there for the first performance of his Concerto for Piano and Chamber Orchestra. From the start I realized that it would have been absurd to approach him with anything I had done. But, authentic *gaditano* (inhabitant of Cádiz) that he was, he did talk to me about the possibility of composing music for some of my songs from the *Marinero*. (When? When would he do it?) I found myself trembling with excitement. His offer had been spontaneous, but . . . Don Manuel moved very slowly. He would depart from this earth without ever finishing *La Atlántida*, a composition he had begun around that time. In a state of desperation, I accepted an offer that had been made to me months before to give a lecture at the Ladies' Lyceum Club.

I was a fool and what I had seen and continued to see had made me two fools.

That grotesque pedestal which sustained the Dictator and his drunken sword in a ridiculous, puppet-like embrace with King Alfonso was already beginning to crumble. One of the figures was going to fall and the other, the Bourbonic member of this Punch-and-Judy Show, was obliged to push him over the brink, believing that in this way he could silence the cries which were coming from all over Spain and had begun to reach the very balconies of the Royal Palace in the Plaza de Oriente. I consciously considered myself then to be a street poet, a poet "of the dawn with his hands raised high," as I expressed it in writing. I tried to compose poems of three or four hundred syllables so as to paste them up on the walls, as I began to sense how great and beautiful it would be to fall among the ruins with my boots on, just like a hero in that Andalusian poem:

> *Con los zapatos puestos*
> *tengo que morir,*
> *que si muriera como los valientes,*
> *hablarían de mí.*

> *I will face death*
> *With boots on my feet,*

If I die like the brave,
Of me, too, they will speak.

The first poem I committed to paper bore the title "With My
Boots On I Must Die," written in anger and from within the bubbling cauldron that was Spain at that moment in its history. Exaggerated, obscure, sensing but not truly knowing what I wanted,
with a taste of bile and gnashing of teeth, with an undefined sense of
desperation that was pushing me to bite the ground itself, this poem
(subtitled "A Civic Elegy") indicated that I had become an integral
part of a new universe which I had entered blindly without thinking
where it all might lead:

> *Será en ese momento cuando los caballos sin ojos se desgarren las*
> *tibias contra los hierros en punta de una valla de sillas indignadas*
> *contra los adoquines levantados de cualquier calle recién absorta en la*
> *locura.*

> *Vuelvo a cagarme por última vez en todos vuestros muertos, en*
> *este mismo instante en que las armaduras se desploman en la casa del*
> *rey, en que los hombres más ilustres se miran a las ingles sin encon-*
> *trar en ellas la solución a las desesperadas órdenes de la sangre . . .*

> *At that moment, eyeless horses will scrape their ankles against the*
> *pointed spears of indignant chairs raised as a barrier against the*
> *mounds of cobblestones along the streets caught up and absorbed by*
> *this madness.*

> *For the last time, I once again shit on your dead, while at this very*
> *moment the coats of armor are disintegrating in the King's house*
> *and the most illustrious of men look between their legs without find-*
> *ing there a solution to the desperate urgings of their blood . . .*

This was subversive poetry that expressed my inner turmoil and
also darkly forecast the future road I would take. Strange as it may
seem, this long elegy found its way to Azorín who, oddly enough,
praised it highly in an article that appeared one morning in the *ABC*,
the most Monarchist newspaper in the country. With his gift of

prophecy, which at this distance seems chillingly eerie, Azorín pointed the way to the road I would clearly follow two years later.

On that January 16, 1930, Azorín had written: "... and nevertheless the poet (here I suppress certain adjectives which make me blush) needs support for his spiritual life. Where will this come from in the case of Rafael Alberti? Rafael Alberti returns to the origins, to what is fundamental and spontaneous; Rafael Alberti is returning with open arms to the people. With their sense of indifference toward established norms, only the people and only nature can give Alberti the support he needs and requests." This was an astounding comment, and particularly coming from Azorín. And even more so in those terrible days of imminent collapse, because one night during that same month of January he would form part of a group made up almost totally of intellectuals who, having abandoned the café known as La Granja el Henar, walked up Alcalá Street determined to reach the royal palace. By the time it had gotten as far as the Puerta del Sol, that small group had become a huge crowd of demonstrators, which to the accompaniment of shouts such as "Death to Primo de Rivera!" and "Down with the Dictatorship!" proceeded along Arenal Street, eager to pour into the Plaza de Oriente. I was among those demonstrators and was accompanied by Santiago Ontañón—then already a great stage designer—and by the overly refined, pedantic and hypocritical Falangist of today, Eugenio Montes, who was then among the group that shouted the loudest. While the mounted police charged against the main body of the demonstrators, a few of us burst into the peaceful darkness of the Real Cínema, causing the terrified spectators to jump out of their seats. On our way back, that same small group set fire to the newsstand of *El Debate,* with Eugenio Montes contributing more than one match. The fire was finally put out after we had watched that printed message, "To the Greater Glory of God and the Dictatorship," go up in smoke, and saw the fading glow of General Primo de Rivera's drunken sword. Another sword was to rise up, wielded this time by Berenguer and inaugurating that sad period which came to be called the "Dictablanda."* In its final days, this regime was to distinguish itself

---

*The invented "dictablanda" constitutes a word play in Spanish. The ending *dura* in *dictadura* would be translated as "hard" in English. The *blanda* ending in "dictablanda" means "soft" or "bland" in English.

by displaying a cruel harshness which the previous fun-loving Dictator from Jerez had never shown.

Another important event was brewing: the return to Spain of Don Miguel de Unamuno after several years of exile in France, where the other Miguel, his enemy, would march off into exile and death a few months later. Unamuno's entrance into Madrid by train at the North Station was triumphant. A great crowd received him with applause and shouts of "Long live the Republic!," a cry that the police in the service of that "Dictablanda" were not able to repress, since it had begun to zigzag and spread throughout the entire Peninsula. Shortly after his arrival, the ardent Rector of the University of Salamanca was reinstated in his professorial chair. And his classes, which had been cancelled for such a long period of time, met again, and heard Unamuno repeat those words of Fray Luis de León: "As we were saying yesterday. . ."

It was about this time that García Lorca left Madrid for New York, crowned with success by the appearance of a second edition of his *Gypsy Ballads*. Goodbye to the Residencia and to the piano, that Pleyel piano which had accompanied him and his songs during those happy years! Federico left for North America already infected by what was then happening in Spain, and his poetry of the New World was to constitute a strange parenthesis, filled with confusion and shadows. Some of the initial poems of the book that was later to become his *Poet in New York* appeared in journals published in Madrid or in other publications that reached us from Cuba. What a sharp, cutting sword had emerged from the throat of this poet from Granada! Tragic tremors were heard in these poems—forecasts of what was still to come, of what would happen to him in those years following his return to Spain! José Bergamín, now exiled in Mexico but the editor of the first edition of the *Poeta en Nueva York*, illuminates the work with great clarity:

> It is a new and fleeting moment in his life in which the poetic forms of his time are extinguished by unexpected sounds—by painful, dark, vague and distant rhythms; here everything is heard in a voice that silences step by step, verse by verse, the splendor of a world glimpsed unwillingly and seen as ultimately dead. The poet, in this way, offers a self-portrait of a man on the verge of suicide. He predicts a violent death which is like a

suicidal wish to overcome such a fate. Thus he foresees and denounces it, yet hardly mentioning it at all. . . .

I returned to the Residencia only rarely, and Federico had also abandoned it upon his return from America. He had decided to live with his family in a house on Alcalá Street. That exemplary decade filled with love, companionship, youth and enthusiasm was coming to a close . . . But for the moment, we are still back in the early days of the year 1930.

One wintry, rainy night while I was seated at a table on the ground floor of the Hotel Nacional facing a row of wine bottles, all empty except for one that still contained a few drops of sherry, a strange manuscript happened to fall into my hands. The title of the work was *Residencia en la tierra (Residence on Earth)*. The author was one Pablo Neruda—a Chilean poet whom most of us hardly knew. The person who had brought this book to me was Alfredo Condón, Secretary to the Chilean Embassy, whom I had met through Bebé and Carlos Morla; Carlos was an Administrative Assistant at the Chilean Embassy, and the Morlas were also very good friends of García Lorca. My first reading of that work left me amazed and impressed by those poems which were so different in tone and atmosphere from what we were writing at the time.

I learned that Neruda was the Chilean Consul in Java, where he lived a very solitary existence, writing letters which expressed his sense of desperation at being so far removed from his own world and his own language. I circulated the manuscript among my friends. There was no literary group in Madrid that did not know the work, and my own enthusiasm was matched by that of José Herrera Petere, Arturo Serrano Plaja, Luis Felipe Vivanco and other aspiring young writers. I tried to have the work published, since such an extraordinary revelation had to appear in Spain. I proposed this to the few editors I knew, but I had no success at all. I then gave the manuscript to Pedro Salinas so that he might approach the *Revista de Occidente*. Salinas was also unsuccessful, although he was able to convince the editors of this journal to publish several of Neruda's poems. I then began to write letters to Pablo. His replies were full of anguish, and I remember that in one of his letters he asked me to send him a dictionary, apologizing at the same time for the grammatical mistakes I might find in what he was writing to me.

280

Living in Paris in 1931, I still kept trying to have the *Residencia* poems published. An Argentinian lady, Elvira de Alvear, agreed to finance and carry out the project. I obtained from Elvira the promise of a cash advance, and with the help of the Cuban author Alejo Carpentier, her secretary at the time, I drafted a cable to Neruda with the message: "Five thousand French francs." But *Residencia en la tierra* was not any luckier this time around. It was not published. And when I met Pablo in Madrid two years later, he told me that he had received the cable, but not the money. I made up my mind then not to ever fight for other people's books, a promise, naturally, which I have not kept. (How could I not remember Alfredo Condón—that intelligent, crazy, heavy-drinking Chilean, to whom I will always remain indebted for my first contact with the poetry of Pablo Neruda—now in this *Lost Grove* of mine? We used to go out frequently together at night, sometimes drinking until dawn. He was a very unhappy man, and committed suicide after his return to Chile.)

Our generation suffered a very great loss that same year. I did not know that Villalón was in Madrid. I met him unexpectedly one freezing afternoon toward the end of February when it was already getting dark and we both happened to be walking along the same street in the Salamanca district. He was alone. He looked extremely sad, his face hidden beneath his hat and scarf behind the raised collar of his overcoat.

"But Fernando! What a pleasant surprise! How come you haven't told anybody you were here?"

Speaking softly and slowly, he replied, "At this very moment I must have a temperature of at least 105 degrees—right at this very moment."

I didn't know what to say. I took him by the arm and we continued walking. When we reached the corner, he suddenly stopped and pleaded with me: "Wait for me here in the street. I'll be down in a minute."

I stood there waiting in a doorway for more than fifteen minutes. When he finally appeared and we had started walking again, I got up enough nerve to ask him what was wrong.

"I have to have an operation. I've just borrowed one hundred and fifty *pesetas* from a friend to pay the hospital bill."

Villalón had been in a state of bankruptcy for some time. Those poetic activities which had been admired throughout all of Andalusia had left him penniless. We were walking along very slowly. I didn't know what to talk to him about, seeing him so withdrawn, so depressed and incommunicative. He had always been so full of life and ideas, as strong as a bull.

"What do you think about the political situation?" I asked, just to say something.

"I see no cause for harboring any great illusions. Until the day the Civil Guard begins to shout 'Long Live the Republic!' everything will stay the same."

I laughed. He was right.

"The world is in a sad way," he continued mysteriously, after a long silence. "Up until now it has been ruled by Kutumí. But maybe things will change and it won't be long before Señor Maitrellas gets his turn to govern."*

I left him at the door of his building.

A few days later he checked into the hospital. Bergamín, some other friends and I, accompanied by Eusebio Oliver, a young doctor who spent a lot of time with us, witnessed the operation. In Fernando's kidneys were embedded many stones of various shapes and sizes which we later saw in the bloody handkerchief Oliver held out to us. We, of course, expected him to pull through in spite of everything. Very late that night and quite upset by what I had seen, I returned home to get some sleep. But a few hours later they called me from the hospital. Fernando Villalón was dead. He had just celebrated his forty-ninth birthday.

I was shocked and left the house immediately to go to the hospital. The cattle-breeding poet was stretched out on his bed dressed in a dark suit and wearing black shoes. I couldn't help but notice that a long silver chain was stretched across his vest from the left pocket to the right. This had been his last wish: that he be buried with his watch in working order. Conchita, the gypsy girl who had been his lover for many years, was crying quietly to the accompaniment of that mysterious ticking sound, Fernando's dying pulse that was to continue to beat in the earth for more than twelve hours after his burial. When his brother Jerónimo arrived, the girl refused to see him and insisted that he not be allowed into the room. That brother,

---

*These references to *Kutumí* and *Maitrellas* are obscure. Aitana Alberti has indicated that Villalón often mentioned these two names and, according to Rafael Alberti, they were related in some way to Villalón's belief in theosophy and reincarnation.

a typical spoiled and dull-witted Andalusian playboy, so different in character from Villalón, had recently taken advantage of the poet's extravagances, contributing in this way to Fernando's financial ruin. Fernando had departed this earth leaving behind very few works: *Andalucía la baja, Romances del 800, La toreada (A Bullfighting Epic)* and some long stanzas from *El Kaos* which he had read to Federico and me the last time we had been together in Sevilla. He had also written a poetic drama called *Don Juan Fermín de Plateros* which was about the "Picadores" of Bailén, an Andalusian episode in our war against the Napoleonic troops. But his best poem—his last will and testament—was still unknown. This document had the impact of a bomb, but at the same time it was full of tenderness.

They opened it one morning before a notary and in the presence of his brother Jerónimo, the gypsy girl, Bergamín, and Sánchez Mejías, who later told me about the will. Its contents were more or less as follows: "I curse my brother Jerónimo to the fifth generation. He has been the cause of much of my misfortune. I leave him nothing. But to Conchita, to that admirable woman who has been my lifetime companion and who accompanied me through the fields as we searched for *collejas** to make our salads, to that good woman to whom I one day gave a rifle to hunt birds, but whose gentle heart made it impossible for her to ever use it, to her I leave several paintings by Murillo and other Andalusian painters."

An ingenious poet, this Fernando Villalón, perhaps more so in his life style than in the poems he left behind, and I will speak of him often, always finding in his memory a source of admiration and joyful laughter!

I dedicated a long elegy to him, "Ese caballo ardiendo por las arboledas perdidas" ("That Burning Horse of the Lost Groves") which I wrote a few weeks after his death and which contained lines of up to one hundred syllables. That impressive detail of his watch ticking underground against his chest served as the principal refrain. It seems as if all this happened only yesterday.

But suddenly something else happened in my life which must be written down.

Collejas is a type of herb or plant with white, tender leaves which at one time was harvested and eaten as a vegetable in certain parts of Spain.

CHAPTER VIII

Cuando tú apareciste,
penaba yo en la entraña más profunda
de una cueva sin aire y sin salida.
Braceaba en lo oscuro, agonizando,
oyendo un estertor que aleteaba
como el latir de un ave imperceptible.
Sobre mí derramaste tus cabellos
y ascendí al sol y vi que eran la aurora
cubriendo un alto mar de primavera.
Fué como si llegara al más hermoso
puerto del mediodía. Se anegaban
en ti los más lucidos paisajes:
claros, agudos montes coronados
de nieve rosa, fuentes escondidas
en el rizado umbroso de los bosques.
Yo aprendí a descansar sobre tus hombros
y a descender por ríos y laderas,
a entrelazarme en las tendidas ramas
y a hacer del sueño mi más dulce muerte.
Arcos me abriste y mis floridos años,
recién subidos a la luz, yacieron
bajo el amor de tu apretada sombra,
sacando el corazón al viento libre
y ajustándolo al verde son del tuyo.

Ya iba a dormir, ya a despertar sabiendo
que no penaba en una cueva oscura,
braceando sin aire y sin salida.

Porque habías al fin aparecido.

When you appeared,
I had been suffering in the shadows
Of a deep cave where there was no air, no exit.
I thrashed about in the darkness, agonizing,
Hearing a death rattle that pulsated
Like the beating heart of an unseen bird.
Your hair spilled over me
And I ascended to the sun,
Discovering that these strands were the dawn
That spread out over the high tide of Spring.
It was as if I had arrived
At the most beautiful of southern ports.
The brightest of landscapes were reflected in you:
Clear, sharp mountains
With their crowns of pink snow,
Fountains hidden among the curled forest shadows.
I learned to rest against your shoulder,
To descend the rivers and the slopes,
To become entangled in the outstretched branches,
And to make of dreams my sweetest death.
Triumphant archways were opened to me,
And my flowered youth, brought sudddenly into the light,
Lay still beneath the palpable shade of your love,
While my heart emerged into the open breeze,
Beating to the green rhythm of your own.
Now I could sleep, now awaken
Knowing that I suffered no longer, struggling
In a dark cave with no air and no exit.

It was because you, finally, had appeared.

*T*HIS POEM was called "Retornos del
amor recién aparecido" ("Remembrances of Love Recently Appearing"). In this work I attempted to recall, twenty years later, the cave-

like state in which I had been living, and the shining light whose golden strands fell into my hands, allowing me to reach the sun and feel that spring had not died in the world.

It happened at someone's house, where I had been invited by a friend. She appeared there before me; blonde, beautiful, solid and erect, like a wave that some hidden sea had sent crashing against my chest. That very night, wandering through the streets, among the shadows of the city's gardens, or sitting back in the secret darkness of directionless taxis, the air I breathed was filled with her. I was in a state of happy delirium, and the sound of her engulfed me and impelled me toward something I felt was security itself.

I was trying to tear myself away from a tortured love affair that was still tugging at me, and I hesitated to seek refuge in another port. But now it was beauty, the lifted shoulder of Diana, the bright, golden, open and full-blooming flower of Venus, the likes of which I had only seen before in the fields of Rubens or in the bedroom scenes painted by Titian. How could I let her go, how could I possibly lose her if she had already defeated me, penetrated my heart with her spear, leaving me totally in her power; helpless, exhausted, and without any wish to escape? But nevertheless I struggled, I shouted, I wept and I dragged my heels—but finally, after such a frantic struggle, I let myself be willingly carried off and I awoke one morning on the beaches of Sóller, gazing out at that unique blue of the Mediterranean. Malignant echoes from those people in Madrid who thought this was merely another fleeting love affair reached us there. Notices even appeared in various newspapers and magazines, and one of the most amusing comments of all read as follows: "The poet Rafael Alberti is repeating the Mallorcan episode of Chopin with a beautiful George Sand from Burgos." There was apparently some wish to create a scandal, since this particular George Sand—a married author not yet divorced—was quite well known. But we, in the meanwhile, laughed at all the gossip, rather proud that our names were being bandied about by people so far removed from our happiness, from our barefoot youth among the rocks and beneath the umbrella pines, or sailing languidly over the surface of the sea.

On returning to Madrid by plane from Barcelona, a severe storm over the Iberian Mountains caused us to make a forced landing in Daroca, an Aragonese city surrounded by Roman walls, harsh and isolated like a line of verse that had fallen from the Poem of the Cid. We were received at that snow-covered emergency airport by a group of shepherds all bundled up in their sheepskins, looking themselves like a flock of immense sheep. We spent two days there at an inn, and made friends with the priest who showed us around the magnificent Collegiate Church. When the plane took off again we were the only passengers, and we had also become intimate friends with the pilot who was kind enough to offer us a display of aerial acrobatics—such a thing would be impossible today—as we approached the Madrid airport. It was the first time I had ever flown, but María Teresa had been up in a plane before and we were not in the least frightened by those hi-jinks. She was very brave, as if her last name—León (Lion)—served to defend her and make her even bolder.

My mother, who had suffered from a heart condition for some time, had taken advantage of a brief improvement in her health to travel south to visit my sister (I was never to see her again). Agustín was already married. The only one left was my brother Vicente, also married, and with whom I continued to live in the apartment. I felt a certain sadness and wondered what I was to do there in my room, in that happy Triclinium of an earlier time. With María Teresa I spent hours working on some poems or helping her make revisions in a book of short stories she was preparing. One night after we had come to a serious decision, I did not return home. She and I were now to embark definitively on a new life, free of prejudices, without caring about the gossip—that fearful, priggish brand of Spanish gossip we both despised.

During all this time, that other Spain continued to seethe and could not be repressed. Its deep longings for freedom, which were becoming stronger and more contagious by the day, were spreading everywhere. Even the most unlikely people, those who actually spoke in familial terms about "Our Isabel, Our Victoria, Our Alfonso," suddenly discovered that the splendid theater known as the Royal Palace was nothing more than a gaudy street-fair booth inhabited by grotesque dolls like those drawn by the pen of Valle-Inclán. Sincere and pure friendships began to develop chinks. For the first time during this period, writers joined with each other because of political affinities rather than professional ones. All of them began to understand that they had accounts to settle with the Royal House, governed by a king who was quite illiterate and had never consulted the intellectuals of his own country. Unamuno, Azaña, Ortega, Valle-Inclán, Pérez de Ayala, Marañón, Machado, Baeza, Bergamín,

Espina, Díaz Fernández (to mention only a few) were now working furiously and openly "in the service of the Republic." Under this title there would later be formed a political party whose most visible leaders—Ortega, Marañón, Ayala—deserted on the 18th of July, 1936, when they became convinced that a white-glove policy would not do, and that such gloves would eventually have to be sullied by the bloody faces of the enemy if the Republic was to be truly saved.

That shout which was powerfully but silently zigzagging throughout the country was to explode suddenly, bursting with valor and heroism, in the throat of the Pyrenees one snowy morning in Jaca. "Long Live the Republic!" It was Fermín Galán, a young soldier, who shouted it to the winds; Fermín Galán, whose name was soon to become part of the street poetry, brought there by a growing popular fervor. The people of the nation, filled with illusions, sensed the coming of a second breath of freedom. The bloodied ashes of Galán and García Hernández were to remove the sleeping body of Liberty from the Pantheon where it had lain for fifty-seven years. This figure was to come alive again and be displayed in banners everywhere. The bloody signal had been given, although the right moment had not yet arrived.

It was a December morning. María Teresa and I, like the rest of Madrid, looked up at the cold sky, hoping that the conspiratorial wings of "Cuatro Vientos" would make the final decision. But the wings, sensing that they would become the target of many rifles aimed at them, were forced to fly off in the direction of Lisbon. (One of those planes carried Queipo de Llano and another had as a passenger Ignacio Hidalgo de Cisneros: two opposing Spains in flight which were later to become totally separated from each other. Queipo, the Monarchist, rebels against the King; Queipo, the Republican, rebels against the Republic. On the other hand, Hidalgo de Cisneros, a man of courage and irreproachable behavior, never removed the Republican insignia from his combat plane. On July 18th, during the decisive battles in defense of the Republic, the nation was to appoint him Commander-in-Chief of the Air Force.)

During the first months of the year 1931, the echoes of the executioners' bullets that had cut down Captain Galán and Captain García Hernández were still heard throughout Spain, and such terrorism momentarily obscured the path along which people had begun to move. With almost the entire future government of the Republic in the Model Prison, no one could imagine that a tidal wave was forming beneath the surface and that the water would burst forth, like a fountain and fireworks display, on that fateful April 14th.

At the beginning of February, the Mexican theatrical company of María Teresa Montoya appeared in the Zarzuela Theater. After the unsuccessful presentation of some play which formed part of their repertory, this great actress wanted to try her hand with the work of a Spanish author. My María Teresa, who had known the actress in Buenos Aires, took me to see her. She was a pale, interesting woman, not particularly refined, but possessed of a great dramatic temperament. She asked me if I had any play which might be suitable for her. I told her I did—*El hombre deshabitado*—but that it was not totally finished. The following day I read the work to her, and she was able to confirm that in addition to the role of The Man, there was also an important feminine character: Temptation. She was very enthusiastic, but would I be able to quickly write the missing act? I felt the sky open up above me. That same night I began again to work on the play, and I finished it about a week later while rehearsals were in progress and posters had been distributed all over town. It was a kind of "auto sacramental," a Biblical play in honor of the Sacraments, but naturally without the existence of any Sacrament or, as Díez-Canedo suggested in his flattering critique written on opening night, it was a morality play which had more in common with the works of the Spanish-Portuguese author Gil Vicente than with those of Calderón de la Barca. The direct influence of my *Concerning the Angels* was clearly apparent, although there were no actual angels in the play. The characters were: Man with his Five Senses in allegorical reincarnation, The Maker (represented by a night-watchman), and two women—the Wife of Man, and Temptation, the latter plotting the downfall of both protagonists in complicity with the Senses.

I will not say that the first night was a repetition of the famous *Hernani* opening, but there *was* a rather noisy battle launched on that opening night of February 26th. I was still the same angry young man, half angel and half fool, that I had been during my anarchistic years. For that reason, when the audience called out my name at the end of the play and asked me to speak, I shouted to them with my most challenging smile: "Long Live Extermination! Down with the putrefaction of the Spanish theater of today!" The reaction took on rather scandalous proportions. The theater from top to bottom split up into two separate groups. The putrefied and nonputrefied members of the audience insulted each other threateningly.

289

Students and young critics, standing on their seats, contributed to the great uproar. Benavente and the Quintero Brothers abandoned the hall to the accompaniment of loud, sustained catcalls. None of my works of poetry had ever received more praise than *The Uninhabited Man*. The critics—except those writing for the Catholic newspapers, who accused me of disrespect, impiety and blasphemy —were unanimous in their praise, but they did condemn the imprudent and unnecessary words I had tossed into the audience from the stage.

The work was even discussed extensively outside of Spain, and it was translated almost immediately into French by the great Hispanist Jean Camp. That literary battle which had erupted on opening night was converted into a political battle the night the play closed. Under the pretext that María Teresa Montoya was Mexican and a representative of that prospering country in America, a great homage was organized in her name. The theater was filled to the rafters. Petitions were signed by all sorts of people, in support of this testimonial. Alvarez del Vayo took advantage of the occasion to speak from the stage about the theater in Russia, with clear allusions to and a criticism of our muzzled Spanish existence.

José María Alfaro—that same José María, friend and incipient poet who was later to become a member of the Falangist National Committee and who is now Franco's Ambassador to Argentina! —stood up to read the names of the Republican leaders who had been condemned to prison and whose support for our cause we had carefully obtained that very morning: Alcalá Zamora, Fernando de los Ríos, Largo Caballero ... The spectators loudly acclaimed the reading of these names. The telegram which Unamuno had sent from Salamanca, which we had kept for the last, brought everyone in the hall to his feet. The audience, by now excited and inflamed, marched out as a body into the streets of Madrid. When the police arrived it was already too late. The theater was empty. The only thing left in the wings was the merry-go-round of the uninhabited men which in the play symbolized lifeless human beings, those empty suits of clothes with no one in them that stand on the street corners of the world blocking the way and making it difficult for others to pass.

The tensions during that month of March caused people to utilize the most unusual pretexts to demonstrate their hopes for change. Anything at all would do: a joke told in a café, a couplet with a double meaning, an acrostic sonnet published in the most widely read newspaper, and even public outcries. It was a time of sarcastic nicknames. "Gutiérrez," the name by which the people in the street had baptized their King, was trembling in his palace. Valle-Inclán, and not far behind him the young Republican writers of the journal *Nueva España (New Spain)*, converted their table in the Café La Granja into a political tribunal. Azaña and his friends, serious and reserved, no longer frequented the neighboring Negresco Café. We knew that the Spanish intellectuals fully supported and were working for the realization of our goals. Mysterious journeys, meetings held in elegant bars or taverns in an attempt to throw people off the trail, all these things were aiming in the same direction. Even at the elegant monarchical country club in the Puerta de Hierro, the old rebellious cowbell of the Republic could be heard. And the Duchess of Victoria, in the middle of a patriotic cocktail party, hauled off and gave a white-gloved slap to a young lady, the daughter of a marquis, who in a semi-drunken state had tried to place a small tricolor flag in her hair. Those Republicans who had always been considered somewhat common and vulgar were now philosophers, illustrious professors, great poets and academics, all of whom were democratically involved with student and workers' organizations. The proletariat, which during the first Republic had caused its downfall by trying to precipitate the coming of a free Utopia through their provincial insurrections, was more politically sophisticated in the year 1931 and fully supported this new movement, particularly with its vast number of Socialists, a group that was soon to figure prominently in the political arena.

I also traveled, but not for political reasons. I went first to Sevilla, alone, without María Teresa, to pay homage to Fernando Villalón, on the first anniversary of his death. There, where we had been once again called together by Sánchez Mejías, we found ourselves with Bergamín, Eusebio Oliver, Pepín Bello, Santiago Ontañón, Miguel Pérez Ferrero, and others. The testimonial was simple and almost intimate. In the morning we dedicated a plaque which had been installed in the house where Fernando lived, and in the evening there was a prose and poetry reading in one of the university classrooms. There were no great repercussions, and the events were attended only by the group of young poets from the magazine *Mediodía*.

During this brief stay in Sevilla, we did meet the congenial Rafael Ortega, the wild gypsy dancer and singer. He was the son of an old gypsy whose sister, Gabriela, was the mother of those famous bullfighters known as the Gallo Brothers. Rafael insisted that we meet his mother, whom he deeply loved. It was a strange visit. This gypsy lady, who by that time had become a huge, witch-like character with double chin and moustache, round as a table and with a harsh whiskey voice, received us without any signs of enthusiasm. She remained seated in the center of the room while Rafael raced back and forth introducing all of us to her. He was incapable of standing still, and his attentiveness toward his mother was extremely exaggerated. He kept kissing her, stroking her hair and chin until his mother began to call him "fairy" every two seconds. As we were leaving, Ignacio told us that one day this imposing woman had gotten fed up with her son's friends and in anger had thrown them all out as if they were so many cats, to the accompaniment of these strange words: "For the little combs that my cousin Elvira lost in the throes of death, you young fairies and you old fairies, get out of here! Shoo! Shoo!" Every time I went to Sevilla, Ignacio had new, strange things to tell me.

Immediately thereafter, I made another trip through Andalucía, but this time accompanied by María Teresa. We had to rest a little after *The Uninhabited Man*. We decided to go to Rota, a small white village located on the Bay of Cádiz. On the way we passed through the Puerto. This was a nocturnal visit, unannounced, and we had time to eat our fried fish accompanied by large glasses of that special Fino Coquinero wine. There in Rota—sparkling whitewashed walls flashing in the sun, and sandy pumpkin patches—I began to work on a new play, *Las horas muertas (Dead Hours)*, now that I had been encouraged by my recent success as a playwright. At the same time I began to compose a ballad on the life of Fermín Galán, the romantic hero assassinated in Jaca, who had actually been born near Rota on the island of San Fernando.

But our eagerly sought tranquility was not to last very long. We had only been strolling along the beaches for a week when Sánchez Mejías appeared and suggested that we accompany him to Jerez. Igancio was at that time involved in organizing an Andalusian dance company which was later to be directed by La Argentinita. With the help of García Lorca, this group was to become world-famous. He was searching for pure gypsy dancers and singers who had not yet been contaminated by what was known in Madrid as "Flamenco Opera." And there was no better place than Jerez and the villages along the bay to find what he wanted. What fantastic discoveries our friends made on that journey! Together with the monumental figure of Espeleta, who looked like a singing Buddha, Ignacio was able to extract from the town squares and hidden patios a whole group of young children, bronzed and flexibly graceful, whose extraordinary contortions at times bordered on scandalous obscenity. He made his greatest acquisitions in Sevilla, where he discovered La Macarrona, La Malena and La Fernanda, three old and almost forgotten ladies who in their day had represented the very best of Flamenco dancing. La Fernanda was so ancient that she could hardly stand up, but she had once danced with La Gabriela and La Mejorana in the famous Café del Burrero. All of them were practically starving, and they accepted with their heads filled with fantastic notions of international travel and success. Only one gypsy refused, and that happened in Jerez the day after our arrival.

We were in the hotel room getting ready to leave when someone pushed open the door and asked: "Is this where I can find Don Rafael Alberti, the most important musical comedy impresario in Spain?"

This was one of Ignacio's jokes. It was perfect. At that moment, laughing hysterically, someone appeared behind the first gypsy. He was a vivacious type, about forty years old, thin, graceful, with extremely white teeth and bursting with good will.

"I am Chele—olé, olé!—and I am here to sign a contract."

"Fine," I responded in all seriousness, very much caught up in the role that Sánchez Mejías has assigned to me. "And what can you do, Chele?"

"Me? The dance of the brush!"

And grabbing a clothes brush that was on the bed, he began his fantastic *zapateado** while at the same time he rhythmically and gracefully brushed his jacket and pants.

"Bravo!" I said to him. "That will be a magnificent number. You're hired on the spot."

Ignacio interrupted: "Very good, Chele, but listen to what I have to say. We will pay you, in addition to costumes, travel expenses and room and board, fifty *pesetas* a day just for your dance of the brush. What do you say to that?"

Zapateado is a Spanish flamenco dance step in which the performer strikes the floor with his or her boot heels in complicated rhythm patterns.

"Fifty *pesetas*?" And he stood there meditating for some time. "Do you have a pencil, Don Ignacio?"

The three of us looked at each other in surprise. Ignacio, without saying a word, gave him a pencil. Chele, suddenly very serious took a torn piece of paper from one of his pockets and began to make strange calculations, seeming to perform some complicated mathematical operations. He then declared quite decisively, with the air of a successful businessman: "That doesn't suit me. I'd lose money."

"Oh, so you would lose money?" said Ignacio slowly, almost without being able to control his laughter.

"No doubt about it. You can see my figures," answered the gypsy, handing him the paper which contained some unintelligible scribblings. "I'd lose money. You see, Don Ignacio, that position you offer me couldn't possibly be a lifetime job. And the thing is, I make a living just by being amusing and by reciting sermons I learn from the priests in church. When the job you offer me is finished and people see me in Jerez with a new suit and smoking a cigar, they'll all say that Chele is rich, swimming in gold, and then who will hire Chele to hear his funny remarks? So you see, Don Ignacio, it wouldn't work. I'd end up losing money. Good morning. Olé! I'm off."

And he strutted out of the room after returning the pencil to Ignacio.

Our eagerly sought privacy turned out to be impossible, and on returning to Rota there was a telegram from the Ateneo in Cádiz inviting me to give a reading of my poetry. We were once again traveling along the coastal roads of my childhood.

Cádiz, the city of freedom, of romantic conspiracies and the first Masonic lodges; Cádiz, where no workman could be found to remove from its walls the plaque that commemorated the Constitution of 1812,* that same Cádiz which I used to see from my schoolroom windows like some unattainable blue stamp, was now being battered from one end to the other by the winds of Republicanism. The political folklore which had existed under the First Republic was reborn, and in the dark corners where *cante jondo* was sung, in little out-of-the-way bars and taverns, its musical sounds could be heard. It was there that I learned this little ballad:

*The Constitution of 1812 was approved by the Cortes (Spanish Parliament) in Cádiz and later abolished by Fernando VII in 1814, soon after his return to the throne. It was reinstated in 1820 and abrogated once again in 1823.

Republicana es la luna,
republicano es el sol,
republicano es el aire,
republicano soy yo.

The moon is Republican,
Republican is the sun,
The air is Republican,
Republican am I.

The great bulk of Cádiz seemed to be seething at the water's edge as if waiting for something to happen. On the afternoon of my reading, the audience in the Ateneo—the majority of whom were students—could not sit still in their seats. When I was about to begin, a young man suddenly jumped onto the stage and shouted:

"Rafael Alberti will not be allowed to say anything in this hall as long as Pemán is present."

That poet of Jerez, a partisan of the Monarchy, was in the audience. I had never seen him before. When I decided to ask him to leave, I discovered that he had already walked out. He had shown enough tact to leave immediately. My recital became more heated when I read the "Elegía Cívica" ("Civic Elegy"). The doors and walls began to vibrate. At the end of my reading I even dared to recite one of those ballads I had written in honor of the hero from Jaca:

Noche negra, siete años
de noche negra sin luna.
Primo de Rivera duerme
su sueño de verde uva.
Su Majestad va de caza:
mata piojos y pulgas
y monta yeguas que pronto
ni siquiera serán burras.

Dark night, seven years
Of dark and moonless nights.
Primo de Rivera dreams
His dream of the green grape.
His Majesty is off to the hunt,

He kills lice and fleas,
And mounts his mares that soon
Will not even she-asses be.

That ballad met with great success. It was greeted with applause and shouts of *Viva!* as well as with consternation on the part of some members of the audience. The following day, a street demonstration was organized by those same Ateneo students and I was asked to recite another episode from the Ballad of Fermín Galán. I shouted it out at the top of my voice, standing on a table of a café where we had all gathered while the authorities, represented by some poor uniformed guards referred to in our operettas as *guindillas* or "little red peppers," listened to me in a daze, not even considering that their sabers could have dispersed us all.

Filled with happiness and the sense that something new and serious was imminent, we returned to Rota. We remained there resting, working, lying in the sand dunes, running barefoot along the shores, far removed from the political and electoral worries that had all of Spain in a state of anxiety.

But suddenly everything changed. Someone called us by telephone from Madrid, shouting: "Long Live the Republic!"

It was high noon and the sun shone brilliantly. Written on a page of the sea was the date of a fine spring day: April 14.

Surprised and excited, we raced into the streets and saw with astonishment that up there in the little tower of Rota's City Hall an old flag of the Republic of 1873 displayed its three colors against the Andalusian sky. Groups of peasants and other peaceful inhabitants of the town had gathered on the street corners, commenting on the sudden appearance of that flag and listening to a scratched version of the *Marseillaise* which some impatient Republican had put on his phonograph, turning the volume up full blast. We knew that Madrid was celebrating the event with festivities and that people were teeming through the streets satirizing in poems and effigies the dynasty which was traveling by car toward Cartagena. A poor member of the Rota Civil Guard who was leaning against the sun-and-fly-covered wall surrounding his little headquarters shook his head and repeated dejectedly: "There's no way! No way! I'll never get used to it! Never!"

"What is it you'll never get used to?" asked his companion, another member of the Civil Guard.

"What do you think? I'll never get used to being without a king! Something will always seem to be missing."

Once again and as always, I began to see clearly that there were two Spains: this was the same wall of incomprehension that continued to keep us apart, a wall that one day would collapse and leave behind a great river of blood. María Teresa and I talked about this on our way to Madrid. The new flag had been raised only an hour ago, and yet the one which had been vanquished had already begun to tremble and create vibrations of civil war. The Republic had just been proclaimed amidst fireworks and clear displays of jubilation. The people had forgotten their sorrows and former hunger and had joyfully banded together in infantile groups and parades, attacking as if in a game the bronze and granite kings who remained impassive beneath the branches of the trees. The Queen and the royal family, abandoned in the Oriente Palace, were protected by these same, noble people who formed a human chain around the royal mansion. No one can say that they assaulted the palace, stole the treasures, plundered the banks, or even killed a hen. The only serious incident I can remember is a stone that had shattered the windows of a car belonging to the poet Pedro Salinas as he drove through the Cibeles Circle accompanied by the French author Jean Cassou. All was relatively peaceful, sensible and civil. As people repeated with a sense of satisfaction, the Republic had arrived in an atmosphere of complete legality. The words of Azaña struck the right note:

> It is truly exciting to think that the Republic of 1931 had to come so that for the first time the Constitution could offer a truly constitutional guarantee (a guarantee of freedom for the individual) which the people of Castile had demanded back in 1529.

In general, intellectuals, authors and artists celebrated the event. Works that had been prohibited could now be produced. Irene López Heredia praised the Republic by presenting Valle-Inclán's play *La farsa de la reina castiza* (*The Farce of the Pure-Blooded Queen*). The actress who best epitomized the new Republic was Margarita Xirgu, always the true friend of poets and writers. She presented Azaña's *La corona* (*The Crown*) and my *Fermín Galán*.

Almost immediately upon my arrival in Madrid, I dashed off, filled with civic enthusiasm, to propose to Margarita my plan to convert those ballads of mine dedicated to the hero of Jaca into a play which would be a simple, popular work in which I would not stick so much to historical truth as to the events that had already been somewhat deformed by the people and were beginning to spread in the form of a legend. This was a rather dangerous enterprise, since the truth of what had happened was still very much alive and the fictional version was not yet well defined. I began to work very seriously at this adaptation. My plan was to write a *romance de ciego*,* a colorful spectacle similar to those presented at country fairs to describe the latest crimes. I was innocently and almost unconsciously writing my first political work. Margarita had accepted the first two acts, and while I was preparing the third one the posters announcing a performance of *Fermín Galán* appeared outside the Teatro Español.

In the meantime, and in the midst of rehearsals of my play, I had the opportunity of coming into direct contact with Don Miguel de Unamuno, whom I had met one morning in the Café La Granja el Henar. I invited him to our house on the Paseo de Rosales, with its balcony that overlooked the evergreen oaks of El Pardo and faced the Escorial framed in the distance against the celestial blue of the Guadarrama Mountains. But our invitation had been extended on the condition that Don Miguel would read us something, whatever he preferred, from his latest works of poetry.

"No, I won't do that," he had replied at the time, "I would prefer to read you my latest play, still only in draft form, which is called *El hermano Juan (Brother John)*. I think you will be interested in hearing it."

I remember this as a marvelous afternoon. The only other person we had invited was César Vallejo, the sad and profound "half-breed" Peruvian poet who had become a political refugee from his own country and was then living in Spain. I was not as concerned with the meaning of *Brother John* as I was by the magnificent figure of Unamuno himself, the noble expression on his face and the way in which he zealously carried off the interminable reading of his draft in which the pages were often out of place or actually missing, so that Don Miguel was obliged to fill in with his own words. No, I didn't pay much attention to the play, and never even bothered to find out

---

*A *romance de ciego* ('blind man's ballad') often deals either with a historical theme or recent event and was recited by a blind beggar in the streets of villages or at country fairs.

if he later published it. What is vivid in my memory is the spectacle of that powerful old man, his magnificent example of health and energy, of fecundity and enthusiasm.

When more than three hours later he had concluded the reading of his drama, he still possessed enough wit and vigor to search with his fingers through the pockets of his vest in a playfully childlike way for those little slips of paper on which he had scribbled his poems. These were poems that had suddenly assaulted him while he was walking down the street and which he wrote down while leaning against a street-lamp or standing in some other unlikely spot. So on that afternoon in our house and by the light of the late afternoon sun coming from the mountains, he deciphered for us a harsh and beautiful poem dedicated to the bisons in the Caves of Altamira and a lullaby he had written for his new grandchild, a delicate musical cadence which was like a strange plant in his garden of esparto grass and harsh winds.

On June 1st, a few days after that meeting with Unamuno, *Fermín Galán* had its opening night. Margarita played the role of the hero's mother, and Fermín was played by Pedro López Lagar, who was just then beginning to achieve renown and prestige as an actor. As was to be expected, the Republicans turned out to see the performance that night, but there were also large groups of Monarchists scattered throughout the theater and prepared to make trouble. The first act went well, but when during the second they performed the scene in which I had the wild idea of having the Virgin appear with rifle and bayonet to defend the battered group of rebels and demanding the heads of the King and General Berenguer, the entire theater protested violently. The atheistic Republicans objected to the very appearance of the Virgin, and the Monarchists were horrified to hear such criminal feelings expressed by the Mother of God whom I had invented. But the worst was still to come: the scene in which Cardinal Monsignor Segura appeared drunk and sputtering Latin phrases like a character straight out of Molière, during a party held at the palace of the Duke and Duchess. The enemy could not take this "blasphemy" sitting down. They moved forward in waves from everywhere in the theater, advancing toward the stage with shouts and clubs. Fortunately someone in the wings ordered the metallic curtain, the one used only in case of fire, to be lowered as soon as possible. In spite of this, and since the audience was still willing to see the work through to its conclusion, Margarita—who was a real Agustina of Aragón that evening—had courage enough to perform the epilogue. She was greeted at the end of the play with a bombardment of insults and applause, both for her extraordinary courage and her well-earned reputation.

The critics were not as favorably disposed toward *Fermín Galán* as they had been with *El hombre deshabitado*. The Catholic newspapers practically demanded my head, and the Republicans, although praising certain passages of the work, also pointed out its evident failings, considering the main one to be a lack of historical perspective that was evident in the presentation of episodes that had just only recently occurred. In part their objections were valid. But my greatest error undoubtedly consisted in my having presented a *romance de ciego* —whose stage setting should have been some village square— before a bourgeois, aristocratic and in some ways sectarian audience whose nails were still quite sharp and pointed. Although I didn't realize it then, latent in them were all those germs which in the course of a very few years would multiply and develop until they created that bloody explosion which would finally bring about the collapse of the new Republic.

Only a few days after the opening, an elegant horse-drawn carriage came to a stop along the Carriage Path of the Retiro Gardens. A very severely dressed lady, black *mantilla* covering her head, prayer book in hand, descended from the vehicle. Under the shade of the trees a simple and rather ordinary-looking lady was calmly strolling. The woman of the carriage approached her. "Are you Margarita Xirgu?" And, before the actress could even reply: "Take that! That's for *Fermín Galán!*" she said, slapping Margarita across the face and then dashing off.

The play had a run that lasted the whole month of June. It may not have affected anyone else, but in spite of its rather limited success, *Fermín Galán* allowed me to give vent to feelings that were surging within me and it stirred me to make my choice and my sacrifice. I now clearly and sharply saw before my eyes the common cause of the people.

The earlier storms were receding . . . Step by step, tenaciously, the Lost Grove continued to advance, overtaking my own footsteps.

EPILOGUE

AT LAST this second book of *The Lost Grove*, begun so long ago (how long has it been?), is finished. And here it stands. Many branches have been lost along the way. Many leaves, which subsequent breezes later swept before my eyes, could not be grasped nor affixed to these pages. There are, therefore, numerous blank spaces that are in no way indicative of my forgetfulness. I would have had to go back to what had already been done, to make a clearing in the thick underbrush of its sentences, in order to place here and there other names, events or commentaries that I remembered afterwards. But the job of interpolating such things in their suitable places would have had the ultimate effect of making it impossible for me ever to reach the longed-for conclusion to this period of my memories. Perhaps some day in a future edition, and with the possible help of enthusiastic readers, they will occupy the space I have reserved for them. Will such a future work be written in Spain or will I still be here in Argentina, where the final section of the first part and the entire second book were written? I cannot say for sure, but there is something in my country that is on the verge of collapse. Among us, the Spanish exiles, there are breezes circulating which sing to us a song of return. In the meantime . . .

I have planted a new grove, but it is not like the one from my Andalusian childhood that is lost forever. This grove is located in the woods of Castelar, an hour's train ride from Buenos Aires. It is there

I wish to conclude this epilogue, but first I also want to speak about it, about my lovely American Lost Grove.

The woods of Castelar—or the Leloir Park, which is the name of its most beautiful section—are huge and filled with unexpected wonders. How many people and friends of mine are unaware of the existence of these forests! They are amazed when they see them for the first time. More amazing still are they for one who lives in the midst of them and awakens surrounded by the wintry mists, or by the almost burnished gold of its autumn season or the audible musical green of its spring and summer. This dense shade at first seems to be deserted, but it is criss-crossed by roads that ask to be explored. The shadows are filled with houses and mansions scarcely glimpsed behind the curtains of branches, flowers and thick vines. Here in these murmuring thickets some time ago, I chose the isolated place I needed for my incessant work, some spot far removed from the city, from the tremendous city which nonetheless continues to advance voraciously, perhaps with the hidden thought of assaulting these woods one day with axe in hand in order to erect its hideous buildings there and replace those pure and perfumed paths with noisy, unhealthy streets. But that can never happen. Or at least *I* will not see it happen.

Here among these thick branches I chose, or perhaps found, my new Lost Grove, a beautiful rectangular strip of land with its orderly stands of cypress and poplar trees, a secret simple garden that is as classical as that of an ancient Roman villa. Along the one side that is lined with yellow *huisache* trees is a street called Receros; on the other side, with its growth of dark oak, is Vidalita Street. Inside, in a clearing which is like an intimate enclosure, I have planted my house. It is a prefabricated house of wood, full of brightly varnished charm with its white trim, doors, and shutters. A long violent storm brought unexpected floods just when we had planned to erect it. The engineer, Israel Dujovne, a great enthusiast of my new Grove, had already laid the cement foundation on which the house was to rest, an extended plinth that had arisen from the grass as if awaiting the arrival of some work of classical sculpture. But the heavens, which had dissolved in torrents of water, had declared war against us. Many of the roads were like rivers, and the forest floor seemed to have drowned after having swallowed so much water. Every morning in Buenos Aires we looked up at the sky with great impatience. But it continued to rain furiously while our house, in bits and pieces, waited in a storage shed in the village of Ramos Mejía. What could we do? Autumn was coming to a close, and we had dreamed of bidding it farewell from our new house in the Grove. But the rain continued to fall indefatigably, although now with less intensity. Finally one Monday morning the sun pushed its way between the clouds, and two days later, very early in the morning, Dujovne phoned us: "Be ready in a few minutes. They're going to deliver your house."

The three of us drove off at top speed to witness the great event, and were soon at the Lost Grove. The ground had begun to harden, but we were still under an overcast sky which could at any moment again dampen our illusions. We had already begun to feel restless when a huge truck made its triumphant appearance on Vidalita Street, loaded with its cargo of wood. Six determined men got out of the vehicle. This pile of stacked lumber was to be our future home! It was necessary to work rapidly, since the weather was still unstable. Working in pairs and with the help of hooks, the workers placed on the ground—in their corresponding places around the platform— those huge pieces of a puzzle or stage set that a few days later would comprise our forest refuge. The most urgent thing was to get the roof on. Rain was strictly prohibited; the water could not be allowed to damage the inside of the wood.

With this new problem preying on our minds, we returned to Buenos Aires. How horrible were those three nights we spent there, filled with frightful nightmares of cyclones and rainstorms! I was in a state of almost uncontrollable hysteria. When we returned to Castelar with Dujovne that Sunday, the cypress and poplar trees of the Lost Grove, which seemed to be standing stiffer and straighter than ever, appeared to be saluting our house, whose polished virginal wood gave it the look of a strange ship which had been brought to the center of the forest to be painted. A ship? Such was the delirium of a poet.

After I had partially gotten over my sense of anxiety, I devoted myself to imitating Dujovne's enthusiasm for the house. Along those paths and roads he found workers who were to give shape to the structure and complete its construction. The first one to appear, mounted on a huge white horse, was Martínez, the foreman, a talkative and amusing individual who came with his helpers— masons and bricklayers—who gave the impression of a band of squires accompanying their noble knight on foot. Next came two young men on motorcycles, but looking like peasants—they were the painters. One of them had previously been a trumpet player in a military band. Two days later the drainage engineer came, and he was later followed by the carpenter who was to build the floor. It was an intimate and charming spectacle complete with *mate* and outdoor barbecues, all of which gave the scene a popular and festive air.

And now, in spite of rainstorms and high winds, the Lost Grove is finally finished. Dujovne smiles with satisfaction as he might have at a group of children whom he had helped to construct a delightful playhouse. Martínez, the foreman, somewhat sad and gloomy and mounted on his white nag, which for me had become a truly marvelous beast, has disappeared into the forest. On their winged motorcycles the painters have taken their leave.

But what was still missing was the pool, a mirror of water where the clouds would be reflected and the birds could bathe. Around it we would plant orange trees, lemon trees, *quinotos.** Everything was going to turn out perfectly. We look upward. There is no sign of rain. The sky is a dazzling blue, almost like the blue of Cádiz. The sun moves peacefully across my Argentinian Grove. With it go my greetings to that other distant Lost Grove of my youth.

The Lost Grove, July 1959

*The *quinoto* or *quino* trees are the source of quinine; they belong to the Rubiacea family.

GLOSSARY OF
NAMES AND PLACES

ALCALÁ ZAMORA, NICETO (1877–1949): leftist Republican political figure who became President of the Republic in 1931. He was forced to resign near the beginning of the Civil War.

ALEIXANDRE, VICENTE (b. 1898): Spain's finest surrealist poet and one of the most important poets writing in Spain today. His works include *La destrucción o el amor (Destruction or Love)* and *Sombra del paraíso (The Shadow of Paradise)*.

ALEMANY Y SELFA, BERNARDO: a prominent academic literary critic and historian. He was held in contempt by the younger "Gongoristas" for the unimpassioned and academically analytical approach he took to the poet's works. This approach is manifested in *El vocabulario de 'Góngora*.

ALONSO, AMADO (1896–1952): philologist, linguist and literary critic. His works include *Materia y forma en poesía* and *Estudios lingüísticos* as well as studies on Pablo Neruda and Valle-Inclán. He was a professor in Buenos Aires and later at Harvard.

ALONSO, DÁMASO (b. 1898): one of Spain's most erudite and incisive literary critics and a poet in his own right. His poetic work *Hijos de la ira (Children of Ire)*, published in 1944, describes Madrid as a cemetery where more than a million cadavers are rotting in their niches. He has written many essays on the poetic generation to which Alberti belonged.

ALTOLAGUIRRE, MANUEL (1905–1961): Spanish poet whose work is distinguished by its delicacy and ingenuity. The main themes of his poetry are love, nature and solitude. He translated the *Adonais* of Shelley and was the founder of several poetry journals.

ALVAREZ DEL VAYO, JULIO (1891–1975): the last Foreign Minister of the Second Spanish Republic, he continued in exile to write about the events of the Spanish Civil War and its aftermath. *Freedom's Battle* (1940), *The Last Optimist* (1950) and *Give Me Combat* (1973) are the English titles of his three books on the subject.

ANGUIANO MANGADO, DANIEL: Socialist Party leader who took part in the Cuatro Vientos rebellion. He later served as Spanish Socialist delegate to the Second Comintern.

ANNUAL: The Morrocan site of a 1921 battle which was a disastrous defeat for the Spanish in their effort to subdue the Moroccan rebels. It also marked the beginning of the decline of popular confidence in the Monarchy.

ARANJUEZ: a city near Madrid on the banks of the Tagus River which became the summer residence of the Spanish monarchs. The Royal Palace, begun by Felipe II and completed by Felipe V and Carlos III, is set among magnificent gardens and unusual fountains.

ARCONADA, CÉSAR MARÍA (1900–1964): Spanish author and essayist who at one time was the Managing Editor of the literary journal *La Gaceta Literaria*. From 1939 until his death, he lived in Moscow where he devoted himself primarily to translating the works of Spanish classical authors into Russian.

ARNICHES Y BARRERA, CARLOS (1866–1943): Spanish dramatist especially noted for his comedies depicting the life of the people of Madrid.

ARTIGAS FERRANDO, MIGUEL (1887–1947): an erudite investigator and professor of literature, he was appointed Director of the Biblioteca Nacional in 1930. He is the author of several critical works on Góngora and Quevedo.

ASTRANA MARÍN, LUIS (1889–1960): literary critic and historian, he edited the works of several authors of the Spanish Golden Age, particularly Quevedo and Lope de Vega. He is perhaps best known for his monumental seven volume biography of Cervantes.

AUB, MAX (1903–1971): novelist, essayist, and playwright who was educated in Spain and wrote only in Spanish, although he was of German background. He came to Spain in 1914 and left after the Civil War to settle in Mexico. He wrote many short stories and novels, his last being *Jusep Torres Campalans,* an ingenious tale about a painter who seems to be a cross between Picasso and Gaugin. Aub himself painted all the works which are reproduced in the novel and are attributed to Campalans. His brief return to Spain is described in his diary *La gallina ciega (Blind Man's Buff),* published in Mexico in 1971.

AZORÍN: pseudonym for José Martínez Ruiz (1873–1967), novelist, playwright, critic and essayist of the Generation of 1898 who moved from a rebellious youth to a solidly conservative and rather traditional approach to both politics and literature in later life. His works include *Castilla, Los pueblos, La ruta de Don Quijote, Brandy, mucho brandy* and *Doña Inés.*

BAROJA NESSI, PÍO (1872–1957): prolific novelist of the Generation of 1898—although he himself denied the affiliation —whose dark vision of human nature dominated by cruelty, dishonesty and violence permeates many of his novels. His better-known works are *Zalacaín el aventurero (Zalacaín the Adventurer), Camino de perfección (Road to Perfection)* and *El árbol de la ciencia (The Tree of Science).*

BASTERRA, RAMÓN DE (1888–1928): a Spanish diplomat, poet and essayist, he was a firm believer in the supremacy of Spanish culture over that of the Anglo-Saxon world. Basterra was convinced that Castile was destined to play the role of ancient Rome and that Spain should be viewed by contemporary society as the modern equivalent of classical antiquity.

BÉCQUER, GUSTAVO ADOLFO (1836–1870): Spanish Romantic poet little known during his own lifetime but whose *Rimas (Lyric Poems)* are now famous throughout the Hispanic world.

BERCEO, GONZALO DE (1195?-1264): the earliest Spanish poet whose name is known. He wrote on religious themes but in popular language, and his poems were often utilized by the Church to popularize religious legends. A prolific writer, his works include *Santo Domingo de Silos, El sacrificio de la misa (The Sacrifice of the Mass)* and *Milagros de Nuestra Señora (Miracles of Our Lady).*

BERENGUER, DÁMASO (1878-1953): Minister of War in 1918 and during the Spanish defeat at Annual, after which he retired from active service. Alfonso XIII appointed him Prime Minister during the last months of the Monarchy, but he could not put down the rebellious Republicans and was overthrown along with the king in 1931. During the next year he was condemned to death, but was pardoned in 1934.

BERGAMÍN, JOSÉ (b. 1894): literary critic and essayist of Alberti's generation. His works include *Las fronteras infernales de la poesía (The Infernal Frontiers of Poetry), El arte del birlibirloque (The Art of Bullfighting)* and *Al volver (Return).* This last work was written after his return to Spain following an absence of twenty years.

BESTEIRO, JULIÁN (1870-1939): reformist Socialist who became President of the UGT and served in the Cortes, or Spanish Parliament, during the Republic.

BLASCO IBÁÑEZ, VICENTE (1867-1929): a regional novelist of the Naturalist School who wrote mainly about the area of Spain known as the Levante. He achieved international fame as a result of his novel *Los cuatro jinetes del Apocalipsis (The Four Horsemen of the Apocalypse)* which appeared in 1916. In addition to being a novelist, he was a staunch and politically active anti-monarchist with equally strong anti-clerical views.

BOCÁNGEL, GABRIEL (1608-1658): Baroque poet.

CALDERÓN DE LA BARCA, PEDRO (1600-1681): dramatist of the Spanish Golden Age whose most famous works are *La vida es sueño (Life is a Dream), El alcalde de Zalamea (The Mayor of Zalamea)* and *El mágico prodigioso (The Prodigious Magician).* He was the author of approximately two hundred dramatic works, including eighty "auto sacramentales" or one act plays dealing with the sacrament of the Eucharist.

CARLIST: this term refers to the followers of Don Carlos, the claimant to the Spanish throne under the Salic law on the death of Fernando VII in 1833. Carlos was Fernando's brother, but Fernando had wished his daughter Isabel to inherit the throne. There have been three Carlist wars and the issue of succession is not entirely dead, even today. In the province of Navarra and among the Basques, the Carlist movement has been extremely active.

CARPENTIER, ALEJO (b. 1904): Cuban poet, musician and writer, author of *El reino de este mundo (The Kingdom of This World)* and other novels dealing with Negro themes.

CARRERE, EMILIO (1881–1947): novelist, poet and critic.

CASTELLANA, PASEO DE LA: one of the major boulevards in Madrid; it was once a fashionable place to walk or ride along in carriages. It is still a beautiful, tree-lined street, but the residential aspect is disappearing as the traffic and high-rise construction increase.

CASTRO, AMÉRICO (1885–1972): formerly a distinguished professor at the University of Madrid, whose long period of exile in the United States was spent primarily as a member of the faculty of Princeton University. Although he began his academic career as a philologist, he extended his fields of investigation to include the literature and history of Spain. His extremely fertile and highly productive period of exile led to the publication of his book *España en su historia: cristianos, moros y judíos* (1948) in which he presented an original and controversial theory of Spanish history and culture, which has had an incalculable impact on subsequent research in Hispanic studies. A second version of this work was published in 1954 under the title *La realidad histórica de España (The Structure of Spanish History)* and still another augmented version in English, *The Spaniards,* was published by the University of California Press in 1971.

CAUDILLO: the popular term used to refer to Generalísimo Franco, the most recent dictator of Spain. The word means leader, chief or boss.

CERNUDA, LUIS (1902–1963): one of the most interesting and complex poets of the Alberti generation, whose works are receiving critical attention at the present time. Cernuda has affinities with Bécquer, but his poetry is more varied and elegiac, with classical overtones. He translated Shakespeare and Hölderin and published several essays on various national literatures. He lived outside Spain in an unhappy exile and taught in the United States; he died in Mexico. His better-known works are *Perfil del aire* and *La realidad y el deseo*.

CERRO DE LOS ANGELES: a hill near Madrid on which there is a huge statue of Christ. This is reputed to be the exact geographical center of Spain.

CHURRIGUERA, JOSÉ (1665–1723): the most famous member of a family of Spanish architects, he created an exuberant and complicated architectural style which came to be known as "churrigueresco." His highly ornamental architecture was a blend of gothic, plateresque and baroque styles. His brother Alberto (1676–1740) drew up the plans for the Plaza Mayor of Salamanca.

EL CID: the name given to Don Rodrigo Díaz de Vivar (1040–1099), a Spanish warrior whose deeds are recorded in the *Cantar de mío Cid* (anonymous), an unusually realistic epic poem which portrays the Cid as a faithful vassal to his king, loving husband and father, and a cunning warrior against the Moors. One of the interesting aspects of this work is that it was undoubtedly recited to people who had known the historical figure of Rodrigo Díaz. As a result, the legendary aspects of the Cid are not as predominant in the poem as they were to become in later versions of his story.

CUATRO VIENTOS (FOUR WINDS): an airport near Madrid which was captured by the Republicans, who had begun their rebellion at Jaca. The uprising, which was swiftly crushed (for the time being) by Monarchist troops, took its name from that of the airport.

DARÍO, RUBÉN: pseudonym for Félix Rubén García Sarmiento (1867–1916), Nicaraguan poet, journalist and diplomat who spent many years abroad, living in Chile, Argentina, Spain and

France. He founded and led the Modernist movement in Hispanic literature and had an important influence on contemporary poetry in Spanish. Author of *Azul, Prosas profanas, El canto errante* and numerous other works.

DATO IRADIER, EDUARDO (1856–1921): Conservative Party leader and the President of the Council of Ministers 1914–1918 and 1921–1922. He was killed by an assassin.

DIEGO, GERARDO (b. 1896): Spanish poet, contemporary of Alberti and leader of the *Creacionista* and *Ultraísta* literary movements in Spain. *Creacionismo* and *Ultraísmo* constituted important poetic "schools" during the second and third decades of the twentieth century. *Ultraísmo* affirmed the urgency of an art free from ties with the past, claimed a relationship with Dadaism, and wished to liberate Spanish poetry from the false trappings of an exaggerated modernism into which the *ultraístas* felt it had degenerated. The *creacionistas* were followers of a poetic doctrine elaborated in 1916 by the Chilean poet Vicente Huidobro and closely related to the ideas of the French poet Pierre Reverdy. The basic principal was "to create a poem as Nature creates a tree." In *Creacionismo* there was a desire to escape from the limits of social reality and moral purpose in literature.

DÍEZ-CANEDO, ENRIQUE (1879–1944): Modernist poet and critic. He was one of the most influential critics in Spain, writing on literature as well as art. He wrote a biography of Juan Ramón Jiménez, translated Verlaine and published many journal articles. He also served as Spanish Ambassador to Uruguay and Argentina.

D'ORS, EUGENIO (1882–1954): known primarily as an essayist and interpreter of the Generation of 1898. His influence on the youth of Spain was at one time as great as that of Ortega y Gasset. He wrote first in Catalan under the pseudonym of Xenius and was a novelist, art historian and philosopher. Some of his works include *El arte de Goya, Cézanne, Picasso, Las ideas y las formas (Ideas and Forms)* and *El secreto de la filosofía (The Secret of Philosophy)*.

ECHEGARAY, JOSÉ (1832–1916): Spanish mathematician and

playwright who won the Nobel Prize for Literature in 1904. His works were extremely popular with the general theater audiences of Spain.

ESPINOSA, PEDRO DE (1578–1650): Spanish Baroque poet, contemporary of Lope de Vega, Cervantes and Góngora, and author of *La fábula del Genil*.

FELIPE CAMINO, LEÓN (1884–1968): Spanish poet whose long period of exile is captured in a series of poems that are almost biblical in tone. He has come to be known as *El español del éxodo y del llanto (The Spaniard of Exodus and Lament)*, the title of his most famous collection of poems. He was a great admirer of Walt Whitman, whose *Song of Myself* he translated into Spanish as *Canto a mí mismo*. His poetry often shows mystical and prophetic qualities that are reminiscent of Whitman, but he was also greatly influenced by the Spanish mystics as well as by Unamuno and Antonio Machado. He died in Mexico.

FRAY LUIS DE LEÓN (1528–1591): a mystic, a poet and a great humanist. He was a member of the Order of Saint Augustine in Salamanca and taught at the university there. Fray Luis de León was involved in a series of bitter controversies fomented by personal rivalries and by other religious orders. He was accused by the Inquisition of being a *judaizante*, or sympathetic to Jewish culture, because of his interest in the ancient Hebrew biblical texts. He was also condemned for having translated the *Song of Songs* and was imprisoned for five years (1572–1576). He was eventually vindicated and returned to Salamanca, where he is purported to have renewed his classes at the university with the words "Decíamos ayer" ("As we were saying yesterday . . .").

GALÁN, FERMÍN (1899–1930): soldier and social critic who began the rebellion at Cuatro Vientos airport and was the first to proclaim the establishment of the Second Republic on December 12, 1930. He was court-martialed and shot two days later. Galán was the author of a radical utopian treatise on social problems called *Nueva creación (New Creation)*.

GARCÍA HERNÁNDEZ, ANGEL (1900–1930): a Republican soldier under Galán who was sent to negotiate with the government troops. They detained him, and after a summary war tribunal he was shot.

GARCÍA LORCA, FEDERICO (1899–1936): although all the details are not known even to this day, García Lorca was shot to death in Granada in the Spanish Civil War. Throughout Lorca's *The Poet in New York* are scattered phrases and images evocative of the violence and bitterness which characterized his death.

GARCILASO DE LA VEGA (1503–1536): Spanish poet from Toledo who, after a youth as the perfect Renaissance "courtier," fought with the troops of the Emperor Charles V, was wounded in battle and died in Nice. He is famous for his eclogues, which have their inspiration in Virgil. He adopted Italian metric forms in his poetry and was already considered a classic poet during the Spanish Golden Age. Interest in the poetic style of Garcilaso had a kind of rebirth among many members of Alberti's generation, including such poets as Pedro Salinas, Manuel Altolaguirre and Miguel Hernández, as well as Alberti himself.

GARDEL, CARLOS (1903–1935): a popular Argentine singer famous for his tango interpretations.

GENERATION OF 1898: The designation given to a group of important writers and intellectuals whose work concentrated on revitalizing Spanish culture through the rediscovery of what they considered to be the country's great heritage. Its members included such figures as Unamuno, Azorín, Machado, Baroja and Valle-Inclán.

GIBRALFARO: a fortress in the old quarter of Málaga which was built by the Moors and served for centuries as the basis of the city's defenses. The view from its ramparts is spectacular.

GIMÉNEZ CABALLERO, ERNESTO (b. 1899): dynamic author and critic, he was a leader of several unorthodox literary movements in Spain during the second and third decades of the twentieth century. His own works of fiction were filled with irrational and surrealistic qualities which have been attributed to the influence of Franz Kafka. He founded *La Gaceta Literaria* in 1927, and this literary journal was to have a profound effect on many members of Alberti's generation. Giménez Caballero was a great admirer of Italian Fascism and became active in the Spanish Falange.

GÓMEZ DE BAQUERO (1866–1929): a journalist and critic who

wrote under the pseudonym "Andrenio". His works include *Literatura y periodismo (Literature and Journalism)* and *Letras e ideas (Letters and Ideas)*.

GÓMEZ DE LA SERNA, RAMÓN (1888–1963): novelist, dramatist and biographer influenced by the Ultraist and Surrealist movements.

GÓNGORA Y ARGOTE, LUIS DE (1561–1627): One of the finest of Spain's Baroque poets. He wrote in a style characterized by the use of obscure and archaic language; this style, known as *culteranismo*, was responsible both for the disfavor with which his work was viewed and for the later admiration expressed by Alberti and the poets of his generation. His works include the *Fábula de Polifemo y Galatea* and *Soledades* (Solitudes).

LA GRANJA: a palace in the town of the same name located near Segovia. It was built by Felipe V in imitation of the Palace of Versailles, and is famous for its splendid fountains and gardens. Felipe V retired to La Granja after his abdication.

GUADALQUIVIR: an Andalusian river, mentioned often in Spanish literature, which flows through Sevilla and Córdoba.

GUERRERO, DOÑA MARÍA (1868–1928): Spanish actress celebrated throughout her own country and in Latin America.

GUERRERO RUIZ, JUAN (1893–1955): editor of *La verdad* who published the works of many of the poets of Alberti's generation and was a friend to many of them as well. *La verdad* later became *Verso y prosa* when Guerrero Ruiz began collaborating with the poet Jorge Guillén. García Lorca once called Guerrero Ruiz "the consul general of Spanish poetry."

GUILLÉN, JORGE (b. 1893): one of the most durable and better known poets of the so-called Generation of 1927. His poetry is distinguished by its clarity of expression and its overall tone of affirmation. His principal work is *Cántico* (1928) which has been published in various augmented editions that span many decades and is primarily a joyous hymn to life. The fourth and complete version of *Cántico* was published in Buenos Aires in 1950. His second collection of poems bears the title *Clamor*. This work was also to grow "organically" and it eventually appeared in three parts: *Maremágnum* (1957), *Que van a dar en la mar* (1960) and *A la altura de las circunstancias* (1963), all of which were originally published in Argentina. Guillén's third book of poetry, *Homenaje*, completes the series and it was published in Italy, together with *Cántico* and *Clamor*, under the collective title of *Aire nuestro* (1968). Jorge Guillén has also written works of literary criticism and has taught extensively at various universities in France, England and the United States since his exile from Spain in 1938.

GUTIÉRREZ SOLANA, JOSÉ (1886–1945): Spanish painter whose style and pictorial themes are reminiscent of Goya's "dark paintings." He was also a writer and his literary works share this somewhat grotesque quality so apparent in his canvases. ·

HERNÁNDEZ, MIGUEL (1910–1942): a self-educated poet born in Orihuela (Alicante) where, as a child, he was a goatherd. He died of pulmonary tuberculosis in a prison hospital.

HIDALGO DE CISNEROS, IGNACIO (1894–1966): an aviator who took part in the Cuatro Vientos uprising. During the Popular Front regime he was Commander of the Air Force and he joined the Communist Party in 1937.

HUIDOBRO, VICENTE (1893–1948): Chilean poet and novelist, originator of *Creacionismo* and author of *Altazor* and *Canciones en la noche (Songs in the Night).*

ISABEL II (1830–1904): Queen of Spain from 1833 until the rebellion of 1868 when she abdicated in favor of her son Alfonso XII. Her grandson Alfonso XIII, the last King of Spain before the establishment of the Second Republic in 1931, married the English Princess Victoria in 1906.

JÁUREGUI Y AGUILAR, JUAN DE (1583–1641): Baroque painter and poet, adversary of Góngora and *culteranismo.*

JIMÉNEZ, JUAN RAMÓN (1881–1958): one of the greatest Spanish poets of the twentieth century. He was originally influenced by Darío and the French Symbolists, but later developed an intensely individual style based on a poetic search for purity which engaged and sustained him throughout his career. He went into exile in the United States and Puerto Rico. Jiménez was awarded the Nobel Prize for Literature in 1956. His most popular work is the prose poem about an Andalusian donkey, *Platero y yo (Platero and I)*.

JOSELITO: together with Belmonte, he was considered to be one of the greatest bullfighters of all time. His real name was José Gómez; he was also called Joselito el Gallo. He was the youngest Spaniard ever to receive the title of *matador*, at the age of 17, and died in 1920 at the age of 25.

DOÑA JUANA LA LOCA (LADY JOAN THE MAD) (1479–1555): Queen of Castile in 1504, the daughter of Queen Isabella and Fernando of Aragón whose marriage united the two kingdoms and, eventually, gave rise to modern Spain. Juana was the mother of Carlos V. Her madness was partially caused by the death of her husband, Felipe el Hermoso (Phillip the Beautiful), in 1506.

LARGO CABALLERO, FRANCISCO (1869–1946): Republican leader who took part in the anti-monarchist rebellion at Cuatro Vientos in 1930. He later became the leader of the Socialist Party, and served as Minister of Labor, Minister of War, and Prime Minister during the Republic.

LARREA, JUAN (b. 1895): Spanish poet, novelist and friend of Gerardo Diego who settled in Paris while young and whose work was closely associated with *Ultraísmo*, *Creacionismo* and Surrealism. He went into voluntary exile in Mexico as a result of the Spanish Civil War and founded the literary journal *Cuadernos americanos*.

LAZARILLO DE TORMES (author anonymous, c. 1550): the first of the "picaresque" novels; it remains an almost archetypal work in the history of Spanish fiction. Its hero, Lazarillo, is a poor boy who recounts in autobiographical style the adventures and hard times he experiences in his struggle for survival. As the original *pícaro*, Lazarillo has served as a figure for numerous heroes and anti-heroes throughout Western literature.

LEÓN, RICARDO (1877–1943): Spanish novelist who exalted Castile and traditional Spain.

LIMONAR: one of the most beautiful of Málaga's residential districts. Its name signifies "lemon grove".

LITORAL: The Spanish literary journal, edited by Emilio Prados and Manuel Altolaguirre, which frequently published works by the members of Alberti's generation. Its October 1927 issue was devoted to a tribute to Góngora organized by Alberti and his friends. It has recently resumed publication (1968) in Málaga under the editorship of José María Amado. Number 43–44 of *Litoral*, dated March 30, 1974, is dedicated to Alberti. This was the second issue of the new *Litoral* to be dedicated to the "poet of Santa María."

LÓPEZ HEREDIA, IRENE (1894–1962): one of Spain's most popular actresses. Her fame extended to Buenos Aires, where she was greatly admired by the theater-going public. She had an unusually extensive repertory and performed in works by Shaw and in contemporary Spanish plays, often written especially for her, as well as in classical Greek drama. She formed her own theater company in 1928 and toward the end of her life played the title role in *La Celestina* (1499) by Fernando de Rojas, in a production that was also presented in Paris to great critical acclaim.

MACHADO, ANTONIO (1875–1939): Spanish poet and member of the Generation of 1898. He was perhaps the greatest poet of his generation, and continues to exert a strong influence on Spanish and Latin American poetry. His works include *Soledades, Campos de Castilla* and *Nuevas canciones*.

MARAÑÓN Y POSADILLO, GREGORIO (1887–1960): a prolific investigator, essayist, historian and medical doctor, Marañón had an encyclopedic knowledge and he wrote extensively on various themes related to the culture and literature of Spain. He is best known for his theories on the Don Juan figure in literature as well as for his books on El Greco, Antonio Pérez and Luis Vives.

MARQUINA, EDUARDO (1879–1946): Catalan playwright of historical verse dramas such as *Las hijas del Cid (The Daughters of the Cid)* and *En Flandes se ha puesto el sol (The Sun Has Set in Flanders)*.

MARTÍ, JOSÉ (1853–1895): Modernist poet and prose writer from Cuba; he was the only Modernist who participated actively in politics and he met his death fighting for Cuban independence. Martí was imprisoned and later exiled because of his political views; he spent more than twenty years in Spain, France, England, Mexico, Guatemala and the United States. His works include *El presidio político en Cuba, Ismaelillo, Versos sencillos* and *Versos libres.*

MARTINFIERRISTAS: a term referring to those who wrote with the style and themes introduced by José Hernández, a nineteenth-century Argentine poet, in his narrative poem *Martín Fierro* which tells the story of a *gaucho* (a type of cowboy of the Argentine *pampas*) very much within the "Noble Savage" tradition.

MAURA Y GAMAZO, GABRIEL (1879–1963): historian and statesman and author of many erudite monographs, among them *Vida y reinado de Carlos II (The Life and Reign of Carlos II).*

MEDINA, FRANCISCO DE (1544–1615): Baroque poet and author of *Anotaciones de las obras de Garcilaso (Annotations to the Works of Garcilaso).*

MEDINILLA, BALTASAR ELISIO (1585–1620): Baroque poet whose style imitated that of Lope de Vega.

MENÉNDEZ PIDAL, RAMÓN (1869–1968): philologist and literary historian whose extensive research into medieval Spanish literature and the origins of the Spanish language are regarded as the most authoritative and definitive in the field.

MIRÓ, GABRIEL (1879–1930): a highly lyrical novelist, Miró's distinctive prose style has a spiritual and poetic quality not often found in the writings of the more intellectual Spanish novelists who were his contemporaries. Critics have characterized him as an author of Mediterranean sensitivity whose works contain luminous descriptions of nature that are religious in tone. In the novels of Miró, almost all aspects of reality, however sordid, are transformed through language and imagery into a world of sparkling beauty. Among his many works of fiction are *Nuestro Padre San Daniel, El obispo leproso* and *El humo dormido.*

MONTES, EUGENIO (b. 1897): Spanish writer, author of *El viajero y su sombra (The Traveler and His Shadow).*

NEGRÍN, JUAN LÓPEZ (1887-1956): a professor of physiology at the University of Madrid who became a key figure of the Republican Government. He served under Largo Caballero as Minister of Finance and became Premier in May 1937. He retained this title and position during the Civil War and with the Republican Government in Exile until 1945.

NERVO, AMADO (1870-1919): Mexican poet and novelist, popular in his time but now regarded with critical disfavor. He also served as a diplomat in Spain and as the editor of various literary journals.

ORTEGA Y GASSET, JOSÉ (1883-1955): Spain's leading twentieth-century philosopher, who is also known as an art and literary critic. Author of *La rebelión de las masas (The Revolt of the Masses)*, *La deshumanización del arte (The Dehumanization of Art)*, *La misión de la universidad (The Mission of the University)* and numerous other works.

LA PASIONARIA: the popular name of Dolores Ibarruri (b. 1895), an Asturian Communist leader during the Spanish Civil War. The name bestowed on her is indicative of the ability she possessed to inflame the political feelings of the leftist Republicans.

PEMÁN, JOSÉ MARÍA (b. 1898): monarchist poet and dramatist born in Cádiz. In spite of his advanced age he continues to be a powerful, popular and controversial literary figure in Spain. He is admired by the general public and scorned by the younger writers and intellectuals.

PÉREZ DE AYALA, RAMÓN (1880-1962): novelist and poet who brought the "psychological novel" to its full importance in Spain. He also served as Spanish Ambassador to the United Kingdom, 1931-1936. Author of *Belarmino y Apolonio, Luna de miel, luna de hiel (Honeymoon, Bittermoon), Tigre Juan (Tiger John)* and many other novels.

PÉREZ GALDÓS, BENITO (1843-1920): one of Spain's very greatest novelists. He wrote over sixty novels and more than twenty dramas in a realistic style which has often been compared to that of Dickens.

PRADOS, EMILIO (1899–1962): a poet whose work is characterized by a passionate intimacy which often brings to mind the
work of García Lorca. He lived in exile in Mexico after the
Spanish Civil War, writing poetry and serving as an editor and a
teacher there until his death.

PRIMO DE RIVERA, MIGUEL (1870–1930): a general in the army,
he was Commander-in-Chief of the military dictatorship from
1923 to 1925, and Prime Minister from 1925 to 1929.

QUEVEDO Y VILLEGAS, FRANCISCO DE (1580–1645): One of
the most interesting and complex figures in the history of
Spanish literature. In his life and his writings he personified the
conflictive tensions of the Baroque period. He was a poet, a
novelist, a statesman, a humanist and a philosopher. His satirical
writings and dark humor have earned him the epithet of "a
literary Goya." The *Historia de la vida del Buscón llamado don
Pablos* is a picaresque novel which Quevedo is thought to have
written in 1603. It is filled with grotesque deformations of reality which emphasize the overall vision of moral decay and the
devaluation of human actions.

QUEIPO DE LLANO, GONZALO (1875–1951): a general in the Republican Army who became one of Franco's key military oper-
atives during the Civil War. His headquarters were in Sevilla
and his broadcasts from that city became infamous. He had a
reputation for extreme cruelty and is mentioned by Arthur
Koestler in his *Dialogue with Death.*

QUINTA DEL SORDO (The Deaf Man's Villa): Goya's residence on
the outskirts of Madrid, where he retired after he went deaf. The
walls of this house were covered with his most hallucinatory
paintings, many of which were removed before the house was
eventually destroyed.

QUINTERO, SERAFÍN ALVAREZ (1871–1938) and QUINTERO,
JOAQUIN (1873–1944): two brothers who wrote comedies of
manners about the Spain of their time, particularly Andalusia,
which were extremely popular throughout the country.

RÍOS, FERNANDO DE LOS (1879–1949): Republican Socialist who
took part in the Cuatro Vientos rebellion; he later served as

Spain's Minister of Education and as Ambassador to the United States. After the Spanish Civil War he migrated to the United States to pursue his career as a professor, historian and social critic.

Romero de Torres, Julio (1880–1930): Spanish painter of Sevilla whose portraits of gypsy types from Andalusia are highly romanticized and almost constitute a form of calendar art.

Rueda, Salvador (1857–1933): Andalusian poet, precursor to Rubén Darío as a proponent of Modernism. He made use of distinctly Andalusian themes and motifs in his poetry as well as in his plays and novels.

Ruisiñol, Santiago (1861–1926): Spanish painter who used brilliant colors and softly edged figures to create a suggestive impressionistic style. He was also the author of several novels and plays.

Saborit Colomer, Andrés: Vice President of the UGT *(Unión General de Trabajadores)*, the Socialist Workers' Union, when Besteiro was President of this organization.

Salinas, Pedro (1892–1951): poet of Alberti's generation who pursued a distinguished academic career and taught for many years in the United States. His work is characterized by its clarity, intelligence and serenity of spirit. Author of *El contemplado, La voz a ti debida, Fábula y signo* and other works, he was also an outstanding literary critic and wrote extensively on Spanish literature.

Signac, Paul (1863–1935): French painter, a master of Divisionist and Pointillist Impressionism.

Torre, Guillermo de (1900–1971): literary critic, historian and aesthetician who wrote extensively on the "vanguard" literary movements of the twentieth century.

Unamuno, Miguel de (1864–1936): the greatest writer to emerge from the Generation of 1898. He worked in poetry, drama, novels and essays. His lifelong concerns with the revitalization of Spanish literature and culture as well as his personal vitalist philosophy, which stressed the ascendancy of life over

321

logic and intellectualization, are constantly evinced in the tremendous body of work he produced. Among his writings are *Del sentimiento trágico de la vida (On the Tragic Sense of Life)*, *Vida de don Quijote y Sancho (The Life of Don Quixote and Sancho)*, *La agonía del cristianismo (The Agony of Christianity)* and *Niebla (Mist)*.

VALLE, ADRIANO DEL (1895–1928): poet, critic and lecturer, he was one of the leaders of the *Ultraísta* movement in Spain. In collaboration with Fernando Villalón and Rogelio Buendía, he founded the literary journal *Papel de Aleluya* in Huelva, and he was the Editor of *Primer Plano*, a magazine devoted to film criticism.

VALLE-INCLÁN, RAMÓN DEL (1869–1936): Modernist poet, playwright and novelist. He was prominent in literary circles in Alberti's youth and remains one of the primary literary figures of the time. He was a highly eccentric individual whose *esperpéntico* or grotesque prose style makes him an important precursor of much that has been written in the Hispanic world in the last two decades. His novel of a Latin American tyrant, *Tirano Banderas*, is an important and highly influential work which continues to receive critical attention.

VALLEJO, CÉSAR (1898–1938): a Peruvian poet whose works are often incoherent but highly personal expressions of pain and desperation. His poetry is a testimony to his own sense of precariousness in the world, and it is filled with anguish, rebellion and resignation. He is considered by many critics to be one of the most authentic poetic voices every heard in Latin America and he exerted a great influence on the poets of Alberti's generation in Spain as a part of the *Ultraísta* movement. His most important works are *Los heraldos negros* (1918), *Trilce* (1922), *Poemas humanos* (1923–1938) and *España, aparta de mí este cáliz* (1939).

VALLEY OF THE FALLEN (VALLE DE LOS CAÍDOS): the site of a monument supposedly in honor of those who died in the Spanish Civil War. It is located near the Escorial, the monastery and palacial retreat built by Phillip II where many of the Spanish Monarchs are entombed. In the central rotunda of the

Chapel, deep inside the underground monument of the Valle de los Caídos, is the tomb of the founder of the Falange, José Primo de Rivera. Francisco Franco was buried there on November 23, 1975. An impressive structure built in the side of a mountain, it has become a tourist attraction for Spaniards and non-Spaniards alike.

VENTA DEL AIRE: a famous restaurant in Toledo, known for its regional dishes, particularly partridge and lamb.

VICENTE, GIL (1470–1536?): Portuguese poet and dramatist who wrote both in Portuguese and Spanish. He was one of the most perfect cultivators of traditional lyric poetry in the sixteenth century, and the most popular elements in his verse were highly admired as well as imitated by several Spanish poets of Alberti's generation.

VILLAESPESA, FRANCISCO (1877–1936): Spanish poet and playwright, a Modernist and a friend of Darío.

XIRGU, MARGARITA (1888–1959): one of Spain's greatest actresses. She was admired for her performances of the works of Shaw, Wilde, Galdós, Benavente and Lorca, with whom she shared a close friendship.

ZORRILLA Y DEL MORAL, JOSÉ (1817–1893): popular Romantic poet of Spain whose works were filled with color and musicality.

ZULOAGA Y ZABALETA, IGNACIO (1870–1945): Spanish-Basque painter of the Realist School who made use of somber colors to dramatically portray the harsh and stern character of Spain and its people.